Praise for *The Empowered Wife*

"Laura Doyle truly understands how the modern marriage works. Her modern approaches are eye-opening and marriage-saving!"
—John Gray, Ph.D., author of *Men Are from Mars, Women Are from Venus*

"Laura Doyle does it again with *The Empowered Wife,* and this time, she's not alone. The anecdotes from other women underline her lesson: women hold the key to improving our marriages."
—Fawn Weaver, *New York Times* bestselling author of *Happy Wives Club*

The Empowered Wife

The Empowered Wife

Six Surprising Secrets for Attracting Your Husband's TIME, ATTENTION, and AFFECTION

Updated and Expanded Edition

Laura Doyle

New York Times Bestselling Author of
The Surrendered Wife
The Surrendered Single
Things Will Get as Good as You Can Stand

BenBella Books, Inc.
Dallas, Texas

BenBella

BenBella Books, Inc.
10440 N. Central Expressway, Suite #800
Dallas, TX 75231
www.benbellabooks.com
Send feedback to feedback@benbellabooks.com

BenBella is a federally registered trademark.

Printed in the United States of America
10 9 8 7 6 5 4 3 2

ISBN 9781637742266 (trade paperback)
ISBN 9781944648602 (electronic)

The Library of Congress has cataloged an earlier edition as follows:
Doyle, Laura.
    First, kill all the marriage counselors: modern-day secrets to being desired, cherished, and adored for life / Laura Doyle.
        pages cm
    Includes bibliographical references and index.
    ISBN 978-1-940363-86-8 (paperback) — ISBN 978-1-940363-96-7 (electronic) 1. Marriage—Psychological aspects. 2. Wives—Psychology. 3. Husbands—Psychology. 4. Man-woman relationships—Psychological aspects. 5. Interpersonal conflict. 6. Interpersonal relations. I. Title.
    HQ734.D788 2015
    306.81—dc23
                                                                    2014046311

Editing by Erin Kelley and Alexa Stevenson
Copyediting by Oriana Leckert
Text design by Publishers' Design and Production Services, Inc.
Proofreading by Amy Zarkos and Cape Cod Compositors, Inc.
Cover design by Sarah Avinger
Cover photo © Adobe Stock / Parilov (couple) and Andrey Kuzmin (burst)
Author photo by Tara Shannon
Printed by Lake Book Manufacturing

For all the certified coaches who have trained with me because of their passion and commitment to their own relationships and their desire to help other women. You move me every single day. I couldn't do what I do without you. Thank you for sharing my vision to end world divorce and standing shoulder to shoulder with me.

And for John, whose steady presence has helped me become my best self.

Contents

Introduction to the
New Edition

Ever since I got my hands on the Six Intimacy Skills, which you'll find spelled out step by step in this book, I've felt both joyful passion and burning obligation to make sure that as many women as possible are able to get their hands on them too. I hate to see *any* woman struggling in her marriage because I remember how painful and lonely it was before I learned what I know now about how to have a lasting, thriving marriage. So I wrote a book describing the life-changing secrets I learned from women in happy marriages.

And while tens of thousands of women have gotten their hands on the Six Intimacy Skills and used them to transform their marriages, thousands more women *still* have never heard these secrets. This will not do! So I started blogging, and I wrote another book (the one you're reading now). I started group and private coaching programs, where my coaches and I have guided thousands of students who wanted more support than they could get from the books alone, as well as a relationship coach training school, where we've trained hundreds of coaches to become experts on the Six Intimacy Skills. I created the *Empowered Wives* series on Amazon Prime, launched *The Empowered Wife Podcast*, and offered the Adored Wife Challenge, which still runs twice a year. I continue to search for ways to more impactfully and effectively spread this work I care so deeply about.

I've learned that inspiration and hope are indispensable in opening up possibility for those who want a lasting, thriving marriage but feel stuck wondering how that will ever happen in their current circumstances. And I've seen how hearing other women tell the personal, intimate stories of their marriage breakdowns and breakthroughs can be a powerful source of those critical ingredients. Hearing the other side of the story from the men who are married to these students further validates that, to paraphrase Thomas Wolfe, miracles not only happen around here; they happen all the time.

So in this updated edition of *The Empowered Wife*, I've included even more of these real-life stories. You'll find examples throughout, as well as excerpts from podcast interviews (including the episode number, so you can listen to them yourself).

I've also included two new chapters in this edition. One covers the problem of a distant husband—and the techniques I've seen women use to get their disinterested, absent, or wandering husbands back.

The second new chapter introduces the most powerful and effective structure for practicing the Six Intimacy Skills: the four pillars of the Connection Framework. The Connection Framework can help you put this book's lessons into practice right away without feeling overwhelmed.

It continues to be my sincere desire that every woman feel empowered to make her marriage last and thrive. *Every* woman—that means you, even if the challenges in your marriage make you feel alone, like an outlier whose problems are terminally unique and incurable, like I used to. In my experience with thousands of students, there's every reason to be hopeful that you can transform your marriage. You wouldn't be reading this right now if you didn't have at least a bit of that hope yourself. So let's trust your hope and get started on the wondrous journey of making your marriage a playful and passionate one.

PROLOGUE

The Breakdown Before the Breakthrough

"Every master was once a disaster."

—T. Harv Eker, Author and Motivational Speaker

My Husband Was a Loser

At the lowest point in my marriage, I was absolutely convinced that I had married the wrong person. I was sure that my husband, John, was not as smart, spiritually evolved, or capable as I was. I believed I had made a bad choice. Secretly, I was embarrassed by him.

(Maybe it wasn't so secret.)

In the early years, I thought that as his wife, well, I would just help him become a better person!

Armed with recommendations from experts who encouraged me to be direct about my complaints lest they fester into resentment, I explained to John that it would be a lot more romantic if instead of watching so much TV, for example, he'd surprise me by taking me out.

I let him know that I was deeply concerned that he wasn't initiating much activity in the bedroom, and that he wasn't making enough of an effort to spend time with me.

I showed him how he could be more ambitious at work by telling him what to say to his boss to ask for a raise.

I pointed out the shortcomings in his diet (no veggies!) and made suggestions for how he might cut back on junk food.

As you will no doubt be shocked to learn, none of this motivated my husband to change or improve himself—nor did it improve our relationship. Quite the opposite: He dug in his heels and seemed more committed than ever to doing the things that bothered me.

We argued. A lot.

I understood that my husband didn't like to be criticized—no one does. Of course he wanted to feel a sense of autonomy over his own life—we all do. But what about the things that were important to *me*? He didn't seem to care about those, no matter how much I explained or how hard I tried to make him understand.

My Marriage Was Hopeless

I read lots of articles and books on how to have a better relationship. Communication was supposedly key, but my husband was not responding the way I wanted him to. He didn't even seem to be listening. Most of the time I felt that he was just tuning me out, which was infuriating. How could he be more interested in watching a rerun than talking to me, or even making love?

Six years into the marriage, it was clear that my husband would never do the things that he knew—because I'd told him!—would improve our relationship and make me happy. It was the source of near-constant bickering and several knock-down, drag-out fights.

I insisted we go to marriage counseling, and he reluctantly agreed, but six months later, our problems had only gotten worse.

I realized that my husband was never going to open up about his feelings, or help out more around the house, or make an effort to spend time with me, or say the tender, loving things I craved.

I felt trapped. I was deeply hurt and afraid that I would never have the kind of marriage I'd envisioned, one where we'd have long talks, enjoy lots of physical passion, and laugh together.

At least, not while I was married to *him*.

What No One Ever Taught Us

No one signs up for an "okay" relationship. No one gets married because they don't have enough hard work already. You made a vow because you wanted to love and be loved, to have a sense of family, to know that there's someone in the world who will worry about you if you don't come home at the usual time. You signed up for marriage because you believed you had found someone you could truly count on, and because you felt so good and happy in the company of your beloved that you wanted that person by your side forever.

But most couples struggle. With a divorce every thirteen seconds in the United States, and many more unhappy marriages limping along, millions of couples are at risk for expensive legal battles and crippling heartache.

Maybe some of this sounds familiar. But what if your marriage is in trouble not because you married the wrong person but because, like me, you didn't get any training on how to have a good relationship?

Like anything else worthwhile in life, a happy relationship takes some skill. No one is born knowing how to have a happy marriage. You probably got to see your parents' marriage growing up, but if they were divorced or unhappy, you were following a failed recipe.

Imagine if we gave out driver's licenses the same way we do marriage licenses. What if we just tossed the car keys to a teenager as soon as she turned sixteen, with no instructions? She'd probably crash the car and from that experience decide that driving is hard, scary, and dangerous—and she'd be right.

Of course, that's not what we do. We require our prospective driver to learn the rules of the road, take a written test, practice driving with an instructor, and take a behind-the-wheel test. If she demonstrates proficiency, then she gets a license to drive a car.

When it comes to relationships, most people get no instruction at all—so why are we surprised when so many of them crash?

It doesn't have to be that way. Once you learn the Six Intimacy Skills™, marriage—like driving—can be a pleasant ride over a smooth road.

How I Got Empowered

The road early in my marriage was not smooth, and the ride was anything but pleasant.

Finally, we were at an impasse. My husband wouldn't put in the effort to make things better, and I was already doing everything I could think of—so how could I expect any improvement in the future? It was hopeless.

I'd threatened divorce many times in my desperation to get his attention, to get him to wake up. Now it seemed clear that divorce was truly the only answer. I would never be happy in this marriage.

There was just one problem: I was too embarrassed to get divorced.

My family and friends had been at our wedding not so many years before; I'd been so happy on that day, proud to be marrying such a smart, talented, handsome, and funny guy.

I didn't want everyone to know how bad things had gotten, especially since I'd been acting as if everything was fine. John and I would have a big fight on the way to a party, for instance, then pretend all was well when we got there. It was a big secret that things were falling apart (or so I told myself).

If we got divorced, everyone would find out I'd made a big mistake. They would all see that I had failed—a prospect too humiliating to contemplate.

So, instead of filing for divorce, I made one last-ditch effort: I decided to ask women who had been married for at least fifteen years—which seemed like an eternity—what their secret was. How had they stayed married for so long? How did they make it work? What made a happy marriage?

I went into this inquiry believing that these women had better husbands than I did. *That* was how they made it work, I was sure I'd find out. And that would be the reason my questions were futile. But I was wrong.

It was only the beginning of me being wrong. I was in for a real shock. What these women told me was so contrary to what I thought I knew about relationships that it didn't even make sense. But I was desperate to avoid the cost, pain, and embarrassment of a divorce, so I decided to give their suggestions a go.

When some of their seemingly crazy recommendations actually worked, I was amazed. That's when I had the first clear glimpse of how I'd contributed to the suffering in my home.

The bad news was that I was definitely part of the problem, and not the perfect wife I'd thought I was. This was very hard to swallow, but fortunately it was tied to the good news: I had the power to improve my marriage in ways that I hadn't even imagined.

When I took a different approach, my husband had a much different response. This was a breakthrough! Instead of feeling like a victim of his stubborn, uncooperative behavior and mistreatment, I could finally see how I'd been pressing levers that I didn't even know existed.

This was true empowerment, because I was focusing on my own desires, not on the behavior of someone else. I saw a future where I was no longer overwhelmed and resentful. I saw firsthand how I could begin to feel more relaxed and dignified, and how I naturally attracted my husband's time, attention, and affection like a magnet.

It was a huge "aha!" moment.

I was so excited and hopeful that I could have the kind of marriage I'd always wanted. I could see how we wouldn't have the tense, silent cold wars that lasted for days or those big blowups in the car anymore.

There was just one problem. I couldn't always get myself to do the things that I now knew would make my marriage shiny and amazing again. It's not that the new way was so hard. It was just new.

It wasn't long before we had a big blowup in the car. Again. Argh! I was crushed because I'd thought those days were over, but it looked like they weren't. Yet.

I had the idea that if I could get some of my girlfriends who were also complaining about their marriages to apply the Intimacy Skills with me, it would help me develop the new habits I needed—and possibly help their marriages too. So I started a tiny support group in my living room.

And then, at long last, I got my miracle.

The man who had wooed me was back.

It took time, and some trial and error, but eventually out of this experience I distilled six core skills that greatly improved the happiness of my marriage. I call them the Six Intimacy Skills, because when I practiced them, the connection and passion in my relationship came roaring back. John became more thoughtful, and he started taking more initiative—from taking me out to dinner to deciding on his own to stain the deck. He was also doing the dishes without my having to ask him six times—or at all! He wasn't watching as much TV or looking as depressed and dejected. He even started his own business and took over handling the household bills. I knew that the Six Intimacy Skills were working because we were laughing together, holding hands, and enjoying physical intimacy in a way we hadn't for years.

I felt as though my husband had changed and was finally doing all the things I had wanted him to. But in reality, *I* had changed and he was responding to me the way he had when we first fell in love—because I was acting the way I did back then. At the same time, I felt more authentic, more like myself.

And those friends I had recruited with "hopeless husbands" also saw impressive, dramatic results. One husband came home early from work just to be with his wife, while another started painting the family room—a chore they'd been arguing about for months. Still another friend got to go on the most romantic trip of her life after her formerly unambitious spouse won a sales contest at work.

Seeing their results, which were breathtaking, inspired me. And they kept me motivated.

Every time I heard myself telling a friend how to use one of my newfound skills, it upped my commitment a little more and reinforced my new behavior. When I was tempted to go back to my old ways, I felt the weight of responsibility, knowing that those friends were counting on me to practice what I preached. I knew I had to be accountable to them, and knowing that kept me more focused than I would have been on my own.

Discovering the Six Intimacy Skills was a huge breakthrough, but by themselves, they weren't enough for me. Without the support of a community of like-minded women—seeing myself in their stories and challenges, and hearing myself encouraging them and paying forward what I had learned—I wasn't nearly as good at practicing the Intimacy Skills.

Word spread. Dozens, then hundreds of women came to me for help. I showed them all the Six Intimacy Skills, and the results were always the same. When a woman learned and practiced these skills, her relationship improved dramatically—in about two weeks.

Talk about feeling empowered!

Today there are thousands of empowered wives practicing the Six Intimacy Skills all over the world. These women often say to me, "I feel like I have a new husband!" Of course they don't—what they do have is a new marriage. These women are passionate about the Six Intimacy Skills because these skills have helped them create the kind of marriage they dreamed of having when they said "I do."

To this day, I rely on the influence of the worldwide community of empowered wives to keep my own marriage shiny. They inspire and amaze me, and they remind me what's possible when I practice the Six Intimacy Skills. Every time I interview a success story for *The Empowered Wife Podcast*, meet with our certified coaches, or hear the story of a coach trainee, it lifts me up for days and helps me show up as my best self wherever I go.

Empowering Playful, Passionate Relationships

If you feel like you've been trying really hard to improve your relationship and it's not working, maybe the problem was never you, or your husband, or the two of you as a couple. Maybe the problem is that nobody ever taught you the skills you need to make things work.

You are holding a guide to those skills in your hands, and you'll be able to start using them today.

You're on your way to having your husband's time, attention, and affection—not because you told him you wanted him to make more of an effort to spend time with you and be physically affectionate, but because he naturally seeks you out, puts his arm around you, or steals a kiss when he passes you in the hallway.

The suggestions you're going to read in this book may seem pretty crazy to you at first, just as they did to me. This is not the usual relationship claptrap, like "schedule a date night," "communication is the key," or "go to couples counseling." Contrary to what you hear absolutely everywhere, marriage is not hard work. It felt like hard work before I learned the Six Intimacy Skills, but now it's my soft place to land—to find out I'm beautiful and wonderful and to get love and support.

When you apply the Six Intimacy Skills, your relationship will become more passionate, playful, and peaceful, which definitely feels empowering. Your husband will make bedroom eyes at you again and look for ways to delight you. But it gets better.

Besides having the kind of marriage you've always wanted, you're going to also feel more authentic, more like your best self. You're going to be having more fun and honoring your desires more than ever before. You'll stop hearing yourself nagging or begging to get what you want—because you won't feel the need to do any of that. If you're anything like me, you'll like yourself more.

You'll feel more dignified, more confident, and more relaxed. But it gets better.

Your other relationships will improve, too. You'll have stronger connections with those you care about and get better responses from your kids, your parents, and your friends.

But it gets even better.

You'll have more time and energy for the things that are tugging at your sleeve—your purpose and your passions—as you stop wasting your resources on what I call Needless Emotional Turmoil (NET).

Once I got back all the energy I'd been spending on my struggling relationship, I was able to accomplish some pretty wonderful things, like writing a book that landed on the *New York Times* bestseller list and founding an international relationship coaching organization. Who knows what might emerge in your own life? Wouldn't you like to find out?

To sum up: There was a huge payoff in every area of my life, all for practicing a few skills I discovered only because I was desperate to fix my broken marriage.

Once you incorporate the Six Intimacy Skills into your life, you'll experience the same kinds of benefits. What are you waiting for?

Quiz: Can You Tell the Good Relationship Advice from the Bad Advice?

Can you spot the myths about marriage? Mark each statement "true" or "false."

1. Marriage is hard work.

2. Husbands and wives have to give and take equally for a marriage to succeed.

3. Men tend to be less mature than women, which is one reason women end up taking on more housework and child-rearing responsibilities.

4. Women have more influence than men on whether a relationship will be connected and fun or distant and miserable.

5. Wives who are always saying what they want are more likely to get divorced.

6. A happy wife is often willing to have sex with her husband even if she is not in the mood.

7. When you've been married for a while, you can pretty much predict what your partner is going to say in a given situation.

8. A husband wants his wife to be happy and will go to great lengths to make sure she is.

9. If something your husband is doing is bothering you, it's best to be honest and say so directly.

10. Happy wives tell their husbands when they want more attention or affection.

11. Diagnosis and medication for conditions like ADD, OCD, Asperger's, borderline personality disorder, or narcissistic personality disorder provide insights that can dramatically improve a marriage.

12. If your husband grew up in a dysfunctional family, it may take him years to learn to be emotionally supportive, take initiative, or respond to your needs.

13. Marriages where the wife is feminine and the husband is masculine are highly successful.

14. Once your marriage is in crisis—you're separated, divorcing, or there's been an infidelity—it's probably too late to save it.

15. Couples with happy marriages have learned how to fight fair.

16. If you're in an unhappy marriage, that probably means one of you has changed since you got married, and you may not be right for each other anymore.

17. Most people who get divorced are happier a few years later than they were when they were unhappily married.

18. Happy couples tend to make peace at the end of the day, even if it means staying up late to talk it through.

19. For a marriage to improve, both people have to work on it.

20. Happy marriages are the result of two people being lucky enough to find and marry the right person for them.

Answers:

1. **False.** I've been married twenty-five years, and my marriage is a soft place to land. Waitressing is hard work. Writing a book is hard work. Marriage is a piece of cake now that I have the right skills.

2. **False.** The more women receive graciously from their husbands and focus on their own happiness, the more successful the marriage will be.

3. **False.** Women take on more responsibility because they're afraid it won't be done the right way—their way.

4. **True.** Women are the keepers of the relationship and have much more power over the culture in the home.

5. **False.** The more you express your desires, the more your husband knows how to make you happy, which in turn makes him feel more successful as a husband.

6. **True.** Why would you want to pass up the opportunity to feel desired, to feel pleasure, and to connect with your husband physically, emotionally, and spiritually? Just because you don't start out in the mood doesn't mean you won't end up there.

7. **False.** We'd like to think we can read our husbands' minds, but it's simply not so.

8. **True.** Ask a married man and he'll tell you.

9. **False.** You don't have to suffer indefinitely, but criticism has a chilling effect on intimacy, and there's always a better way to get what you want.

10. **False.** Happy wives are irresistible and don't need to ask for attention or affection because their husbands are drawn to them. Feeling that you need to ask is a sign you've forgotten that, as a woman, you are a magnet for men, especially your husband.

11. **False.** Those diagnoses may give you insights—or they may be a giant distraction from your own feelings and desires—but they don't get you any closer to feeling desired, cherished, and adored, which is about practicing the right skills.

12. **False.** With the Six Intimacy Skills, you'll notice an improvement in two weeks. You wouldn't have married him if he didn't have qualities you admire. Those will come back when you begin treating him respectfully again.

13. **True.** Yin and yang go together beautifully.

14. **False.** No matter what kind of crisis your marriage is in, it can likely be completely revitalized, becoming the best it's ever been.

15. **False.** There's no such thing as fighting fair. It's called "fighting" because it's about hurting another person. Couples with happy marriages don't fight very much.

16. **False.** If your marriage is very strained, you may have forgotten what you were attracted to about him, but he's still the same great guy. It's fun to rediscover those wonderful qualities as you repair the relationship.

17. **False.** Studies show that people are just as unhappy after they divorce as they were in a difficult marriage.

18. **False.** Go to sleep. Things will look better in the morning. In fact, there might not even *be* a problem; you could just be overtired. Sleep first, talk later.

19. **False.** Women have far more power in a relationship, and therefore have the ability to revitalize the intimacy of a marriage singlehandedly. Men rise to the occasion, but women set the tone.

20. **False.** A happy marriage is the result of a woman learning certain skills that, when practiced, result in her feeling desired, cherished, and adored by her husband every day, for the rest of their lives.

CHAPTER 1

Empowerment Wears a Disguise

"When a well-packaged web of lies has been sold gradually to the masses over generations, the truth will seem utterly preposterous and its speaker a raving lunatic."

—Dresden James, author and TV writer

You've Been Lied To

If your marriage is anywhere near as hostile, lonely, and dysfunctional as mine was, I want you to know that it's not your fault. It may not be your husband's fault, either. It's just that no one ever taught you the skills you need to have a happy relationship. Like everything else in life, it's easier to succeed in a happy marriage when someone shows you how.

Before I learned what I know now about how to naturally attract my husband's time, attention, and affection, I had bought into some harmful myths that made my marriage feel like wearing ankle weights in the middle of the ocean.

You may be subscribing to some of these same myths, because they are everywhere and often repeated as indisputable fact. But they're not—they're lies, like "To save your marriage, go to marriage counseling," "You have to be honest and get the problems out in the open to work on your issues," and "Marriage is hard work." In this book, I'll show you why none of that is true, and how it's been keeping you from having the marriage you signed up for, just as it did for me.

Here's one example: When there was a serious breakdown in our marriage, I told my husband, John, that we needed to go to counseling—because that's what you're supposed to do when your marriage isn't working. Counseling didn't make things better, but we hung in there for a long time, hoping that it was going to, eventually. We had spent more than $9,000 on our counselor when I got a rare glimpse of the inside of her marriage. I was shocked and horrified to see that she had plenty of hostility and tension in her relationship, too.

It stands to reason that taking marriage advice from someone with a troubled relationship not only won't help, it might actually do harm. If I hadn't gotten a glimpse of our counselor interacting with her husband, I might never have known that her seemingly happy marriage was riddled with anger and resentment—just like mine.

I felt as if I'd been getting the equivalent of personal training from a couch potato with a spare tire, or financial advice from someone who was about to file for bankruptcy.

That was when I first realized that no marriage and family therapist credential could guarantee that the bearer would have a happy, lasting, intimate marriage. Marriage counselors take a theoretical, academic approach to marriage. They've learned things from textbooks and in classrooms and have degrees hanging on their walls, but they don't necessarily have the most important credential of all: a happy, passionate, thriving marriage of their own. And you'll never know how many couples your counselor has helped—or hurt—because that information is confidential.

That's one way that the Six Intimacy Skills are different. They were created in the trenches—with real women in real marriages—and they have worked for more than 150,000 women all over the world. You can hear wives sharing their inspiring stories in their own voices on *The Empowered Wife Podcast* at https://LauraDoyle.org/podcast.

Now that I know how to naturally attract my husband's time, attention, and affection, I can definitely see why marriage counseling wasn't working. You could argue that our situation is just one example, an outlier from the norm, but I'm not the only one who didn't get the desired outcome. Our coaching students and podcast guests tell the same story over and over: "We went to marriage counseling, but it didn't make us feel closer," "It only made things worse," or "That's when we separated/filed for divorce."

In this book, I'll show you the difference between traditional marriage counseling and what actually works to restore the hand-holding, the connection, and the physical intimacy. You'll be able to see for yourself why counseling seldom helps. You'll wonder why no one ever told you before.

I Felt Like Such a Sucker

For a long time after we stopped going, I didn't connect the dots between the prevalence of marriage counseling and the high divorce rate in this country—or maybe I just didn't want to believe that something I'd spent so much time and money on could be not just useless but potentially harmful. I figured our marriage counseling experience must have helped in some way, even though I couldn't figure out how. After all, it wasn't that we'd had a bad counselor; she was caring and attentive. But, looking back, I was forced to admit that while our marriage survived the experience, counseling only made our problems worse.

At first I assumed we were an exception—that our experience was not typical of the entire multibillion-dollar marriage counseling industry. But as I heard story after story of marriage counseling that left the relationship no better than it was to begin with or even ended in separation or divorce, I started to get a sinking feeling about the state of so-called "therapy" for couples or individuals in unhappy marriages.

One student, Stephanie, told me she went to a marriage counselor every week for a year. During the sessions, she told the counselor everything that was wrong with her husband. Each week the counselor listened carefully, sympathized, took her money, and said, "Same time next week?" Stephanie's marriage never improved. In fact, after a year of counseling, she was seriously contemplating divorcing the father of her four children.

After Stephanie learned the Six Intimacy Skills, she made changes that resulted in a dramatic improvement in her marriage—within a couple of weeks. Suddenly her husband was going out of his way to be thoughtful, showing a lot of affection, and spontaneously doing the things she had nagged him to do for years.

That was over a decade ago. Stephanie's marriage has remained loving and happy since, and she still gets tears in her eyes when she talks about how tragic it would have been had she continued focusing on her husband's faults in counseling every week, or acted on her impulse to throw him out and find someone new. There's no question in her mind now that he is—and always was—the man of her dreams.

Christine met and married a terrific guy she was crazy about after adopting the Six Intimacy Skills. She also gained insight about the demise of her first marriage when she looked at it through this new perspective. Back then, when she revealed to a marriage counselor that she and her husband had been sleeping in separate beds for a year, the counselor told her, "Can't you see your marriage is over? It's dead! You need to get out of there." The counselor made no attempt to help Christine improve her marriage, nor did she ask her if she wanted to leave—she just insisted that Christine should. She even implied that Christine was naïve or stupid for staying in her marriage for as long as she had. In Christine's vulnerable state, it was hard for her to argue with this strong-minded counselor who seemed to know best. She went home and announced to her husband that she wanted a divorce. He said he was willing to work on the marriage, but Christine refused. "It's over," she told him, repeating what the counselor had said. She tore apart her young family, even though deep down she sometimes wondered whether the marriage could have been saved.

Another student, Bridget, told me, "I worked really hard on my marriage in couples counseling, but I felt hopeless that it would ever change, so I told my husband I wanted a divorce. At first he tried to talk me out of it, but then he became resigned to the situation. Now I've asked him if we can try to reconcile, but he refuses." After Bridget discovered the Six Intimacy Skills, it was devastating for her to realize that the hard work she had done was the wrong kind of work. "I can't accept that there's more I could have done to save my marriage," she told me, filled with grief. "It's just too painful." Bridget didn't get the help and information she needed, and it cost her dearly.

These stories are both real and representative of what I hear from women every day.

Marriage Counselors Are Marriage Cancelers

Of course, in any profession there are a few bad eggs—the mechanic who "fixes" what isn't broken, the plumber who overcharges for parts, the dentist who pushes expensive unnecessary treatments. Marriage counseling is no different: There are a few bad eggs out there who knowingly take advantage of their clients, but they make up only a small percentage of the people in the field. Most marriage counselors are good people who genuinely want to help. Unfortunately, it ultimately doesn't matter whether your counselor's intentions are good or bad; the entire premise underlying marriage counseling is destructive in my experience.

For one thing, there is no respectful way to complain about your husband in front of a stranger. No matter how carefully you word your grievances, you will still be putting down the man you chose to marry in front of someone who doesn't know him, while he sits there and listens. I'm guessing you wouldn't feel especially warm and open after hearing him outline your shortcomings, either. It's humiliating and adversarial. That's the very opposite of creating the emotional safety that intimacy needs to thrive.

The results we're collectively getting from marriage counseling tell the story: Marriage is down. Divorce is up. In most developed countries, the chances of having long-term marital success are only as good as the chances of getting tails on a coin flip. One law firm that specializes in divorce refers to marriage counselors as "marriage cancelers," because so many of their clients are fresh from the office of a marriage and family therapist or psychologist.

You might argue that marriage counselors have a nearly impossible job, because by the time a couple arrives in the professional's office, the marriage is already broken. You might think it's too late to save most relationships when there's so much hurt, blame, and anger built up. But my experience is that almost all marriages are completely fixable, no matter how long the couple has been separated and no matter how hopeless it seems. I see marriages come back to life after one or both parties have filed for divorce. I see women who came to me skeptical and believing their husbands would never be able to meet their needs return smiling to gratefully admit that the Six Intimacy Skills really did work. Even affairs, mental illness, and addiction have proven no match for the power of a committed wife armed with the Six Intimacy Skills and the support and encouragement to implement them.

There are proven, practical ways to turn your marriage into the one you've always wanted, even if it's been dead for years. But most marriage counselors don't know them. Marriage counseling often focuses on your partner's weaknesses. This book will show you how to focus on your strengths and feminine gifts instead.

If you're a marriage counselor or therapist, I know you and I are on the same team: We want to cultivate and support stronger, happier marriages. The fact that you're reading this tells me that you're open to new ideas and always looking for ways to better serve your clients and help them achieve success. I admire that. I invite you to train with me to explore the Six Intimacy Skills in depth and learn how to share them with those who come to you with troubled relationships. If you're ready to deliver more effective results, visit the "Become a Coach" tab at lauradoyle.org. You won't be the first marriage counselor to join the ranks of our certified relationship coaches.

Of course, you don't have to be a marriage counselor or a psychologist to join our team of coaches. Most of our coaches are regular women who were so inspired by their own relationship transformation that they felt driven to help other women have the same experience. We have coaches in North America, Europe, Asia, and Australia, and we're training new ones every year. No matter where you are, I invite you to join our mission to make your relationship more intimate, make your work more inspiring and effective, and end world divorce.

Is Marriage to an Addict, Abuser, or Adulterer Tolerable or Terminal?

As a relationship coach, almost every day I hear from a woman who is in excruciating pain and on the verge of divorce because her husband is having an affair and refuses to end it.

Or his chronic, excessive drinking has put her over the edge, and she is afraid of what the kids are seeing.

Or even because there is physical abuse in their home.

There was a time when I would have urged every one of these women to leave. I wrote as much in my first book.

I presumed I knew what a woman in one of these situations should do—as if I were the expert on her life.

Only I'm not.

Here's the problem with what I wrote about husbands who are actively addicted, physically abusive, or chronically unfaithful: I said, *If your husband is not one of those, he's a good guy*—which implies that those I singled out are *bad* guys.

One of my coaches called me on this. She explained that her husband identified as an alcoholic and had setbacks from time to time with his sobriety, but it didn't make him a bad guy.

I couldn't argue with that. Of course her husband was a good guy; she wouldn't have married him otherwise.

Here's what I didn't want to admit about marriages to addicts, abusers, or adulterers:

I chose my fear over my faith.

When I was suffering in my marriage and thinking seriously about ending it, I believed our challenges were insurmountable.

I was wrong. And I saw firsthand that even marriages that seemed beyond saving could be saved by practicing the Six Intimacy Skills.

But my husband was not physically abusive or drinking excessively, nor has he ever been unfaithful. I had not lived through those particular hells, and those situations scared me.

So when I initially shared what I had learned to help other women, I defaulted to conventional wisdom about "deal breakers," wisdom that says no self-respecting woman should stay in a marriage to a "bad" man—an addict, abuser, or adulterer.

I made one exception, and that was for abuse that was verbal and/or emotional.

I knew that wasn't insurmountable because I'd experienced it myself. My husband and I stopped saying terrible, hurtful things to each other once I learned the Intimacy Skills—and I saw lots of other marriages where verbal abuse completely cleared up thanks to the Intimacy Skills as well.

So, whenever I heard a woman talking about this particular challenge, I felt safe expressing my conviction that her relationship could be magical again.

In other words, when it came to verbal abuse, I was able to choose my faith over my fear.

But I am not the expert on your life—you are. So if you feel that your marriage challenge *is* insurmountable or makes life unlivable, I absolutely trust that you know what's best for you.

And it is only logical that I extend that same trust in the other direction, which is why I never should have presumed to tell women married to alcoholics, physical abusers, or chronic cheaters whether *their* challenges were unsurmountable.

That was arrogant and bossy of me, and I regret it.

But, as it happens, lots of women ignored me on that point anyway.

As a result, I've had the honor of hearing the stories of courageous women who were married to alcoholics, physical abusers, or cheaters but used the Six Intimacy Skills to heal their marriages.

There was the woman who used the Spouse-Fulfilling Prophecy with her alcoholic husband, who subsequently (and to her amazement) quit drinking as she repeated what felt like a bold-faced lie: that he "didn't drink much."

Then there was the young wife devastated by her husband's affair.

"People told me that I would never be able to trust him again, but I now know that's a lie. I trust him because I decided to trust him, and he's living up to that trust I give him," she told me.

Another wife explained that it wasn't until she stopped focusing on the other woman that her husband's mistress disappeared from their lives and he turned his affection and attention back to her.

And this week, a wife—who once separated from her husband because she believed he was both physically abusive and an alcoholic—confessed to me that, back then, she had been looking for an excuse to leave him.

She found her excuse when he was drunk, and she pulled out her phone to videotape him so that later she could show him how stupid he was being. Her husband hurt her hand wresting the phone from her to smash it to bits.

It was bad behavior, by any measure. But now that they have reconciled, she says she would use neither "alcoholic" nor "physically abusive" to describe her supportive, hardworking, thoughtful husband.

He's the same guy. Though she no longer calls him an alcoholic, it isn't because he gave up alcohol, but because she now feels safe and connected in her marriage.

If you are one of the millions of women facing challenges like these, and you want to preserve your family by working to make your marriage vibrant again, I'm here to offer you hope that you can do just that.

I've seen it happen too many times to doubt it.

Of course, *safety still comes first*. If you believe you are not safe or that your children are not safe, then please know I support you in becoming safe, whatever that looks like for you.

I'm not suggesting that women with abusive, alcoholic, or adulterous husbands should just suck it up. Not at all.

I'm simply allowing for the real possibility that even these challenges can be resolved as tender, connected marriages arise in their place. Nothing more, nothing less.

I am choosing faith over fear.

When my fear arises, I question it. I tear it down by gathering evidence to the contrary.

So even though I feel some fear about coming out in favor of *all* women who want to use the Six Intimacy Skills to save their marriages— including those married to alcoholics, cheaters, or physical abusers— I've decided to focus on how many have already come forward after successfully turning what once seemed like a nightmare into the relationship of their dreams.

They've paved the way for thousands more to create the marriages they've always wanted—with the men they chose in the first place.

You Can't Work on Your Relationship

So, let's get down to business. In reading this book, I'm asking you to set aside everything you think you know about relationships. That's what I did, back when my marriage felt hopelessly broken and I went looking for answers. I won't lie—it wasn't easy.

I started asking women who had been married for a long time about their secrets for a happy marriage, and their answers were like nothing I had ever heard. Their advice didn't even make sense to me at first.

One woman told me that she tried never to criticize her husband, no matter how much it seemed that he deserved it. That was a new one for me, and I was sure I could never manage such a thing. Another woman said it was a huge relief for her that her husband handled all the finances for them both. As a career woman and a feminist, I couldn't fathom that working for me, either. I asked them both, "Have you got anything else?"

Other advice I got was less dramatic but still hard to swallow. I couldn't see, for instance, how focusing on my husband's strengths instead of his shortcomings wasn't "giving up," or how calling a girlfriend instead of arguing wasn't being dishonest. But over time, desperation won out and I decided I was ready to give their suggestions a try. After all, I reasoned, I didn't have anything to lose. I told myself I could experiment, and if something didn't work, I'd just throw it out. Through this process of trial and error, I began to see that when I took certain approaches, I reliably found myself enjoying greater intimacy and connection with my husband. I also saw that when I reverted back to my old, well-worn habit of trying to improve him through constructive criticism...well, let's just say the results of my little marriage experiment were very convincing.

For the first time, I saw a pattern that had eluded me. I had been convinced that my husband was being actively stubborn or distant or lazy, but as I experimented with these new approaches, I came to see that many of his actions were simply *re*actions to what I said and did. All at once, the consequences of my old approach were clear, as though I had on a new pair of glasses. And while I didn't think I'd been such a bad wife, it was startling to realize how much of the conflict and tension in our marriage had been my own doing. By applying these insights, I gained a new way of looking at the problems in my marriage—and a new means of solving them. Instead of feeling like a victim of my husband's lack of interest or hostility, I felt empowered to make my relationship what I wanted it to be. Instead of complicated and tedious, that relationship began to seem simple and straightforward. I could see the causes and the effects, and I was able to use my newfound skills to make our marriage sweet, playful, and passionate. My husband transformed back into the man I fell in love with.

I was astonished to learn that there's no such thing as "working on your relationship." There's only working on yourself—and then your relationship improves. No matter what he was doing or not doing, the Six Intimacy Skills I'd developed showed me how to trust and respect my mere mortal husband, which felt surprisingly good. As I practiced the Intimacy Skills, I became more dignified, humble, and grateful.

I Had the Power All Along

Because we haven't gotten into the details yet, your mind may be running wild, but don't get the wrong idea: The Six Intimacy Skills aren't about bending over backward to cater to your husband's every whim. If anything, I was spending *less* time thinking about my husband and *more* time thinking about my own needs and desires. My husband, in turn, found me irresistible. This was the surprising pathway to becoming a wife whose husband can't do enough to make her happy—from putting gas in my car to telling me how beautiful I am.

I didn't recognize the empowerment in the Intimacy Skills at first because it came disguised as accountability. Where I had previously looked to my husband to do the things that I believed would improve our relationship, practicing the Six Intimacy Skills meant looking only at what *I* could do differently. It meant being willing to suspend long-held beliefs about the way I thought things should be and to take an uncomfortably unfamiliar approach to our conversations. I began to take responsibility for my own behavior and the damage I was doing, no matter how justified I felt in screeching, nagging, or rolling my eyes. I reluctantly found the humility to admit that I don't always know what's best, even when I think I do.

I felt terrible when I realized how much I was doing to squash the emotional connection in my home, especially because at first I couldn't figure out how to stop. But being accountable for what I was bringing to the table was also exciting, because it meant I was no longer helpless and hopeless. Blaming my husband for being defective and believing that he just "wasn't good at relationships" may have consoled me in my loneliness, but it never matched the thrill of having butterflies in my stomach again, or the return of passion and playfulness. Focusing only on what I could control showed me that I had more power than I'd ever dreamed.

When you practice the Six Intimacy Skills, your relationship will begin to feel easy and fun again. You are going to feel more like yourself, and you'll like yourself more. (And watch how quickly the chores get done, *without* having to remind your husband to do them.) But I know that at first it can feel like walking off a cliff. Making the choice to set aside everything you think you know about relationships in general—and your relationship in particular—can be scary. It means looking inward, giving up your long list of accumulated resentments, and trying something new. But I know you won't regret it—it's been more than twenty years now, and I never have.

CHAPTER 2

Wives, Marriage Is Up to You

There's Nothing Wrong with You or Him

I am not saying that no one should ever get help with her marriage from an expert. Just having someone listen and acknowledge your painful situation can be a huge relief. But instead of assuming that you're well and just looking to improve your skills in the area of relationships, marriage counseling often assumes there is something wrong with one or both of you. A counselor may be trained to ask if you come from a dysfunctional family, or to look for an undiagnosed mental health condition, or to address your inner child. Those kinds of conversations may *feel* productive, and they can certainly be interesting. However, based on my experience and the experiences of thousands of students, those conversations don't get you to happily-ever-after as effectively as learning the skills that contribute to connection in intimate relationships. Rather than therapy, a more modern approach is to get relationship coaching from someone who has had the transformation herself. You may think I'm just using slightly different terminology, but counseling and coaching are definitely not the same.

How Marriage Counseling Is Different from Relationship Coaching

Marriage Counseling	Relationship Coaching
Assumes there is something wrong with you that needs to be fixed or medicated	Assumes you want to become proficient in nurturing intimacy
Focuses on the problem	Focuses on the solution
Provided by someone who has achieved academic (theoretical) mastery	Provided by someone who has had a personal transformation and enjoys the benefits of having the desired skills
Explores past hurts	Provides specific actions for the present and future
For men, women, and couples	For women only
Promotes blaming the other person or parents	Promotes personal accountability
Invites you to say hurtful things in front of your husband and a stranger	Promotes emotional safety and respect
Talk-oriented	Action-oriented

Until very recently, there hasn't been anywhere to go when you needed relationship help except marriage counseling. It's not like there's an option to take "Relationships 101" at school. So where do you go to learn the skills that contribute to an intimate, passionate, peaceful relationship?

That's what this book is all about: a new perspective and a new way of approaching your relationship.

I am *not* talking about learning how to suck it up and stay in an unhappy marriage year after year. As women, we want and deserve to be cherished, desired, protected, and adored for life. The point of learning the Six Intimacy Skills is to make your relationship so sweet and satisfying that it wouldn't even *occur* to you to go to marriage counseling—much less get divorced.

The "Worst Relationship Advice of the Week" Award

The reason I can confidently say that marriage counseling is downright dangerous is because once you know the Six Intimacy Skills, you'll see that the prevailing wisdom of marriage counseling is the *opposite* of what actually fosters intimacy, trust, and connection.

To be fair, it's not just the counselors who are confused. The wrongheaded messages are everywhere. This makes me furious and sad because I still remember what it was like when I was confused, hurting, and lonely in my marriage. I still remember putting bad advice into action only to find myself even more miserable and hopeless. I remember dismissing or not recognizing good advice because it sounded so contrary to the conventional wisdom I heard over and over again.

Now I go out of my way to jab at popular relationship advice for the purpose of pointing out that:

- *Only people with good marriages have valuable advice on how to have a good marriage. A diploma is no guarantee that someone has a good relationship.*
- *Divorce is not inevitable or random. Most divorces are unnecessary and result from lack of training.*
- *A warm, tender, passionate relationship isn't just a matter of luck— it's a matter of learning the skills that contribute to intimacy.*
- *Women have much more influence over the culture and happiness of a relationship than men do.*
- *No matter how you spin it, divorce is not just "part of life" but a failure and a tragedy for everyone concerned. A few are necessary, but most are not.*
- *Any woman can learn and practice these skills to have the intimate, passionate, peaceful relationship she deserves.*

There Is No *Groom Magazine*

Marriage and relationships are up to women—when and if they happen and whether they're fun and connected or stressful and distant.

It's all up to us. It's also within our power to make them the gratifying unions we crave.

Women think about, dream about, and agonize about marriage from an early age. We play bride, we play house, and as we grow up, we talk a lot about boys and our relationships with them.

When we're old enough to date or marry, we have the power position because we are the ones who audition suitors for the part of our boyfriend. As women, we're all magnets for men, and it's the men who must take the risk of pursuing us if they want the opportunity to impress us. Then we get to accept or reject them as we see fit, the same way the director of a Broadway show would hire or reject dancers who want a part.

Women have a lot of power right from the beginning, and it continues for the duration of the relationship.

We're also more willing to walk away from our marriages. Surprisingly, wives initiate two-thirds of all divorces, and among college-educated women, as high as 90 percent of them according to a study reported in the *American Law and Economics Review*. In any negotiation, the person who's willing to walk away always has more power. When you're buying a car, if you walk off the lot during the negotiation, there's not much the car salesman can do to close the deal. The statistics suggest that women are constantly evaluating their husbands to determine if they are worthy, even after years of marriage.

Women Are the Sexier Sex

One of the reasons women are so powerful in intimate relationships is because we are the sexier sex. We're the ones with the fancy tail feathers. That's a big part of the reason men pursue us in the beginning: to have sex. Once we're in a sexual relationship with a man, we are still the gatekeepers of sex, because in general, men need sex more than women do.

But it's not just sex that gives us power. Men are driven to please women, to make them happy. Men feel successful as partners when their wives or girlfriends are happy and smiling. They not only want to do chivalrous things for us in order to make us smile, they also want the feeling of fulfillment they get from succeeding at bringing us joy.

It's also up to us if we will get married. When I meet a couple who's been together for years without ever saying "I do," I know that it's because *she* doesn't want to get married. She's content with just being boyfriend and girlfriend, because if she wasn't, she wouldn't be happy in the relationship, and then *he* wouldn't be very happy either, and something would have to give.

Most men are not commitment-phobic, but they seem that way to women who don't know how to use their power. Take the following couple, for example.

Paula was incredibly happy with her boyfriend of two years, but as they were thinking of moving in together, she realized that she couldn't kick her strong desire to be a wife, even though she and her boyfriend had each had two failed marriages already. She knew the topic would be a sore one, because she'd already brought the issue up: Before his second divorce was final, she had asked him if he would ever get married again. His answer was a swift and short no.

Still, Paula's desire was not going away, so two years later, she simply presented the facts to her boyfriend: "I really want to be a wife," she said. "I'm the marrying kind, and I just know I would be so happy to be married."

Her boyfriend shocked and surprised her when he said, "I've been thinking about that lately. I don't have a good reason not to marry you. I just need some time to adjust to the idea." They were married a few months later.

By taking a different approach, Paula got a different response. The first time she brought up the topic, she was premature, asking what he was planning while he was still married to someone else. In the second scenario, she simply expressed her desire at the right time without trying to manipulate or control the outcome.

Naturally, her boyfriend wanted her to be happy, and when he didn't feel controlled or pressured, that desire to make her happy took precedence over his previous reservations.

Paula held the key in her relationship. For two years she thought her boyfriend was a commitment-phobe. When she used her gift—the feminine gift of expressing pure desire without control or manipulation—she was happy to find that she was wrong.

As women, we always have this power, right from the start and right up to the end.

Your Man Is No Exception

If you don't see evidence of your man being eager to please you, that doesn't mean he's an exception. It may mean that he feels like he *can't* please you, or didn't get the message about how he could please you, or has been busy defending himself against your inadvertent control or complaints, which he hears as criticism instead of instructions about how to please you.

This was the case with Ellen, who thought her husband was lazy and insensitive. One of the things that drove her nuts was that when she came home with the groceries, he didn't offer to help bring them in. She would sigh in exasperation and mutter about carrying everything herself, but her husband stayed planted on the couch and barely responded to her.

After learning the Six Intimacy Skills, Ellen took a different approach. When her husband happened to carry a bag in, she mentioned how much she loved that.

"You do?" he said, perking up. She assured him that it made her very happy. The next time she came home with groceries, he ran out to the garage and told her to go in and relax while he carried them all in.

Now Ellen and her husband have a new routine: She calls him when she's leaving the store, and he's there waiting for her in the garage when she comes home so he can bring in all the groceries while she goes inside to relax. He's proud to make his wife happy, and she feels well taken care of. Everybody wins.

That's just one example of the thousands I've heard from our students about the lengths men will go to for the delight of their wives.

This was quite a culture shift for Ellen's relationship, which had previously been filled with bickering and conflict. Now she feels cherished and taken care of, in this area and many others. Ellen wrote me to say, "I believe in ghosts, astrology, and the afterlife, but I *never* believed I would feel so happy to be married to my husband!"

Even if it's not evident to you now that your man would be happy to do thoughtful things for you, I'm willing to bet that he is, and that you've got the power to create the same kind of relationship Ellen enjoys—once you learn how.

I'll explain what the feminine gifts are and how to benefit from them in the next chapter.

Take My Husband—Please!

Recently we got a call from a woman named Alison who wanted to set an appointment for herself and her husband. When she heard we only coach women—not couples or men—she asked if we had anyone who does see couples. One of our senior coaches asked why she preferred being coached as a couple, and Alison answered, "Because the problem in our relationship is my husband. *He's* the one who needs to change."

That's what I once thought too. And nearly every woman whose marriage is in trouble feels the same way.

Deanna was sure that her husband was the one making things so tense and distant between them. They were separated under the same roof, barely speaking to each other for eight years despite raising five kids together. She was sure there was nothing she could do to end the cold war. When I asked her if she wanted to regain the connection in her marriage, she shrugged reluctantly. "I don't see how that's going to happen because it's not up to me," she said. When I asked her again if it was what she wanted, she hesitated and fidgeted, but finally agreed that yes, she did want to have a husband again and not just a silent, brooding roommate who slept in the guest room.

"But what can I do about it?" she asked.

"Have you thought about letting your husband know that you miss him?" I asked.

"I couldn't do that," she said unequivocally.

"Why is that?" I asked.

"It's just too awkward," she told me. "You have no idea what my husband is like!"

"You're right, I don't," I agreed. "But I do know this: His wife misses him on some level, and that might be helpful information for him to have if you're ever going to have intimacy, passion, and ease again. And it sounds like you *want* that."

Deanna reluctantly agreed that she did want that, but she still didn't want to deliver the three-word message: "I miss you."

When I probed further, she admitted, "It feels scary, and I'm a big chicken."

I could understand why she was scared. The message I suggested was a vulnerable one and left her open to the possibility of further rejection.

"Well, if you're okay with the way things are now—" I started to say, but she interrupted me.

"Can I write him a note?" she asked.

"It's a start," I agreed.

It took her a few days to deliver that note, which turned out to be the beginning of a slow dance of reconciliation between Deanna and her husband.

There was no obvious response when he got the note, but when he saw her he smiled at her for the first time in a long time. Then there were more notes, then they spoke, and a few months later she emailed to tell me they were fully reunited.

> Thank you for getting me over the hump, challenging me to become vulnerable (even though I thought I already WAS being vulnerable—WRONG!). And thanks for encouraging me to not ever give up...and assuring me of the possibility of regaining our lost love affair. David and I are still enjoying the newness of wanting to make the other feel loved (me), respected (him), and cherished (both!). I can't thank you enough. I'm looking forward to the mistletoe this year!

It was only once Deanna decided to use her feminine gifts to heal her marriage that a dead relationship came back to life. That's because she had been holding the power to reconcile all along. Her husband never stopped wanting to make her happy, but he didn't see his opening, and he didn't feel successful as a husband until she gave him that first tender message.

Relationships thrive or struggle, rise or fall, are easy or hard based on the wife and her skill level. You may have been taught, as I was, that marriage is 50/50, or even 100/100. But it wasn't until I became aware of my enormous power as a wife and how to use that power—the way I did when we were dating—that I started to enjoy the kind of playful, connected, sweet romance I'd had then and that I'd always craved.

Ready to learn the skills you need to make that happen in your marriage? Let's dig in.

Replenish Your Spirit with Self-Care

This skill is about recognizing that only you can make yourself happy, and that your happiness doesn't depend on your husband. If you devote yourself to your own enjoyment and delight, you'll not only have more reserves to deal with everyday upsets, you'll also become more attractive and pleasant so that you start to resemble the woman your husband fell in love with. Plus, you'll be happier!

Make tending to your own happiness a part of your daily routine, which will give your marriage the chance to be gratifying.

PRESCRIPTION

Make a list of at least twenty things that you enjoy doing just because they make you happy. This is not a list of things you feel you *should* be doing, but things that delight you. The more frivolous the better!

Carve out time to do three things from your list tomorrow, the next day, and every day after that, both to make yourself happy and to focus your energy on what you can control: yourself.

CHAPTER 3

You Are Not a Smaller, Less Hairy Man

"I spent my young adult years postponing many of the small things that I knew would make me happy. I was fortunate enough to realize that I would never have the time unless I made the time. And then the rest of my life began."

—Dr. Chris Peterson, Author, Professor, and Cofounder of Positive Psychology

Your Birthright as a Woman

My whole life, I was taught that men and women are the same. Sure, there are some obvious physical differences, but I believed those were superficial. I pretended that biology didn't affect my mind and spirit. I also denied that I had any special gifts as a woman—as if the world and I would be just fine without acknowledging those gifts.

To me, it was vital that men and women be the same, because I thought that was how it had to be for us to have equal opportunity in the world. I was also angry when anyone said I was different than a man. How dare they!

That's embarrassing to think about because I couldn't have been more wrong. That sort of thinking seems so old-fashioned to me now! I've relegated it to the "It seemed like a good idea at the time" column, along with preparing for a nuclear attack by hiding under a desk.

Fortunately, the idea that men and women are the same is not the prevailing wisdom anymore. There are books on how to market to women (because their buying habits are different from men's and they do most of the spending), how women manage employees differently than men, how having women's input affects investment portfolios (better returns than portfolios with only men's input), and how female brains are hardwired differently than male brains.

It turns out that sameness isn't important in the workplace anyway. Women have demonstrated that we're capable and professional, but we bring different strengths and a different culture with us to work. Of course we do—we're not smaller, less-hairy men; we're an entirely different gender. And admitting that doesn't mean we lose; my experience has been just the opposite. Tuning in to and exercising my feminine gifts has been exciting and gratifying and has provided a sense of ease and relief that I was missing before I discovered the skills and applied them in my relationship and at work.

The Gifts of the Feminine

We're all a unique mix of feminine and masculine characteristics to varying degrees, of course. But there are some big advantages to being a woman that have been downplayed over the past fifty years. Here are some things that I sort of knew but didn't fully understand or embrace about my power as a woman:

1. Magnetism

We are the sexier sex, which means we get to enjoy the power of feeling desired and pursued.

2. Emotional Brilliance

We're better at identifying and expressing our emotions, which is vital for creating long-term commitment.

3. Receptivity

We deserve special treatment, and men like to give it to us—if we let them.

4. Pleasure

We have the only organ on the human body created *expressly for pleasure*. Which tells me that female pleasure is pretty important—and I don't mean just sexual pleasure, although that's important too.

5. Desire

Because men want us to be happy and our pleasure is very important, our desires are a powerful force in the world and often serve as the North Star by which a couple navigates.

The Power of a Woman's Pleasure

I'm always encouraging every woman to "tend to her own pleasure," which means focusing time and effort on activities (or non-activities, in some cases) that make you feel good. I'm not talking about things you feel you *should* do, but things you are drawn to just for the fun of it. Only you know what that means for you, so your self-care list will be unique.

I know that yoga is good for me. It helps with flexibility and strength, and people who practice it have beautiful bodies. But I don't *like* doing yoga. I find it tedious and boring, and no one keeps score, so where's the fun in that? I might decide to do yoga (rarely), but it wouldn't count as tending to my pleasure. Sure, doing it means caring for my body, but I'm not drawn to that activity the way a child is drawn to a swing or a ball.

This is the difference: Doing something pleasurable means it feels good in the moment you're doing it, not afterward. Some activities may be both. For me, volleyball on the beach is both super fun while I'm doing it *and* makes me feel healthy and strong after I've stopped sweating and breathing heavily. I happen to get health advantages from that particular pleasure, but many things on my list have no such fringe benefits and are *only* beneficial because they *make me happy in the moment.* Talking to my sisters on the phone, for instance, or singing in harmony, getting a facial, listening to my favorite podcasts, lazing on the couch and watching a movie, or having coffee with a girlfriend. None of those things improve my aerobic capacity, help prevent diabetes, reduce greenhouse emissions, or declutter my house. They simply give me pleasure, which puts me in a good mood. That's reason enough for me to make sure that I spend time doing those things—three of them, at least—every day.

In my early days as a relationship coach, I used to say that an activity counted as self-care as long as it made you feel good afterward, but I've changed my position on that—now it has to feel good *in the moment*. The reason for my reversal was my student Marni.

When I suggested to Marni that she make a list of things that bring her pleasure and plan to do at least three a day, she agreed to try it. But when I checked in with her the following week and asked her what she had done for self-care that day, she said, "I folded a basket of laundry, which made me feel good because it was bugging me."

There's no way folding laundry should qualify as self-care.

Yes, checking things off your to-do list makes you feel good and accomplished, but let's face it: the laundry was going to get done eventually anyway. It was a stretch to say that it brought her pleasure or delight.

In reality, Marni didn't think it did either, but it was taking a lot of focus for her to switch from always taking care of everyone else to really focusing on her own pleasure. She felt she didn't really have the time, given all her other responsibilities, to get out the art supplies and paint, or have lunch with a girlfriend instead of at her desk. So when I asked her about it, she punted and said she folded laundry. Nice try, Marni. But no dice.

Housework is not and never will be self-care. Not like singing and dancing, or going to a party, or getting a massage, or sneaking off to read, or having a piece of chocolate and coffee—whatever it is that gives you that happy lift.

Self-Care Expands Your Time

After a few weeks, Marni was doing a lot better at finding time to do pleasurable things, and a funny thing happened. She told me her time had expanded.

"What do you mean 'expanded'?" I asked her.

"I mean that I have enough time to get everything done *and* enough time for self-care too," she said, "which seemed impossible to me before when every second was taken up. The only explanation is that my time has somehow expanded."

Marni isn't the only one who has had that experience. Many of our students report the same phenomena, and I've noticed it myself too. It may sound a little nutty, but isn't it true that when you start work relaxed and happy, you get more done? Whereas when you're frazzled and stressed, you get next to nothing done because you're so depleted already.

Have you ever had the experience of being so slammed that you feel hopeless before you even start? Me too. But a fresh pedicure, or a quick walk around the block, or even laughing at a cat video for a minute can go a long way toward restoring my can-do point of view. When my energy and attitude are positive, I get more done. Or, as Marni put it, my time expands.

Therefore, to have more time, be able to do what you enjoy, *and* be a responsible person who gets her work done, start by taking a bubble bath. Unless you don't find that enjoyable, in which case you can go mountain-biking, or gab with your mom on the phone, or knit a scarf.

Or do yoga if you like it. I understand some people do.

Plan Pleasure First

Does that seem impractical or unrealistic to you? That's what I thought too. I'm actually a big fan of practical, and it turns out that pleasure planning *is* a very practical thing for a woman to do. The indispensable first step to having a great relationship is to make yourself happy by practicing self-care.

This may sound pretty obvious when I say it that way, but it wasn't obvious to me when I was newly married to John. I thought it was *his* job to make me happy. Don't ask me where I got that idea, but I was convinced of it. So instead of thinking, "I'm not very happy, what should I do about it?" I thought, "I'm not happy and it's because he's not making me happy." I imagined that I would be happy if he would just do what I wanted him to—or if I had gotten married to somebody else.

It turns out my happiness doesn't depend on my husband, and I wouldn't have been any happier with the next guy. Here's what I've learned: If I make myself happy, if I'm smiling and relaxed and enjoying myself, John responds to me by looking for ways to make me even happier.

I also see this with my students every day. Marilyn's experience is one of the more entertaining examples. She began practicing the Six Intimacy Skills, starting with self-care, in order to save her marriage. Shortly thereafter, she received flowers at work from her husband, who hadn't sent her flowers in years. They came with a card that said: WIFE POINTS BONUS ALLOCATION.

He also sent her the following text:

Congratulations on your reward from your wife points bonus scheme. We'd like to update you on why we feel you deserve this reward:

- *Lovely wife-like behavior*
- *No bipolar mood swings*
- *Distinct lack of shoutyness*
- *General kind, friendly attitude toward husband.*

Well done once again and thank you for your dedication to the loyalty scheme.

Marilyn emailed me a screenshot of the text and added: "P.S.: You saved my marriage. Thank you!"

That's just one example of the many I hear from women who put their own pleasure first. It's hard to argue with the results, and why would you want to?

I practice self-care religiously. Sometimes I disappear in the afternoon for a catnap. Nobody looks for me Saturday morning because everybody knows I'll be playing volleyball on the beach with a smear of sand on my cheek and a gleam in my eye.

I put substantial time and energy into self-care, which used to make me feel guilty and uncomfortable. I notice that many of my students face the same challenge. One woman asked me to clarify whether it's still self-care if she dropped off a letter at the post office while she was on her walk, even though it was the endorphins and the change of scenery she was after. Another asked if playing games on her phone still counts as self-care even though she only spent ten minutes doing it.

There's just one measure of whether you're getting enough self-care: your state of mind. If you're grumpy, you haven't had enough. If you're feeling good, you're doing a great job. Only you know what's right for you, but whenever you're finding fault with your husband, consider checking to see if you've gotten some self-care in. Nothing is going to look right—including your marriage—until you do.

One more benefit to self-care—in addition to giving you the reserves you need to have a good relationship, signaling to your husband that you're pleaseable, and spending more time doing things you love—is that it teaches other people how to treat you. A woman who takes good care of herself sends out a signal that she enjoys being treated well. That's bound to give you more self-confidence as people begin to see you as a woman who is well taken care of.

Why We Man Up at Work

When I talk about feminine gifts, I want to be clear that I'm not talking about manipulation or taking advantage of anyone. Those are not qualities that anyone wants in a partner. I'm talking about simply relaxing into your femininity so that you naturally receive the pleasant things your man wants to give you.

In our efforts to be successful at work, we sometimes forget what it's like to be feminine, because part of success at work involves showing that you need no special treatment. At work, you want to show that you can pull your own weight.

I think of this managerial aspect of myself as my masculine side, and I'm grateful to have it, because it serves me well in business. But for a long time, I was so well-versed in and reliant on my masculine side that it obscured my feminine gifts, which are very powerful too. I found it difficult to switch out of that familiar work mode even once I *did* know about the gifts of the feminine. But I couldn't get all that I wanted in my relationship until I did, so I made a concerted effort. Today I'm more feminine both during *and* after work. In fact, all of the Six Intimacy Skills have contributed to making me more effective and successful professionally, as has the inner strength I get from having a great marriage.

But my goals at work are very different from my goals in my marriage. At work, I want to satisfy my clients, produce results, and improve the bottom line. With my husband, I want to snuggle, laugh, and share my hopes and dreams. I want his face to light up when I walk into the room, and I want to feel desired. Those are completely different goals, and they require a completely different skill-set to attain.

If you're in a job where you're mostly wearing a suit of armor for forty hours a week and you find you have difficulty taking it off to become your softer self when the workday's done, you're not alone. Welcome to the modern woman's challenge! But you don't have to be stuck in that suit of armor. There are some practical ways to peel it off and feel your own lightness and tenderness beneath.

Self-care is a great place to start. Right after work, consider a transition time that includes a few minutes of solitude, for instance. Maybe you'll sit in the car for a while and write in your journal, read, or just zone out and listen to music.

The point is to remind yourself of who you are and all that you want and deserve in your relationship. Showing up as the Girl of Fun and Light that you are will also remind your husband how good it feels to be the man who gets to desire, cherish, and adore the woman he loves.

CHAPTER 4

The More You Know What You Want, the Better

"It's a helluva start, being able to recognize what makes you happy."

—Lucille Ball, Actress, Comedian, and Film Studio Executive

The Embarrassing, True Story of My First Romantic Getaway

Before we were married, John and I went on vacation to Hawaii. We were still a new couple, and I had a big perm, but that's not the most embarrassing part of this story. The most embarrassing part is that I had no idea how to honor my desires or express them. As a result, I was cranky a lot.

We had just arrived on the island for our romantic getaway. It seemed to me that anybody in Hawaii would want to go to the beach because *hello!* We were in *Hawaii*. So we got up in the morning and instead of saying "I can't wait to hit the beach," I asked John, "What do you want to do today?"

I fully expected him to say, "Let's go to the beach."

Instead he said, "I'd like to check out the volcanoes."

Huh?

We'd only been dating for five months, and I was trying to be considerate because I thought that was what you should do to have a good relationship. So instead of saying, "Really? I want to hit the beach," I just said, "Okay."

That was my idea of being a good girlfriend: not telling him what I wanted because it was different than what he wanted. I figured if I expressed my desire, there would be a conflict because we wanted different things. I thought that meant there would have to be a winner and a loser. I didn't want a conflict; I wanted to stay close and connected. And I *had* asked him what he wanted to do, so it seemed rude to say I wanted to do something else.

This was not a good setup, because as we were driving around that hot day looking at all the boring molten rocks, I kept thinking about how we could have been on the beautiful beach playing in the waves. I started getting irritable, thinking about how it was all John's fault that I was stuck in the car. I thought about what a sacrifice I was making for him and how he hadn't even asked *me* what *I* wanted to do. I started to fume and sigh and roll my eyes. Finally he asked me what was wrong, and I let it all out—not in a nice way.

"Why are we looking at ugly rocks when we're in Hawaii and we could be playing in the waves on the beach?" I shrieked. "What's so exciting about looking at stupid volcanoes? Who would even want to do that? Did you think this would be fun? Because I don't! I think it's a huge waste of time!"

I was in a full-blown rage over not getting to go to the beach, *even though I'd never said I wanted to go to the beach*. The poor guy couldn't figure out where he'd gone wrong. He never had a chance.

I know this brings up a lot of questions about how I ever managed to get married, because later when we were reflecting on the trip and laughing about this incident, John told me that my face turned all red and my big hair was sticking up so that I looked like a crazy person. He got to see a volcano all right—just not the kind he'd been expecting.

We did go to the beach right after that (even after the scene I'd caused, John still wanted to make me happy), but I didn't much enjoy it. I felt awful after using that shrill voice and working myself into hysterics. I remember apologizing over and over and asking him if he was mad, if he still liked me, if he forgave me. I had lost my dignity. It was really unpleasant and unattractive, even to me.

It was also terrifying, because I knew that I might drive him away by acting like that, and then I'd be alone. I didn't even want to be around myself when I sounded like that.

The First Step to Making Yourself Happy Is Knowing What You Want

I feel sad for that younger version of me who couldn't figure out how to say what she wanted without making a demand, having an expectation, or starting a fight. Since I didn't say anything about my desires, I knew I wasn't going to get them, and that was frustrating. But just shoving my desires to the side and then exploding later was not a good strategy. Each time I did, it chipped away not only at the intimacy between us, but also at my dignity when my desperate feelings came out sideways.

Now that I know how to honor and express my desires without expectation, demand, or manipulation, I'm less likely to ask someone else what he wants without first turning that question to myself. What do *I* want?

I even keep a list.

When I first discovered the Six Intimacy Skills, I started writing down my desires nearly every day. Now it's a habit. I've kept it up for two decades because I consider my list essential to my happiness, which is essential to having a happy relationship. Plus, it's awfully fun to dream and think about what I want for a few minutes every day.

I update my list frequently because my desires are always changing. That's my prerogative as a woman—to change my mind. I keep updating my list so I've got my finger on the pulse of what I want.

You may have some resistance to the suggestion that you focus on your desires every single day. For one thing, you may be wondering how we got so far off topic. Aren't we supposed to be talking about how to have a better relationship? You might think I'm not getting that you're in an unhappy marriage and that until that changes you won't be happy. Maybe the thing you want most is a happy marriage, and that would be at the top of your list of desires.

That was what I wanted too, for years. But I also wanted a new bed, a weekend getaway to Palm Springs, a pedicure, a tougher volleyball serve, to work from home, to remodel the kitchen, a girls' night out, and time to read with a cup of tea. Until I turned my attention to the things I wanted, my marriage continued to flounder. That's partly because I thought it was my husband's job to make me happy. When I was unhappy, I thought it was because he wasn't making me happy.

I had it all wrong. I was unhappy because *I* wasn't making myself happy. I hadn't been tuning in to the subtle marching orders my soul was giving me. Instead of honoring even a simple desire—that I yearned to go for a walk on a crisp fall afternoon, for example—I'd make myself stay at my desk and get my work done because I thought that was the more responsible thing to do. Then I'd end the day frazzled and irritable. That's no way to have a happy marriage, which flows a lot better when you're in a good mood.

How to Figure Out What You Want

When I started turning my attention to my desires, it was pretty hard for me. At first I came up empty: I had no idea what I wanted. A lot of our students have the same problem. That's how far away we are from ourselves—we don't even know what we want!

But as I focused on my desires more, I realized that as soon as I thought of something I wanted, I almost always had an immediate thought about why I couldn't have it, which made me feel bad. I discovered that I had a habit of dismissing my desires before they even bubbled all the way to the surface because it was no fun to think about what I was never going to get. So instead of acknowledging a desire, I'd squelch it because I was sure I couldn't have it.

As you can imagine, that's not a very empowering approach to life. Here are a few examples of the depressing thought-loops I used to have:

Example #1:

My desire: "I want to live by the beach."

First thought: "We can't afford a house at the beach."

Conclusion: "We can never move and will be stuck in this house forever."

How I felt: Hopeless and stuck.

Example #2:

My desire: "I want to take Mondays off from work."

First thought: "My boss would never allow that."

Conclusion: "I have to keep working five days a week, which means work is going to keep draining me and taking up all my time and energy."

How I felt: Hopeless and stuck.

Example #3:

My desire: "I want to hit harder in volleyball."

My first thought: "I'm too short and don't jump very high or swing very hard."

Conclusion: "I'm stuck playing at the level I play now."

How I felt: You guessed it—hopeless and stuck.

No wonder I didn't want to think about my desires! It made me feel terrible.

It wasn't a very fulfilling way of thinking, but it all happened so fast that I didn't even realize what was going on. I just knew I felt hopeless and stuck...again. I don't even know how I got started dismissing my desires like that, but it was a well-worn habit that was not only keeping me from getting the things I wanted, it was hurting my marriage.

If only I had known how to stop and linger on the desires that were underneath my negative thoughts! That would have saved me years of being grumpy.

Your Desires Are Sacred Marching Orders

When I talk about honoring my desires, I don't necessarily mean that I always make them happen, although I do frequently get what I want these days. Honoring my desires simply means I *acknowledge* them, even if they seem impossible or impractical or that having them would make me lose something else I love. I admit my desires to myself. I tell them to other people. I write them on my list, no matter how outlandish.

Some of the benefits of this habit are:

- *Just entertaining the idea of the things I desire is fun, and it puts me in a better mood than dismissing them does.*
- *I can head toward my desire, trusting that it's leading me in an exciting and gratifying direction.*
- *Knowing what I want makes me feel passionate, which is an attractive quality. The world responds to passion and often rearranges so I get what I want.*
- *Some of my desires are pretty humble and easy to fulfill once I know what they are.*

One of our students, Katie, had a hard time seeing how honoring her desires would make any difference in her life. She and her husband worked together as business coaches, and as a result they were together almost all the time. She longed for some solitude—time to write in a journal or just stare out the window—but she had a hard time recognizing her desire.

Katie's pure desire: "I want some time to myself."

Her next thought: "I can't just tell my husband to go away and leave me alone, because that would be rude. I shouldn't have gotten married if I want to be alone so badly."

Therefore: "Because I'm married, I can never have any time to myself."

How she felt: Trapped and resentful.

As a result of this line of thinking, Katie's husband was getting on her very last nerve no matter what he did. His mere presence was a reminder that she could never have the solitude she craved.

During her coaching sessions, Katie had a hard time acknowledging that she wanted solitude, because she was afraid that her desire meant she wasn't cut out for marriage and that she'd made a mistake in saying "I do." She feared that admitting she longed to be alone would be the beginning of the end of her marriage.

But after weeks of me asking her about her desires and what she was doing for her own pleasure, Katie decided to give herself an entire weekend away from everyone, including her husband, for the purpose of being able to listen to her own voice. She booked a beach house an hour out of town and spent some great solitary time reading, contemplating, meditating, and refreshing her spirit. By the end of the weekend, she was eager to reconnect with the man she loved, who had been completely supportive of her taking the time she wanted.

In the weeks following, Katie's work life took off. She was more connected to her desire to help the businesses in her community prosper, and she planned and executed an industry event that made a powerful, lasting impact on the business community in her city. Katie described the feeling of empowerment that resulted from the process of honoring her desire for solitude as sweeping and thrilling. Every area of her life was improved once she began honoring her desires.

"That's nice for Katie," you might be thinking, "but I have kids and a job and a home to maintain. I could never take a weekend off." That's what Katie thought too. That's what I used to think. But we both discovered that honoring our desire is the first step to getting what we want.

So start by honoring your desire without jumping to any conclusions, even if you think it's totally impossible. Just give your desire its moment in the sun, and don't listen to the voices telling you it's impossible. Just say or write "I want _____," filling in whatever is true for you.

What If You Still Don't Know What You Want?

When you go to write your list of desires, you might come up empty at first. You may be tempted to skip this step. Maybe you think it's silly or pointless. Maybe you think you know what you want and don't need to spend time writing it down or talking about it. Maybe you've spent so long shutting down your own desires that you can't really hear them. Maybe you don't want to commit to a desire because you think you may change your mind. And you know what? You probably will. It's a woman's prerogative to change her mind. You can even have several contradictory desires at the same time if you want, and it won't hurt your intimacy a bit.

Here's another embarrassing story to show you what I mean.

John and I were packing to move to a house I was very excited about—the one by the beach that I had wanted. As I was packing, I started to get sad about leaving behind the purple hydrangeas in our front yard and the back patio where we had salsa danced during our anniversary party. When John asked me what was wrong, I said, "I don't want to leave our house!" and started crying.

John tried to make me happy. He said, "We can tell them that we don't want to buy the new house after all. We can stay here if you want."

"But I *want* to move to the new house!" I said.

At that point there wasn't much he could do for me, because my desires were totally contradictory! So he just patted me on the back and said "There, there." No harm, no foul. I got to say what I wanted and express my sadness, and he witnessed that for me. There was a nice connection between us despite the complete lack of reason on my part.

Sometimes we don't want to acknowledge what we want because we think the price will be too high or the disappointment of not getting it will sting too much. But I've found that it's actually more painful and disappointing to skip acknowledging the desire, and it's much more exciting and delightful to spend time thinking about it.

You may feel some resistance or fear about this, but don't worry—it gets easier with practice, and I've never yet had a student die from writing down her desires.

Here's my list of desires for today:

- *A hula hoop*
- *A clean garage*
- *To sleep in on Sundays*
- *To see a summer concert at an amphitheater*
- *A facial*
- *Sushi for lunch*
- *Two more coaches for the upcoming training*
- *A tougher volleyball serve*
- *To send my book proposal to my agent this week*
- *To go for a walk*

What's on your list? Write it on your phone or jot it in the margins of your book or on the napkin under your latte. Just write it down. You're going to need it for the next chapter when I show you how to express your desires in a way that inspires the man you married, even if it doesn't seem like he cares about what you want right now.

I will also explain why your desires are the North Star of your relationship: an important guide the two of you will use for navigation once you know how to honor them.

CHAPTER 5

Express Your Desires in a Way That Inspires

"You are a living magnet. What you attract into your life is in harmony with your dominant thoughts."

—Brian Tracy, Author and Motivational Speaker

Just Say the Words "I Would Love..."

Imagine if every time you expressed a desire to your husband, he started thinking about how he could delight you by meeting that desire. In this chapter is everything you need to inspire him to do just that.

Your husband really wants to make you happy. If you're wondering how I know that, it's because I've asked thousands of men how important it is to make their wives happy, and they all have the same answer: "It's *very* important."

If you think your man is an exception to this rule, it's likely that you haven't seen that side of him for a while because he's been so busy defending himself from inadvertent criticism, control, or disrespect. That's what I see over and over with our students. But when we wives clean up our side of the street by relinquishing control and being respectful of our guy (I'll explain exactly how to do that in Chapter 8), his desire to make us happy re-emerges stronger than ever.

After I became a relationship coach, I started to have even more respect and admiration for men because our students were constantly telling me sweet stories about their husbands doing chivalrous, romantic things for them. It became so obvious to me that men just want to make us women happy. What's not to love?

I'm willing to bet that your husband wants to make you happy too. If you're not convinced of this, I understand. I was skeptical myself at first. You won't know for sure until you experiment a little with the Six Intimacy Skills and see what happens. Here's the hypothesis to start with: You don't have to persuade, manipulate, argue, nag, or coerce him into doing something to make you happy, because he *already* wants to be your hero. He just needs to know what you want.

When you express your desires, you are giving your guy information that he needs to please you. You can't always get what you want—especially if, like me, you sometimes want two contradictory things at the same time. But when you acknowledge your desires out loud, it's definitely a step toward feeling cherished.

When I talk about expressing your desires purely—without expectation or manipulation—it doesn't mean that you have to figure out how to say them in a specific way so that he'll do what you want. You simply say what you would love, and then let go of the results. The way to express your desires is to simply say "I want…" or "I would love…" and fill in whatever appeals to you in that moment.

For example, instead of "Don't you want to have a big family?" you'd say, "I would love to have a big family." Instead of saying "We should try to get home early because we have to work tomorrow" (which is a nice way of telling him what to do), you could say, "I would love to get to bed early tonight."

Forget the "How" and Focus on the End Result

When you think about your desires, you may have in mind that they should be fulfilled in a certain way. But what if you got that new purse *not* because your husband got a bonus and bought it for you, but because he urged you to buy it for yourself with the tax refund? You still got the outcome you wanted, just not the way you thought it would happen.

Keeping your focus on the outcome, not how or when it happens, is key to expressing your desires in a way that inspires. Sometimes we confuse the message by saying more than we need to. As soon as you specify how something should happen, you squash the inspiration your husband naturally feels when he sees a chance to please his wife. When you tell him *how* to do what you want, your desire goes from being an opportunity for him to feel proud and accomplished to just another chore you've put on his to-do list.

When I first asked Patty to express her desire, she responded with, "I want my husband to get a better job." But that didn't really tell me what *she* wanted, because I didn't know how his better job would impact her. So I asked, "What would *you* get if your husband had a better job?" The answer was that she would have more money to spend. But money is not an end result either; it's just a means to something else we want: security, status, new shoes, a vacation, more free time. So I asked her what she would get if she had more money, and this time I got the real answer: "I would love some new clothes." Finally she was at an end result. She had taken her focus off of *how* it would happen.

Try to figure out what your end result is. Less is more with expressing desires. If it's something like "a change of scenery," "to feel accomplished," "a new coat," or "to work from home"—you've arrived at a pure desire. You'll know you're expressing a pure desire when it's an outcome without an expectation.

There Is No "You" in a Pure Desire

Another common pitfall with expressing your desires in a way that inspires is that often a woman is focused on what she wants her husband to do. She comes up with desires she wants *him* to fulfill, like, "I want you to spend more time with me" or "I want you to help with the housework."

The problem with these desires is that they have the word "you" in them, which immediately changes them from desires to commands. Commands diminish intimacy and lower your husband's motivation to pay attention to what would delight you.

Saying "I want you to spend more time with me" is not only a very thinly veiled complaint ("You don't spend enough time with me"), it's also a trap.

What you *really* want is for him to *want* to spend time with you. You want to feel *desired*. If you tell your husband you want him to spend more time with you and he does, you'll have that worrisome feeling that he's only doing it because you asked him to, not because he really *wants* to. You'll never get what you crave most that way. But if you resist saying it—even when the temptation is strong—then when he *does* come to you, you'll know it's because you're irresistible, and that feels amazing.

Of course, wanting your husband to spend more time with you is a desire, and it's important to honor your desires. But instead of saying it to your husband, which won't yield the result you want, consider bringing the desire to a friend and telling *her* that you want your husband to spend more time with you. That way you're still honoring the desire but aren't hurting your chances of getting what you really want. (I'll show you what to say to him for best results in Chapter 14.)

Let's take another example. Telling your husband "I want you to help with the housework" is not about having a clean house. It's about the process by which the house gets clean, which is that *he* has to do it. And within that is an underlying criticism that he doesn't help out with the housework enough. Now, instead of responding to your pure desire, your husband is busy defending himself against your complaint. He's likely to respond by reminding you that he vacuumed twice recently. This is not getting you any closer to what you want: a home free of dust bunnies.

When you find yourself tempted to express a desire with "you" in it, take a step back and ask yourself what end result you want most before you say it to your husband.

When I asked Sumaya what her desire was, she said it was for her husband to be logical when they fought. Since there's no respectful way to say "I want you to be logical when we fight," I asked her what *she* would get if he were logical when they fought. She thought for a moment and said, "I would get to win the argument!" and then she laughed, realizing that that particular desire probably wasn't worth the price of admission. I asked her to consider the outcome she was looking for in that situation, and what finally bubbled up for her was "I would love to have peace between us. I want to not fight at all." Her pure desire was both moving and inspiring.

Expressing Desire Always Works

When Jill decided to say to her husband, "I would love to cut back on my work hours because I want to be home with the kids more," she thought she was expressing a pure desire. But when we next met she told me, "It didn't work." I asked her what she meant, and she said her husband didn't respond to her desire by agreeing that she should cut back her work hours, so she felt justified in telling him that he didn't care at all about what she wanted.

But saying that expressing her desires "didn't work" told me that she had an expectation lurking underneath what sounded like a pure desire, which turned it into a demand, which her husband likely picked up on instantaneously. Husbands are smart like that.

Since she then insulted her husband for not getting on board with her desire, it appeared she was just trying to get her husband to see things her way. That's not the same as honoring your desires. In fact, that's the definition of an expectation or a demand: when you have a desire and you punish your partner for not delivering on it.

When Jill's husband didn't see things her way, she felt so hurt and disappointed that she was no longer motivated to be respectful or dignified.

I know how it is. I've done that too. But once I learned the difference between a pure desire and a demand, I started to see my husband really respond with enthusiasm at the possibility of making me happy.

Expressing desires is completely within your control, and whether you get the desire or not, honoring it with your words always "works." You may not always get what you want, but you always get to *honor* what you want, which is the same as honoring yourself.

Tess experienced this firsthand when she discovered the Intimacy Skills and learned about Relationship Coach Training. After attending my masterclass on the training, she was excited about the idea of becoming a coach, so she made an appointment to talk to Coach Kathy about the possibility of enrolling.

But on that call, Tess realized that if she was going to take the course, she would have to talk to her husband about the investment, and she felt she couldn't do that. So she apologized to Coach Kathy for taking up her time and said she was not going to enroll after all.

Coach Kathy asked Tess what was stopping her from talking to her husband about the investment, and Tess said that she had done some other professional training recently, so it wouldn't be fair to put her husband on the spot by asking to invest in something else now.

Coach Kathy gently said, "I hear you're afraid to express your desire to enroll in Relationship Coach Training to your husband. Is that right?"

Tess was surprised. She hadn't thought about it that way! After she got off the phone, that question stuck in her craw. She had to admit she was afraid to express her desires to become a relationship coach to her husband, but what was she afraid of?

She couldn't come up with a good reason to not at least share what she desired with him instead of predetermining that he would be against the idea. Regardless of his response, she decided she wanted to honor her desire by saying it out loud.

So she gathered her courage and used the formula for expressing desires in a way that inspires, saying, "I would love to sign up for Relationship Coach Training," and then told him how much the investment was.

To her amazement, her husband was immediately in favor of her doing it. So she did, and today she's a successful relationship coach and a member of our terrific coaching body.

A Complaint Is Always an Unexpressed Desire

Everybody knows you're not supposed to complain. For years I took that to mean that instead of voicing a complaint, I should just keep my mouth shut and suck it up, accepting things as they were even if I didn't like them. But just knowing I shouldn't complain didn't stop me, until I learned how to dissect the complaint and find the desire underneath. Now I know I was missing an important aspect of this wise instruction.

It's true that complaining is a big waste of energy. Now when I feel myself tempted to complain, I know it means I have an unexpressed desire. It's my job to figure out what that is and express it.

It's really easy and requires no effort whatsoever to say "I'm sick of this heat!" That's a complaint, which I now think of as a lazy desire. The desire underneath that complaint is most likely "I'd love to cool off." It takes a little more effort to get to that desire, and sometimes when you're sweltering, that's hard to muster. But once you establish a habit of expressing desires instead of complaints, you'll start to do it automatically. The benefits to your relationship will be far-reaching.

I know it may not sound much different to say "I'd love to cool off" instead of "I'm sick of this heat!" It may seem like I'm saying the same thing in a different way, and to some extent I am. But where complaints just sort of lie there and stink up the place, desires are empowering and full of possibility. They also give your husband an opportunity to please you.

What comes to mind when you say "I'm sick of this heat!" as far as possible solutions?

Not much, right?

But when you express the desire "I want to cool off," does your brain start coming up with ideas? I know mine does. I think of air-conditioned buildings I could visit, like malls or movie theaters. I think of finding a swimming pool or heading to the beach or a lake. I think of a cool shower, a big glass of ice water, or even turning on the sprinkler and running through it. I think of sleeping all afternoon with the shades drawn, and then getting up in the evening when it's cooler. How about visiting a friend with air-conditioning, or going to an ice-skating rink, or making a frozen fruit smoothie for lunch? What about buying an air-conditioner? How about squirt guns and water balloons?

Granted, not all of these possibilities are practical. It's been a long time since I ran through the sprinkler on a hot day, but I have been known to provide squirt guns and water balloons at backyard barbecues.

The point is that there *are* possibilities there, and thinking of them is much more appealing than focusing on how sick you are of the heat. Since everything that happens in this world starts with an idea, thinking about all these potential solutions greatly increases the chances of having an outcome that meets your desire to cool down.

How many possible solutions came out of the complaint "I'm sick of the heat!"? None. Zilch. How many arose from expressing the desire to cool off? About a dozen.

So the score is:

Desire: 12

Complaint: 0

Team Desire clearly has the momentum.

When you're tempted to complain, identifying the outcome that you want and expressing that instead—even if you're the only one who hears it—is more empowering, more fun, more pleasant to be around, and much likelier to result in you getting what you want.

Carly loved going to parties, but her husband was more of a stay-at-home guy. When they got invited to a party, she would start strategizing about how she was going to get him to agree to attend. She would start by complaining about how long it had been since they'd gone somewhere socially and griping that they never did anything fun. She would say, "Wouldn't it be great if we could go to a party?" But she never really came out and said what she wanted. All he heard was complaining, so he would tune her out. And then she would get mad, both because he was ignoring her and because she wasn't getting what she wanted, even though she had never actually *said* what she wanted.

Now Carly has a different approach. She says, "My cousin invited us to his birthday party, and I'd really like to go."

These days, Carly not only has a better connection with her husband, she gets to go to a lot more parties with him. "It saves a lot of heartache," she told me. "He doesn't mind going to a party if he knows it will make me happy."

What's something you're unhappy about right now—something you could easily complain about? It's not hard to think of something, right? Most of us have that habit nailed. With a little practice, it's easy enough to replace the habit of complaining with the habit of expressing your desire.

Start by asking yourself what you want—something more specific than *not* what you have. Instead of saying "This house is a disaster," say "I would love this house to be tidy." Then let the possibilities start to bubble up.

Instead of saying, "I never have enough money," express your desire for whatever you want to spend money on, like "I would love to take dance lessons." You can even start thinking about the kind of dance lessons you'd like to take.

Rather than wallowing in how much you hate your job, say "I want a job that I'm excited to go to." You don't have to know what that job would be yet. Just hang out in that possibility for a moment.

Instead of putting energy into what you don't want and doesn't serve you, focus your energy and attention on the outcome you *do* want.

You Can Still Make Requests

Although expressing your desires in a way that inspires is a powerful practice for restoring intimacy and making you feel cherished, that doesn't mean that everything you say to your husband has to be expressed as a desire. Sometimes you may want to make a request, like, "Would you be willing to go to the store for some milk?"

Charlotte found herself tongue-tied as she tried to write a note asking her husband to move the clothes from the washer to the dryer while she was out. "I started out saying 'I would love it if you—' then stopped myself because there was a 'you' in there and I knew that wasn't right," she told me. "I agonized for fifteen minutes before I finally wrote, 'There are clothes in the washer. I would love it if they were dry when I came home.'"

I thought that was pretty good, and I admit that's how I phrase things most of the time too, just knowing that my husband so loves to do things he knows will make me happy. But Charlotte wouldn't have risked a loss of intimacy by saying "Would you please move the clothes to the dryer for me?"

The difference, of course, is that when you make a request, it's up to him to say "Okay" or possibly "No." You're putting the ball squarely in his court and asking for a response.

A pure desire never ends with a question mark, but a simple request does. Sometimes you may just want to ask him for a hand, and that's absolutely fine. It's a normal part of a relationship. Just today I asked John if he would look at my printer, which wasn't working. He responded by saying he had a brilliant idea.

"What's that?" I asked.

"I'm going to turn it off and then turn it on again," he told me.

"That is brilliant," I agreed. "How did you ever think of it?"

"I Googled it," he admitted.

In marriage counseling, they typically ask you what's not working. With intimacy skills, the first question is, "What do you desire?"

My way is really a lot more fun.

Now that I've been doing it this way for a while, most of the time expressing my desires comes pretty naturally to me. Recently, however, while thumbing through my neighborhood newsletter, I saw an ad for a local dance studio and absentmindedly said to John, "We should go back to dance lessons."

This is a good example of how *not* to express a desire.

Saying "we" instead of "I" is like sneaking a hidden "you" in there. And "should" is not the same as "would love" at all. I made it seem as if learning to swing dance was a vital task we had been shamefully neglecting, when of course it was no such thing.

So my husband heard "you should" instead of "I would love."

John groaned a little and shook his head.

You'd think I'd know better by now, but I dug my hole even deeper: "You don't want to go back to dance lessons with me?"

My husband is practically an expert on what I teach now, because he makes all my videos. So he nudged me by saying, "Laura, how about taking your own advice?"

(See how I can't get away with anything anymore?)

I was busted. "I would love to go back to dance lessons!" I quickly amended.

"Okay," John said.

I was *still* off my game, though, because I responded with, "But you just said you didn't want to go!"

John shook his head. "Don't make me self-examine," he said, sounding like one of my coaches. "If you want to go, let's go."

In other words, he didn't want to think about whether he'd enjoy dance lessons—maybe he wouldn't, but who cares? He didn't want a discussion. He just wanted to take the opportunity to make me happy, something we would both enjoy.

Your husband wants to make you happy, too. If it doesn't seem that way at the moment, it might be because he hasn't been getting the information he needs to do it. But that stops today, now that you know how to express your desires in a way that inspires.

CHAPTER 6

Happy Wives Phone a Friend

"The most daring thing is to create stable communities in which the terrible disease of loneliness can be cured."

—Kurt Vonnegut

Why Girltalk Rocks

My husband can't meet all my emotional needs.

Don't get me wrong—he's a wonderful listener. He's patient and compassionate. But if he were my only support, it just wouldn't be enough. Sometimes when I get really bent out of shape, it takes three friends, two sisters, *and* my husband to put me right again.

That's why girlfriends are so vital. I get to hear myself tell the story of whatever has me fretting four or five times, and each time I get a little closer to that moment where I uncover my desire. Plus my girlfriends and sisters bring something to the table that my husband simply can't: the perspective and shared experience of being a woman.

Talking to other women is critical for my happiness and sanity, and therefore critical for having a happy marriage. Without my friends, I would be relying on my husband to meet my every need to vent, think out loud, process, and just generally hear my own voice. My self-care wouldn't be complete without my friends.

One of the things I often find with students who are not so happy in their relationships is that they're having a tough time getting the girltalk they need.

Here's what I commonly see: A student will say she has a great girlfriend who recently moved away, or her girlfriend just had a baby so they don't talk as much as they used to, or that she just isn't the type to cultivate those friendships with other women.

Even so, it's vitally important to either call the faraway friend or make a new one. Without this crucial girltalk, your marriage has little chance to be the connected one you crave.

One way you can get this kind of connection is to join our community.

When a woman becomes a part of our community, she discovers other women she has a lot in common with. Suddenly she has new friends she can relate to. She feels heard and understood. Her new friends remind her to do her self-care, so she does, and she gets happy. Next, her husband buys her flowers for no special reason and tells her how much he loves seeing her so happy.

She shares with the community about the flowers and the compliment. They celebrate with her because that's what good girlfriends do. They say, "You're doing such a great job creating intimacy in your marriage!"

And they're right.

Are You a Traitor in Your Tribe?

Just as girlfriends can help reinforce the habits that lead to feeling cherished, they can also be powerful agents in scaring the stuffing out of you. And a fearful wife is one of the main ingredients in most divorces.

Kelly walked regularly with three girlfriends for exercise and chatting. They had plenty in common, because all four of them were in various stages of getting divorced. Kelly had told her husband Pete to leave months ago, and she had been to see an attorney. But when she discovered the Six Intimacy Skills, she got a sense of her own contribution to the problems in her marriage in a way that she never had before. Her intuition told her she had to give the relationship another try, if only for the sake of their three children.

A short time later, Pete had moved back in, the kids were excited to be a family again, and Kelly was feeling fortunate that the attorney she'd visited had been too busy to take her case.

But Kelly's divorcing girlfriends were questioning her every step of the way, reminding her of what a jerk she had said Pete was. They were using her own words to discourage her from making what they saw as a terrible mistake: opening herself up to heartbreak again, as well as more years of putting up with a man she said she didn't love or respect.

Kelly regretted all those months of complaining about Pete and tried to convince her pals that her husband of sixteen years was actually a sweet, decent guy and that they'd only been hearing one side of the story. She even shared with them some of the things she'd learned in our coaching program that were working well for her and Pete and encouraged them to try some experiments in their own marriage before filing for divorce themselves.

But none of it was going over well with her walking club.

"I felt like a traitor," she told me. "We had an unspoken pact that we were all going to get divorced. When I strayed from that pact, I wasn't welcome anymore. Nobody kicked me out of the group, or told me not to come back, or was mean. I just no longer belonged."

We all belong to groups with cultural rules. We subtly enforce the rules with each other because that's how community works. The upside is we get to feel like we belong, which is a basic human need. The downside is that it can be hard to change your habits when people around you are encouraging you to stay the same. Kelly managed to buck the trend in her group, although it wasn't easy. But now that she's laughing with her husband again and getting sweet love letters about how beautiful she is, she doesn't regret learning the skills that saved her marriage and parting ways with the newly single women.

Will Women Who Like Their Husbands Please Stand Up?

If you can bring the women in your circle along with you on the great adventure of creating a passionate relationship by showing them what you're learning, that's ideal. The more you support each other in treating your men respectfully and practicing good self-care, the better, right? It's good for you and good for them.

But what if they don't want to learn new skills that will lead to having a gratifying relationship?

If some of your friends or family are in the habit of complaining about their husbands or they say things that are disrespectful of yours, consider keeping conversations with them to other topics: work, the weather, politics, anything but marriage, men, and relationships. Or you can do what Penny did for her friend Leah, when she heard Leah start to complain about her husband for the umpteenth time.

Penny didn't enjoy hearing Leah complain, and since it had been going on for years with no improvement, it clearly wasn't helping Leah either. So Penny bravely said, "Leah, either divorce him or stop complaining about him."

Leah was shocked and hurt, but it made her realize she was sick of hearing herself complain too. She made a decision to stop then and there, and to focus instead on what she could improve in her marriage. Shortly thereafter she learned about the Six Intimacy Skills, and now she has a marriage that any woman would envy, including a husband who plans surprise romantic getaways for their anniversary. Leah has since thanked Penny for her strong words that day. Complaining about her marriage is the furthest thing from her mind now that things are so happy at home.

Even if you don't know them yet, you can always find women on our campus who will cheer you on when you say, "My husband is wearing a shirt with holes in it and I haven't said a word about it" or match you when you say, "I'm taking a nap, eating chocolate, and going to dance class today for my self-care. How about you?" Everyone here is standing for you, for your husband, and for your marriage to last and thrive, whatever it takes.

SKILL
#2

Restore Respect

You may think of respect as something you give to someone in a position of authority, like a teacher or boss. But respecting your husband simply means that even if you don't agree with him, you still honor his decisions for his life. A respectful wife can listen to her husband talk without offering suggestions or helpful tips. And a woman who respects her husband will apologize when she's disrespectful, just like she would apologize for being cranky or being late.

Respect means that you don't dismiss, criticize, contradict, or try to teach your man how to do something better, because you trust him and expect the best outcome from him already. It means you don't make fun of him for doing things the way a man does things, which is often completely different from the way a woman does things.

PRESCRIPTION

Act as if you respect your husband—even if you don't feel respectful, just the way you would act confident at an interview or giving a talk. It's okay to fake it 'til you make it.

A powerful way to quickly restore intimacy is to think of a specific situation where you criticized, insulted, contradicted, or belittled your husband and offer an apology. Use the phrase "I apologize for being disrespectful for..." and reference the specific situation.

If you find yourself wanting to teach your husband something or help him improve, consider using the phrase "Whatever you think" or just giving him the gift of feeling listened to by saying "I hear you" instead.

One big exception is when your husband is asking for *your* preference. If he wants to know your desires, tell him so he can make you happy. But remember to focus on the outcome and the experience you want to have rather than how he should do it.

CHAPTER 7

What Were You Thinking When You Said Yes to the Dress?

You Might Have Selective Amnesia

When I was miserable in my marriage, I firmly believed that it was because I had chosen the wrong husband. I reasoned that I had been too young and made a hasty decision. But in reality, I had rewritten the story of my relationship—and left out most of the good parts.

When John and I first met, I found his sense of humor and playfulness a joy to be around. He was so much fun! But when it came to the serious business of getting housework done, paying bills, and filing taxes, I decided that he was *too* playful and not responsible enough. I wanted things to get done the way I thought they should get done, and I decided that John's laid-back style was a detriment to our well-being. I felt he was leaving me with more of the burden because he didn't react to things fast enough. Dirty clothes littered the floor of the bedroom, bills went unpaid, and our cars were driven well past three-thousand miles before their oil got changed—unless I intervened, which I did constantly.

Around that time I read an article about how people who get married when they're young are more likely to get divorced. I thought about how I had only been twenty-one when John and I met and twenty-two when we married, and I concluded that I'd made a big mistake. It said right in the article that, statistically speaking, our chances of making it were not good.

I figured I'd chosen John for the wrong reasons. It was a carefree time in my life, and I'd been seduced by his singing, his guitar playing, and his boyish grin. I never considered whether he'd take care of his half of the chores (he didn't!), even after I wrote them out for him (which is why he didn't do them, I realized later). Now that it was time to pay back student loans and a mortgage, I was terrified that I'd focused on all the wrong things when I picked him.

It turns out that I married a guy who was fun-loving *and* responsible. I just didn't see it that way because I seized on every responsibility that we had as a couple and did everything myself. That's what good martyrs do, and I was one of the best.

But just today, while I was expressing concern that I wouldn't have enough time to finish some errands and meet my deadline to my editor, my husband came into my office and asked what he could do to help. He had just finished doing the dishes and taking out the trash. I handed off some paperwork that really should have been mine, which he took care of efficiently despite having spent all day running his own business. What a guy! How can he be the same one from those early years?

John wasn't making those kinds of offers in the bad old days for one simple reason: I didn't respect him enough to entrust him with important work, and he knew it. To avoid rejection and a potential conflict, he didn't ask if he could help. And I didn't ask him to help because I was so controlling that I wanted to do everything myself.

Now that the respect is restored in our relationship, John never gets tired of doing whatever he can to take care of me and make me happy.

He's the same guy, but I get a totally different response because I have a totally different attitude. I see how smart he is, how hardworking and conscientious.

But I had forgotten for a while.

Did You Rewrite Your Relationship Story?

In case *you* forgot, let me remind you that you fell in love with your husband because he has some great qualities too. You may look back at that courtship time and wonder—like I did—what you were thinking when you said yes to the man standing next to you. You might have chalked up your marriage struggles to having been too hasty or just plain making a mistake.

But my experience with thousands of students is that they chose their husbands for really good reasons—and then forgot what they were. These women rediscover those valuable qualities as soon as they restore their respect for their husbands. And with the restored respect comes all the excitement and joy that they felt in the beginning of their relationships. They really are completely thrilled again. They're not just sucking it up because it's best for the kids or because it would be too embarrassing to divorce. They're genuinely happy to be married to their husband again.

See if any of these rationales sound familiar. Have you been telling yourself that you made a bad choice of husband because you were:

- *Anxious to get away from your parents?*
- *So needy at the time?*
- *Looking for a good father for your kids?*
- *Financially insecure?*
- *Too young to know any better?*
- *Going to change him?*
- *In a rush to marry so you could have kids before you were too old?*
- *Rebelling against people who told you he was wrong for you?*
- *Agreeing to marry the guy everyone else thought was right for you?*
- *Not getting any other offers?*
- *Telling yourself anything else that dismisses or nullifies the guy you chose?*

You've almost certainly fallen into what I call the "relationship rewrite rationale," which goes like this:

1. My marriage is miserable.
2. How did this happen?
3. He must be the wrong guy.
4. I must have said "I do" under duress. It was a huge mistake.

The good news is that your story about why you made a mistake is just that: a story. It's not the facts. But if you have such a story you're harboring, you're not alone. Nearly every wife I work with has a story about why it was a mistake to marry her husband.

Serena explained to me that she was young and trying to get out of her parents' house when she married her husband. She just couldn't stand living with them any longer, and then along came a handsome young man—now her husband of fifteen years. Looking back, she felt that she had been hasty and was full of regret now that they had three kids and a house and none of the housework was getting done unless she did it. Her husband was very distant, spending all his time helping his family and not her or the kids.

As part of practicing the Six Intimacy Skills, Serena asked her husband to help their kids with their homework. He agreed, but said he wanted to take them swimming first, as it was a nice day out. He asked her what she thought about that. Serena was very tempted to say, "Homework should come first," which would have been a subtle criticism, but she chose to respect her husband instead. She told him, "Whatever you think."

To her surprise, the homework did get done, right after the kids had a nice afternoon with their dad, leaving Serena blissfully alone to catch up on her work. She reflected that one of her big complaints was that her husband didn't spend time with the kids, and she realized that if she had said what she'd been tempted to say, she would have deprived them all of a good time together.

Serena began to remember what she saw in her husband fifteen years ago but had forgotten about. "I'm grateful for how hardworking, loyal, and generous he is," she told me. "I was mad because he wasn't spending time with me and the kids, but now he's doing so much of what I wanted, I don't feel angry anymore. It's part of his nature to be thoughtful and helpful, and that was part of what I liked about him. He's really very considerate."

How I Know Your Husband Is a Good Guy

The way that I know your husband is a good guy is because you wouldn't have married him otherwise.

That doesn't mean your husband is a perfect man. He has flaws. But he is a man you can have a wonderful relationship with if you make a few adjustments that are within your power. You wouldn't have married a putz. You wouldn't have committed to spend the rest of your life with a jerk. You wouldn't have picked a worthless bozo to start a family with or grow old with.

Given the choice, you would have picked the most attractive, smart, talented person you could find. *So you did.* You chose your man because you saw a lot of good qualities in him.

We really can't marry up or marry down; we wouldn't match. That's one of the laws of nature. We can only marry our match.

Since you're not mean and spiteful, he's not mean and spiteful. You're not a bad person, so he's not a bad person either. And if he seems that way right now, what that tells me is that you're getting hurt a lot, and the reason you're getting hurt a lot is twofold.

The first reason is that your husband doesn't feel respected right now. A man needs respect like he needs oxygen, and when he's not getting it from the woman who knows him best in the world, he's going to respond defensively. As the saying goes, the best defense is a good offense, so at times he may be slinging metaphorical rocks and stones your way in order to restore his sense of self-worth. When he's not having to defend himself, he can focus on protecting you, finding ways to make you smile, bringing you presents, and telling you how beautiful you are. Those are the things that make him feel successful as a husband.

But first, he's got to get his respect. He's likely going to fight for himself every moment that he's not feeling respected. I see that in my coaching practice over and over.

Marge experienced this when she tried to discourage her husband from drinking soda, which she deemed dangerous. Whenever he drank it, she reminded him that he was poisoning himself and making himself sick—to which her husband responded, "What you say doesn't matter." That hurt Marge deeply, because she saw it as her husband dismissing her and saying she wasn't important. But he was forced to dismiss what she said for the survival of his own identity. She was making his choices (and therefore him) out to be bad and wrong, so he had to either take that on or dismiss *her* as bad and wrong.

I'm not saying it's okay for a husband to dismiss his wife and tell her what she says doesn't matter. But when you're trying to blame or shame someone, it's not unusual for that person to try to defend himself. And at times that defense may look like dismissal, which is very hurtful.

The other reason you're getting hurt in your relationship is because that's part of being in an intimate relationship. When we live so close together, it's bound to happen sometimes. Kids hurt each other when they play, not because they mean to but because they bump into each other. Drivers cut you off in traffic, not because they set out to scare you but because they're distracted. Even the happiest couples hurt each other sometimes.

When the culture of your relationship feels strong, safe, and steady, you can easily shrug off that kind of hurt and recognize that it's not intentional. But when there's lots of hurt going back and forth between you, it's hard to separate the innocent mistakes from the ongoing battles. When you're treating your husband with disrespect, it's going to result in a lot of Needless Emotional Turmoil (NET). The result is that the relationship feels hopeless.

But all of that changes quickly when you focus on being respectful.

Your Reasons Were Reasonable

Keep thinking about why you chose to marry your husband. Maybe it was the way he loved you. Maybe it was his book smarts or street smarts. Maybe he was sweet to your kids, or protective of your pets, or generous to your mom. You might have loved how feminine you felt around him or how much you laughed together. Maybe you felt some inner strength around him and a sense of optimism that made you look forward to the future. Maybe you felt drawn to him physically or liked how well he listened. You thought he was considerate, generous, charming. Those are all excellent reasons for getting married.

Those are also the reasons that matter now, because he still has all those qualities. They'll come shining through again as soon as you go back to treating him respectfully—just the way you did when you were falling in love. When you do that, you'll not only eliminate most of the conflict in your relationship, you'll also restore the excitement that you once shared.

If you felt desired, cherished, adored, protected, and excited during your courtship, your marriage has the potential to make you feel all those things again. If you never felt those things during your courtship, now you have the chance to experience them for the first time with your husband.

As an added bonus, his steady presence will help you become the person you want to be. Part of you knew that when you made the choice to marry him.

The Wisdom of No Escape

Pema Chodron has a book by that name, and it instantly made me think of marriage. One of the great things about getting married—about swearing in front of God and everybody that you want to be together until your last breath—is that you wisely give yourself no easy way out.

You were clever to do that. You did it partly because you knew that at some point it might be tempting to walk away. You wanted to give yourself some glue that would bind you and your husband together even when you were hurt or scared.

Now there are probably financial entanglements you share, or maybe children. Your home and your cats would have to be divided up or sold if you split, and you would have to have a lot of awkward conversations with friends and family about how your marriage didn't make it.

You did a good job leaving yourself no good option but to learn how to make your marriage gratifying. I say that with all sincerity, because now that I have these skills, I'm grateful that I didn't leave myself an escape. I would have missed out on the greatest self-improvement project I've ever undertaken. I would never have become my best self.

Once a student confided to me that she would have left her husband long ago except that she didn't want to be alone. "I know it's a terrible reason to stay," she told me.

Loneliness is a huge concern for most of us. Most humans find another person's presence a great comfort, if not essential for their well-being. I have a very low tolerance for loneliness. I feel it acutely when I travel alone for a few days. Imagine the suffering I would have endured from ending my marriage!

Another student told me her reason for not wanting to get divorced was because she didn't want to have to go to work while her children were still small. She too thought that was a bad reason to stay in a painful marriage. But her marriage was only painful because of her lack of Intimacy Skills, and after some training she was able to rediscover the romance that led her to get married in the first place.

I can't think of a bad reason to stay married. Sometimes women tell me that they stay married just because they don't want to be failures at love. That's a very good reason to stay married! No matter how you spin it, divorce is a tragedy and often unnecessary.

When you're learning intimacy skills, you not only preserve your marriage, you make it so that you don't even consider divorce anymore because you're so happy. You feel excited, pursued, and beautiful. You feel desired, cherished, and protected. That's what it means to be in a happy relationship. Nobody wants to get out of that.

Miriam experienced this firsthand when she trained in the Six Intimacy Skills. Early in her training, she believed the only thing that would really change her marriage was if her husband went to marriage counseling so he would be more sensitive to her needs. She told him that, reiterating that a therapist had told her he would never be emotionally available until he worked on healing his dysfunctional childhood. She was unhappy that he wasn't more romantic and attentive, and she told him that often. Eventually she came to see that she wasn't being very respectful. She agreed to practice being more respectful as an experiment, even though she didn't really think it would help.

Over the next few weeks, a series of events led her to look at things differently. She was bursting to tell us about how much her husband had changed. Of course, Miriam was the one who changed—and then her husband started responding to her differently.

First there was an incident where her husband caused them to be late to a family party, even though he knew she really wanted to be there a bit early. Miriam was so moved when he apologized for disappointing her with no prompting whatsoever.

"This is a man who I thought did not consider my feelings," Miriam reported. "I don't remember him ever apologizing to me like that on his own! It was a very special moment for me."

A few days later Miriam had cabin fever from staying home all morning with her little ones. She was feeling overwhelmed by the mess. In the past, that situation had been a recipe for conflict, but this time was different. Her husband not only cleaned up and got the kids to help, he also helped her get out of the house and even prepared a salad for her to eat when she got back.

"Before," Miriam said, "there was a lot of grumbling when he helped me out of the house, and he was always in a rush to leave. He didn't like to be home very much."

Next, Miriam expressed her desire for a vacation, but they agreed that it was not a good time to travel because she was starting a new job. But her husband saw a chance to make his wife happy and planned a romantic night at a local hotel.

"I was so touched that he would want to vacation with me. In the past he would give me reasons we couldn't go, so we almost never took vacations together. When we did, it was because I made all the arrangements," Miriam reported.

She went on, "In the beginning of the year, I was convinced he needed therapy. I learned to change my perspective and *not* my husband. He is so kind and caring and always looking for ways to please me. I know he cherishes me and loves me. He has become so attuned to my needs and loves me so much more passionately. I can't remember why I ever wanted him to go to therapy. I finally have the intimacy I always craved."

You will too, as soon as you begin practicing being respectful in your marriage.

CHAPTER 8

Your Husband Doesn't Want Your Opinion

> "The man may be the head of the household, but the woman is the neck, and she can turn the head whichever way she pleases."
>
> —Nia Vardalos, Actress, Screenwriter, and Director

The Wife I Aspire to Be

One of the most powerful phrases I ever learned for showing my husband that I trust him is "Whatever you think." The reason I like it so much is that it conveys my faith in him and his judgment. I wholeheartedly trust him now, but I didn't always.

In weak moments, I occasionally revert back to thinking that I'm the smarter person in our marriage. But having thought that for years, I can tell you it's a lonely place that I don't like to visit anymore. Today I choose respect regardless of whether I feel that I know better than him. My connection with my husband is a higher priority than needing to demonstrate that I am a smarty pants.

When I say, "Whatever you think," I'm choosing to be the trusting, respectful wife that I aspire to be even if I'm inclined to think my husband is just plain wrong. I use that phrase so much now that it's second nature.

There was a time when my default was to tell John everything I was thinking, including where he was being illogical, ridiculous, or impractical. His response was to withdraw. He stopped sharing a lot of his thoughts with me because he thought I would just shoot them down. And I wondered why he wouldn't confide in me!

When I realized I had been making him feel unsafe to share just about anything, I felt terrible. I decided to accept whatever he thought was best about anything that was his responsibility (his work, his car, his clothes). Then I extended my policy to anything he was handling (bills, tree trimming, tax returns) that affected both of us.

Using the phrase "whatever you think" was a salve to the wounds I had inflicted on my husband. It wasn't long before he was sharing openly with me again. I realized that a lot of what he was saying was just thinking out loud. Some of it was about his to-do list, as in "I don't have time to take the car in for that recall right now" or "Do you think I should FedEx this paperwork to my client or send it through the mail?"

There was really no need for me to comment on these musings, except to reinforce his good judgment with a quick "Whatever you think."

Sometimes it was a flight of fancy, as in "They're talking about sending people to Mars. I think I'll go." Mars, huh? That sounds like he'll be gone a while. But instead of protesting a trip that would likely never happen, I say, "Whatever you think."

Sometimes he was juggling bills, as in "I'm paying the mortgage now, and I'll pay the property taxes at the last minute on Wednesday." Sounds a little dicey to me, but that gets a "Whatever you think" out of me too.

Suddenly I was telling him that I trusted him—even though I didn't necessarily feel like I trusted him—and that was strange. But at the same time, I was showing up as the wife I wanted to be: a respectful one with whom he felt safe to share his innermost thoughts.

Over time, I started to realize that I actually trusted him as much as I was saying I did. My words were an affirmation that changed my reality.

Acquiring a Taste for Respect

It's not easy to say "Whatever you think" at first.

Mandy said that when she first said "Whatever you think" to her husband, it felt like sawdust in her mouth. Over time, though, the words helped her gain so much in her marriage that she now says they taste as sweet as honey. If you don't like using these words at first, think of them as an acquired taste. They might become one of your favorites.

"Whatever you think" were the first words that Kathy latched on to from the Six Intimacy Skills. Like me, Kathy was in the habit of managing her husband Doug and every decision in their household, so he was well trained to check with her about how she wanted things done to avoid getting in trouble later. They had been fighting and distant for years despite—or maybe because of—regular marriage counseling.

On this day, Doug approached her in the usual way with some options about their cell phone plan, asking which one she thought they should pick. Kathy used the magic words "Whatever you think."

Doug was so taken aback that he asked her a second time. "No, really, I need to know what you want me to do here," he said.

But Kathy stuck to her guns. "Whatever you think," she said with a smile. "I trust you."

Things changed that evening. Kathy crawled into the same bed with her husband for the first time in six months. He said, "Gee, you were so nice tonight." Doug felt respected and Kathy felt dignified about having faith in her husband instead of telling him what to do. That night was a symbolic turning point and the beginning of a new, more intimate relationship that they still enjoy more than twenty years later.

Thinking Is Different Than Wanting

Sometimes when I suggest that women use the phrase "Whatever you think," they modify it to say, "Whatever you want." But I see a big difference between those two phrases. Your husband wants to be respected and trusted, but he also wants to know what you want so he can make you happy. When you say "Whatever you want," what he hears is, "I'm not going to tell you how to make me happy. You just have to figure it out. Good luck."

I know it's only one tiny word of difference between "whatever you think" and "whatever you want," but to your husband, that is a big deal. If you don't provide the answer, you're making his job harder.

If your husband asks, "Where do you want to go to dinner tonight?" and you say "Whatever you want," that's not deferring him back to his own thinking or showing respect. That's simply not giving him any clue about what would make you happy and expecting him to figure it out. If the question is about your preference, consider saying "Italian would be great," or "How about that new sushi place down the street?" That would provide him with information he needs to be the hero. Or if you really wanted to, you could say, "How about if you surprise me?" That's also a way of expressing your preference.

In order to feel successful, our husbands need to know what we want. If we don't tell them, they're stuck. They don't really know which direction to go. They have no North Star to navigate by.

When your husband asks for your preference or desire, figure out what that is and let him know. When he's making a decision for his own life or for something he handles for both of you, that's a good time to defer to his thinking.

Hilary learned this the hard way when her husband asked her what movie she wanted to see and she said, "Whatever you think." In that case, he was asking for her preference, but she didn't give it to him. Instead she essentially said, "Let's see a movie you like." So, left to his own devices, her husband picked a prisoner-of-war story with plenty of torture scenes, which Hilary found depressing. Maybe she didn't know exactly what she wanted to see when he asked, but it's too bad she didn't at least say, "I would love to see a comedy," since that was her preference.

Listening 101

Here's a concept that was quite shocking to me at first: I can listen to my husband so that he feels really heard *without agreeing or disagreeing with him.*

Honestly, this idea completely changed my life. I had previously assumed that if he said something—anything—it was up to me to say "You're right" or "Yeah, that makes sense" if I agreed. But if I didn't agree, I thought it was my responsibility to say, "I think you're looking at this all wrong" or, possibly, "You don't know what you're talking about."

I don't have to agree or disagree. I don't have to weigh in. I don't have to share my experience. I don't have to do anything but listen, and the phrase that helps me do that best is "I hear you."

We all have a deep need to be heard and understood. Listening to your husband is both a form of respect and a fundamental part of loving him. The phrase "I hear you" is so fantastically neutral and at the same time so validating, it does the job beautifully. It says, "I'm listening to you. I'm here. What you say matters"—and nothing more.

I started out saying "I hear you" to my husband, and I soon found myself saying it to my sisters, friends, coworkers, parents, and everybody else, as well. It's such a delight to simply listen without having to weigh in. I enjoy deeper connections with everyone I love, and I notice many of them echo the same phrase back to me.

It's not always easy to listen without comment. At my Cherished for Life Weekend, we do an exercise that drives this point home. During the exercise, two strangers partner up and one of them talks for two minutes straight about a problem or a challenge she's having. The other woman's job is to listen to her and say either "I hear you" or "uh-huh," and nothing more. Afterward, the woman who was speaking feels truly heard, and the woman who was listening endured and triumphed over the temptation to comment in some way. One common response after this exercise is "I see what a gift it is to have someone just *listen*." Another is "I feel so connected to my partner," even if the two women only just met.

It may not come naturally to only say "I hear you" to your husband. A lot of women find it challenging to ignore the opinion or knowledge that pops into her head when her husband is talking. It takes some patience and maturity to choose to listen.

One of the coaches on my team recently said, "I have a student who really hates the phrase "I hear you," and she's asking if there's an alternative."

"Yes," I answered wryly. "Tell her to try 'Whatever you think.'"

Honoring Your Inner Smarty Pants

Naturally, neither of those phrases is easy to say when you're thinking "I know the answer. I'm right in this situation. I can fix everything, save time and money, and help him be more efficient." Of course, you always have the option to just say whatever you're thinking—your opinion, your advice, your fears.

But I've found that that inclination isn't as satisfying as I expect it to be. For one thing, I *don't* always know what's best, even when I think I do. I'm an expert on my own life, and my husband is the expert on his. My nephew is the expert on his life, my mom is the expert on her life, and no matter how invested I am, no matter how much I want the world for them, I don't really know what's best for them. Only they do.

Hearing myself say "Whatever you think" and "I hear you" is a good way for me to remind myself that I know only a little. Getting to hear what my loved ones are really thinking about and what matters to them is the prize I want most of all. The honor of hearing their vulnerability because they feel safe confiding in me is worth forgoing the pleasure of saying something really smart in that moment.

I didn't like the idea of saying "I hear you." I wasn't excited to say "Whatever you think" either—until I tried them. I loved the response I got. It was so empowering. And I never would have gotten there without those magic phrases to rely on. Will they work for you? You're the expert on your own life, so only you know for sure. But consider giving them a try to see how it goes.

Your Desires Are More Powerful Than Your Opinions

The other thing to ask yourself when you're really tempted to give your husband your opinion is: *What is the outcome I want?* As a wife, expressing your desire is always going to be more powerful than debating or disagreeing with his thinking, which is disrespectful.

When Jenny heard about a friend's dog having puppies, she found herself wanting one. She came home gushing and told her husband Derrick how much she would love to have a puppy.

Derrick was not excited at all. "Puppies destroy everything," he told her, "and it's so much work to get them housebroken. They wake you up in the middle of the night, and they bark. One of us would always have to be around, and we both work. I just don't think it's a good idea."

Jenny was disappointed, but she didn't argue. She respectfully said, "I hear you," and let it go. She didn't tell Derrick that he was wrong about getting a puppy, but she also didn't stop wanting one. She continued to express her longing for a puppy from time to time as one of her pure desires. But whenever she did so, she was completely respectful, never contradicting her husband.

A little while later, Derrick came home with a puppy from the litter that Jenny had fallen for, saying, "Surprise! I got you a puppy!" Jenny was ecstatic and felt so adored by her husband. The two of them enjoyed bonding with their new dog and Derrick loved knowing he'd made his wife really happy.

At the same time, Jenny's friend Meredith was also craving a puppy from the same litter. Instead of expressing a desire to her husband, though, she said, "I've been thinking, and I decided we really need to get a puppy." She made a case for why she thought they needed a puppy, but Simon didn't agree at all. "I don't think we need one, and I don't think we should get one. I'm not interested," he said. Meredith approached the puppy conversation as a debate instead of a desire, so Simon didn't see it as an opportunity to make his wife happy.

Meredith brought home a puppy anyway, hoping that Simon would warm up to it, but he didn't. In fact, Simon and the puppy were at odds from day one. Meredith was surprised that anyone could be hostile to a cute little puppy, but for Simon, the puppy represented his wife overriding his thinking and proof that she didn't respect him. And Meredith continued to believe that her husband was an uncaring jerk.

So what's the difference between the tales of these two puppies? Jenny approached it from an emotionally honest place: her authentic desire. She got the puppy, as well as her husband's blessing and participation, and everyone was happy. Whereas Meredith approached it first as a debate by giving her opinion, and then like a steamroller, insisting that she get her way no matter what her husband had to say about it. As a result of this disrespectful approach, she ended up with tension and hostility in her marriage and a new pet that her husband disdained.

Here's another example of the power of expressing your desire over giving your opinion. Dinner was on the table and Ruth was hungry, but there was no sign of her husband. She found him in the basement with their washing machine, which was broken and filled with water. He was trying to bail out the water using an old laundry detergent container with a narrow opening.

Ruth's first thought was *This is going to take forever.* She was tempted to tell him her opinion—that he should stop doing it that way and get a better container—but that would have been disrespectful.

Instead she asked herself what she wanted, and the answer was to eat. So she said only, "Honey, I'd like to have dinner now."

Her husband looked up and said, "Yeah, you're probably right. This isn't very efficient anyway. It would probably take forever to do it this way, and I can do it later."

With that, they went upstairs to have a dinner free of tension and bickering, all because Ruth treated her husband with respect.

CHAPTER 9

Why Wives Cause Most Divorces and What to Do Instead

How to Stop Wanting a Divorce

If you have threatened to leave your husband, that threat is terrifying him. You might think he doesn't care, but he does. He's taking it very personally that you're not happy, and it's making him defensive and nervous every day. The odds of regaining a strong connection under those circumstances are very low, which means that things have little chance of getting better. Therefore, one of the first steps to revitalizing your relationship is getting off the fence.

But it can be scary to jump down too. If your goal is to get off the fence gracefully, land on the married side, and feel inspired about doing it, you'll need to know how to turn the clock back to the beginning of the relationship. I'll explain more about that in Chapter 18, but for now, ask yourself this: Would you want to be in a relationship with the man who wooed you? Think back to what your husband was like when you first met and he was always making you laugh, telling you how wonderful you are, and bringing you presents to show he was thinking of you. Would you want to be in a relationship with that guy? Because he's the guy who will show up once you begin implementing the Six Intimacy Skills.

You may be so thoroughly put off by your husband right now that you can't remember what you ever liked about him. If you're anything like I was, you secretly believe that you are smarter than your husband, and you've probably gone around gathering evidence for this, like the time he hired the crooked contractor, the time he overpaid for the car, or the time he missed the freeway exit and took you twenty minutes out of your way. You think of these instances as proof that he is not capable or competent. You quietly make a case that, of the two of you, you're the smarter one.

Because of this, you've been trying to teach him how to improve in certain areas. You tell yourself that you're trying to help. You're trying to save money. You're trying to make sure he has a good relationship with the kids or that you don't run out of propane or that the colored clothes don't get bleached. But the end result is that you're emasculating your husband, who very likely does things completely differently than you would—unless he's trying to do them your way to keep the peace.

But even if he is doing things your way, chances are that he's not happy about it. And you're actually not either, not really. If that's what you really wanted, you could have saved everyone a lot of trouble and just married yourself. But you didn't—you married someone who had a different point of view.

I Wasn't Nagging. I Was Helping!

Men tend to do a lot of things differently than women do. That doesn't make them wrong, but it can be difficult for us women to wrap our brains around their methods.

There are many situations where you and your husband have different approaches, like handling finances, child-rearing, and lovemaking. There are myriad everyday things—kitchen cleanup, car maintenance, retirement planning, laundry—where you might see the world differently than he does.

One way to cope is to decide that your way is right and his is wrong. You can be outwardly tolerant about this, rolling your eyes only to yourself when the bathroom sink is still dirty and the floor is covered with dust bunnies. But when the stakes seem high, it's pretty hard to keep your superiority complex under wraps. After all, it could result in a higher tax bill, disappointed kids, or damaged cars if you don't show him how to do things the right way—your way.

It starts out innocently enough—with a suggestion. If he washed the whites in hot water instead of warm, they'd come out cleaner, you say. You're just being helpful, because you happen to know better in this instance. But so much of what we consider "helpful" in wife language actually comes across as critical to your husband. What he hears is, "I don't like your way. You should do it my way."

Let's say your husband grunts and accommodates your suggestion but goes back to his old ways the next time he starts the laundry. You might decide to remind him again, thinking he just forgot. What's the harm in that? Most women don't see any.

But most men do. They would consider that exchange emasculating and think of you as a nag.

How to Pretend to Stop Nagging but Still Keep Doing It

In 2012 the *Wall Street Journal* ran an article called, "Meet the Marriage Killer" by Elizabeth Bernstein about how nagging causes more divorces than affairs do. I thought of my own marriage when we were on the brink of divorce, and I have to admit, we were a great example of that. I was causing all the damage. There was no need for another woman to entice my husband, because I was already ruining it all by myself.

What was also disturbing about this article was that they had experts give suggestions on how to stop nagging, but, weirdly, the suggestions were just variations of nagging that would not help create better intimacy or get things done. Here's one suggestion from the article: "Explain why your request is important to you. 'I worry about our finances when you pay the bill late. We can't afford to pay late fees.'"

Here's how I know that's bad advice: I've tried it myself. Repeatedly. And it got me wall-to-wall hostility—not promptly paid bills and a grateful peck on the cheek like I imagined. I'm not sure if it was the part where I implied that I didn't trust him to be responsible that irritated my husband or the part where I explained what a late fee is and why I didn't want to pay one (as if that wasn't terribly disrespectful). Either way, indulging my anxiety and doubting him instead of remembering that I married a smart, capable guy didn't serve either of us very well. What I wanted was an intimate, passionate, peaceful partner, but instead I treated him like a child who needed constant supervision.

Now I no longer remind my husband to pay bills, and he doesn't forget to pay them. The guy was making car payments since before I got my driver's license, so I'm not sure where I got the idea that he might stop doing that once we were married. When I started respecting him by expecting the best outcome, my anxiety melted away because it was unfounded.

Here's another "helpful" tip from that same *Wall Street Journal* article: "Set a timeframe. Ask when your partner can expect to finish the task. ('Can you change the car oil this weekend?') Let him tell you when it works best for him to do it."

The suggestion here is that somehow he will feel less resistant to your attempts to control him if you simply ask him when he wants to meet your demands. But it's not my experience that my husband jumps up to do something cheerfully just because I've given him a time frame in which I expect him to do it.

My husband is smart enough to notice me trying to control him like I'm his boss or his mother—instead of his lover—no matter how clever my wording. Experience tells me that if I try to get him to change the oil "this weekend," I'll end up with a husband who is completely committed to *not* changing the oil, because he doesn't want to be controlled, managed, or mothered. It's simply not a respectful or dignified way for a wife to behave.

You Finally Have the Right Instruction Manual

Today I hardly even think about little chores like oil changes and bill paying. My husband takes care of all those things and is always thinking up new and amazing ways to please me every day. I don't ask him to do that—he does it on his own because he wants to delight me. The result is that everything gets done and we both feel loved.

However, it wouldn't be that way if I had listened to conventional wisdom about marriage. It's so sad how we have been so poorly trained to communicate in our relationships! I caused myself plenty of distress by doing the very things that the experts said to do, attempting to reduce the conflict in my marriage. I see terrible advice like that everywhere I look. I even give out the Worst Relationship Advice of the Week Award on *The Empowered Wife Podcast*. Students frequently send me submissions they've run across to consider for the award. No wonder we were all so confused about what to do to make our marriages last and thrive!

One really powerful way to feel hopeful and inspired is to realize that you probably never had the right information about how to get back to a playful, passionate relationship before now. Remember, there's no Relationships 101 in schools. Where were we supposed to learn about how to have a great marriage? From *Cosmo* and *Glamour*?

But imagine what you could accomplish with the right information. What if you had all the skills to really bring back the magic you felt in the beginning? Wouldn't that make you a lot more excited to try?

Never Ask a Man This Question

One common mistake I see women making in their relationships is asking the guy where the relationship is headed. That never works, because we women are the ones who decide the course of the relationship.

Tawnya had separated from her husband but was continuing to see him occasionally, and they were still engaged sexually, which I thought was a great sign for them. When you're looking to revitalize intimacy on an emotional level, having it still exist on the physical level is a good start. But Tawnya wasn't so sure. "I just end up feeling anxious after he leaves, because I don't know if this marriage is going to make it, but he's still getting sex out of it. Sometimes it feels like the relationship is over and we're just friends with benefits. What should I do? Should I ask him how he feels?"

That was her question: "Should I ask *him* how *he* feels?" I redirected her to her own desires by asking, "How do *you* feel? What do *you* want?"

She said, "Well, I don't know if this is going to work out or not," which is not a feeling or a desire.

I asked her again, "What is it that *you* want to happen, if you could wave a magic wand?"

"I want my marriage back," she finally admitted. "I want us to get back together."

Now we had the information that really mattered: *her* desire, not how *he* felt.

Most husbands would rather we never ask them how they feel. It's not respectful to the male culture. Most men don't like to talk about their feelings, because that's not their area of strength. Men tend to be good thinkers, and women are generally better at feeling and expressing their feelings.

If you're not paying attention to your desires and feelings, and instead are saying to your husband, "What do you want? How do you feel?" you're completely lost. And the reason you're so lost is because you're scared. You don't want to admit that you feel lonely or that you miss him, because that feels vulnerable. You don't want to be the first to say "I want to be a couple again," because it's emotionally risky. It seems safer to make him say it first.

I suggested that Tawnya say something along the lines of, "I'm really missing you, and whenever I see you, I enjoy it so much. It makes me wish we could go back to the way it was when we were husband and wife under the same roof. I would be so happy if we could do that."

Tawnya let out a nervous laugh when I said that. "That *is* what I want," she admitted. "But I don't think I can say that."

That's the challenge about being respectful: Sometimes it's pretty scary. In fact, practicing intimacy skills in general takes a heck of a lot of courage. You can't reconnect with your husband by asking him what he thinks is going to happen. Relationships are up to the woman, so if you're asking him, you're asking the wrong person. Your power lies in expressing your desires in a respectful way.

When All the Oxygen Leaves the Relationship

The most common mistake I see women making in relationships is the same one that I made for years before I finally, painfully realized what I was doing. And even then, I couldn't stop right away—not until I developed a system to help me.

The trouble starts the fateful day we decide to be *helpful*. We think we're just giving a useful suggestion, sharing something we know that he apparently does not. But what we're really doing is letting him know we don't think he could figure it out on his own. The "helpful" suggestion is rife with disrespect. But the wife often doesn't realize this. She is convinced that she's just trying to help.

Husbands respond very poorly to disrespect, even if wives don't realize they're being disrespectful.

For men, respect is like oxygen. It's that important. So the minute a wife is disrespectful, her husband gets defensive. He is trying to shore up his own sense of himself. He may do this by dismissing her or demeaning what she said. He might say something like "You don't know what you're talking about" or "Give it a rest" or even "Shut up."

Now the wife—who was only trying to be helpful—is hurt. So she also responds from a defensive position, perhaps by telling him to stop being so mean.

Things are not improving—they are escalating. Now the husband says something mean back, and they are engaged in a full-blown fight. Both husband and wife get hurt.

This happens over and over, so many times that both of them begin to feel totally hopeless. I can tell when women are stuck in this cycle because they usually describe their husband as cranky, cold, or clueless. They talk about what a terrible temper he has or how distant he is—always watching TV, playing video games, or looking at his phone.

They have no inkling, no concept of how much they have contributed to this hostility.

I'm not saying that you're responsible or that it's all your fault. However, you have a lot of influence over the culture of your marriage, and when you change the way you talk to your husband, he will respond to you differently. If you go out of your way to be as respectful to him as possible, you're going to get a much better response. He's going to be a lot less hostile because he has so much less to prove and so much less to defend against.

One of the most tragic situations that I commonly see is a woman saying, "I had to divorce him because he was so mean and grumpy all the time. I was miserable and he was miserable, so clearly we weren't compatible." Really what happened is that she was being unwittingly disrespectful and her husband was responding in an angry, defensive manner.

I call this the "helpful-hurt-hopeless" cycle, and the only way to permanently disrupt it is at the beginning: *Stop being helpful*. Remember, "helpful" in wife language translates into "critical" in husband language.

If that sounds extreme to you, it did to me too, initially. But over time, I've come to appreciate that it's actually more enjoyable to be the Girl of Fun and Light than it is to be the Wikipedia Wife who knows everything. When I stop trying to be helpful, I can relax and have fun with my husband again. The same will happen for you when you decide to keep your helpfulness to a minimum.

CHAPTER 10

Your Husband Is Smarter Than You Think

"Professors at our leading universities indoctrinate impressionable undergraduates with carelessly fact-free theories alleging that gender is an arbitrary, oppressive fiction with no basis in biology."

—Camille Paglia, Social Critic and Professor

Men and Women Are Not the Same

Part of learning the Six Intimacy Skills is acknowledging and celebrating how different men are from women. Just as John Gray said, men really are from Mars and women from Venus. It takes some adjusting to get used to the cultural differences between those two planets.

I became acutely aware of this one day at the beach, playing volleyball with friends. Mike had his eight-year-old son Matthew with him, and in between games he asked Matthew, "Do you want to have a race down to the water?"

Matthew's face lit up. "Yeah!" he said excitedly.

They both crouched like runners at a starting block, and Mike said, "On your marks, get set—" and just as he said, "go!" he shoved his son into the sand and took off running to the water.

My friend Rana and I were both appalled at Mike's behavior. I couldn't believe a grown man could do something so mean to a little boy. But my friend Dave thought it was funny, and so did Mike. In fact, so did Matthew. They were all laughing while Rana and I stood there with our mouths hanging open in shock.

All the males thought this was great fun, and all the females thought it was mean. What a great example of how different masculine culture is than feminine culture.

I asked Mike later if he felt that he was teaching his son something important in that moment. He said, "Definitely. I was teaching him that life isn't fair, and that sometimes it's more important to have fun than to worry about winning. I was also teaching him to be tough—and how to be a guy with other guys."

That reminded me that Mike is responsible for teaching Matthew how to be a man. His mother can't do it, nor can any woman. Only a man can show a boy how to be a man, and this was apparently part of the lesson. Thankfully, now that I have the Six Intimacy Skills, I can appreciate the differences in the male culture where I used to be critical of it and think that I knew better.

A woman could easily witness that interaction and think Mike was a jerk. From the perspective of female culture, he was being mean. A woman would never push a little girl like that! I respect Mike a lot, and it still jarred my feminine sensibilities. I wanted to protect Matthew in that moment, but the truth is, Matthew was fine. He was getting initiated into being one of the guys.

Ellen had a similar experience when she saw her husband playing catch with her sons in the front yard. Her husband was throwing the ball too hard, so she ran out to explain to him that he needed to be gentle with them. "They're still little," she scolded him, "and they could get hurt."

Neither her husband nor the boys seemed to appreciate her comments, and it ended the game of catch altogether. But Ellen was sure she was doing the right thing protecting her cubs from their insensitive father.

Then Ellen learned the Six Intimacy Skills.

Later she told me, "I have to rethink everything I thought I knew. It's not easy to admit, but I think I did the wrong thing that day when they were playing catch. If I want my husband to teach my little boys to be men, I have to let him do it his way. What if other boys throw the ball hard at my sons? My husband was preparing them for that. Plus, they were all having a good time until I inserted myself into the situation and tried to control it, and that was the end of their fun. I was so sure I was right, but there was a high price to pay for interfering with my boys' relationship with their dad. I wasn't respectful of his role in their lives."

In other words, Ellen's husband was a smart Martian, but that wasn't immediately obvious from her Venusian perspective.

How Capable Is Your Husband?

One reaction I had to the cultural difference between my husband and me was embarrassment. I worried that if other people saw his peculiar (read. masculine) behavior, they would think (as I secretly did) that there was something wrong with him. Looking back, that seems like a remarkably self-righteous point of view, but I didn't see that at the time. Instead, I saw it as my job to try to mitigate, correct, or soften that peculiar behavior, or at least the appearance of it to the outside world, so that people wouldn't think my husband was uncivilized.

I'm not the only one. Mandy's version of this same sensibility was to feel that her husband was lazy and irresponsible for not getting his holiday shopping done early. She'd finished hers more than a month in advance, and he clearly hadn't even *started* by then. So she decided to take over his shopping. She even bought her own Christmas present from her husband for herself. She wrapped it and put it under the tree and let him know it was all taken care of—that he'd gotten her something nice for Christmas. That was early on in her marriage, and seven years later she was still buying her own present and putting it under the tree every year, and it didn't feel very good.

She complained to her mother Liz, "It's so hurtful. He doesn't even buy me a Christmas present! I have to do it myself. I really want him to do it, and I just don't know why he won't."

Her mother, well versed in the Six Intimacy Skills, pointed out that Mandy had taught her husband not to get her anything by buying presents for herself for so many years. Liz said that it's not uncommon for men to go Christmas shopping even right on Christmas Eve. She suggested that shopping at the last minute might even be part of male culture.

Liz suggested that Mandy consider not buying herself a Christmas present this year, but cautioned her that since she was changing the rules, it might mean that she wouldn't get anything. But Liz said that Mandy would be opening up the space to allow her husband to feel the full responsibility and delight of being able to make his own decisions about what to buy his wife for Christmas.

For the first time, Mandy understood that she had robbed her husband of that pleasure by buying his gifts for him. She felt vulnerable about not buying her own present for the first time, but she also agreed with her mom that there was no other way to get to a place where she would feel desired and cherished. She was going to have to start respecting his choices about gift buying—when it happened and what she received—in order to get the intimacy she was craving.

Mandy decided to apologize to her husband for being disrespectful by controlling the gifts for all those years—not just the one to her, but what he bought for his daughters and other family members as well. She explained that she didn't want to operate that way anymore and that she was relinquishing the job from there on, starting with deciding what he should get his daughter Brittney for her upcoming birthday. Mandy was nervous and exhilarated telling her husband these things. She didn't know what would happen. Would she and the girls be disappointed? Or would her husband rise to the occasion and pick out nice presents for them?

A short time later Mandy and her husband were at a jewelry store when he excitedly said, "I'll get a birthday present for Brittney here!" Mandy got a glimpse of the joy her husband felt about the prospect of getting his little girl a present of his own choosing. He was so happy when he found the perfect bracelet, and Mandy couldn't believe she had been depriving him of that joy for all these years. It was so moving to see him wanting to express his love for his daughter by getting her a beautiful gift.

"I was so happy for me, for him, and for our daughter that I got tears in my eyes," Mandy said. "I got out of the way and stopped controlling him, and there was so much more pleasure than I ever imagined when I started buying his presents for him so many years ago. I'll never do that again, now that I see what it's been costing all of us. I'm glad I finally trusted my husband."

What Do You Notice about Him?

I had one wife, Laileh, tell me that there was no way she could respect her husband.

"What could I respect him for?" she asked. "In ten years of marriage, he's never *once* taken me on vacation."

I said, "I hear that you're disappointed that he's never taken you on a vacation. I also remember you mentioned that he pays the mortgage, correct?"

"Well, yes—but he has to live somewhere. He lets us live with him, but so what?" Just like that, she dismissed how much her husband contributed to the family by paying the mortgage on their beautiful home in an upscale neighborhood. That's the biggest bill of all in most households, but to her it was nothing.

I asked, "Didn't you also tell me that every day after work he calls you and asks what he should bring home for dinner?"

"Yes," she agreed. "And no matter what I say, whether it's lobster or steak or even SuperMex, which he hates, he will always bring whatever I ask for."

He was starting to sound like a pretty considerate man to me, but Laileh didn't agree. "He's a very selfish man," she insisted.

"That's an affirmation," I told her. "Is that serving you?"

"It's not an affirmation," she insisted. "It's how he is. It's the truth."

From the outside, it looked like she was married to a great guy but chose not to focus on that. Instead she was fixated on how he hadn't taken her on vacation for ten years.

It was clear to me that he likely felt so disrespected around her that he didn't want to go on vacation together. It would have been too painful for him.

Laileh didn't know it, but she held the key to getting what she wanted. But even considering my perception of her husband—that he was generous and provided well for her and her daughter—seemed like too much of a stretch for Laileh.

What would you see if you took a stranger's perception of your husband or looked at him with fresh eyes, as though you were seeing him for the very first time? What qualities do you think a stranger would appreciate or admire about him?

I can understand Laileh's dilemma. When I thought my husband was lazy, I believed my perception was the truth too. I had all kinds of evidence, because that was what I focused on. However, once I started treating him with respect and looking at him through new eyes, I saw a really hard-working, responsible, accomplished guy. And I discovered that I didn't know as much as I thought I did.

Today I don't think my husband is lazy at all. And the only thing that changed was my perspective and my attitude. Once that changed, my husband responded to me with much more generosity, playfulness, and tenderness, just the way I wanted him to.

Now that I realize how smart he is, I look for opportunities to take his advice. Almost every day, I waltz from my home office into his home office and ask him to solve a problem for me, and most of the time he does. He suggests a course of action, or fixes the printer again, or sometimes suggests a different person to get advice from on a particular topic. Often he makes a suggestion that is clearly wise, and I'll think, "Oh, of course. That's it!" He brings another perspective, or he just sees something I don't.

Sometimes he just listens and comforts or acknowledges me. Sometimes he volunteers to complete a task that will ease my challenges. Not only is he insightful and wise, he's always got my back and cares deeply about my happiness. What an amazing resource! But I hardly ever relied on him before I learned the Six Intimacy Skills. Now I ask to "borrow his brain" all the time. I feel less alone, and he feels useful and helpful. We both love it.

It Pays to Be Respectful

Another benefit to changing your perspective and focusing on the ways your husband is smart, capable, and competent is that it's going to improve the prosperity at your house.

When your husband looks into your eyes and sees reflected back that you think he's a loser, that drains his self-esteem. If you reinforce that you think he's stupid with your words, he brings that low self-esteem with him out into the world. That will negatively affect his performance at work and in other aspects of his life as well.

However, if he looks into your eyes and sees that you think he's smart, capable, and competent, that will affect his self-worth in a positive way. If the woman who knows him best in the world believes he's wise and has good judgment, he will be that kind of man. He'll see the evidence of your opinion every day, every time you tell him, "Whatever you think—I trust you" or "That was a good idea. Thank you for taking care of that." All those things reinforce his sense of high self-worth and help him perform better in all aspects of his life.

We hear all the time that when women become more respectful, their husbands come home with raises and promotions. That was true with Renee's husband, who kept getting one promotion after another when she started practicing the Six Intimacy Skills. We also see a lot of husbands starting their own companies once their wives trust them to take that kind of risk.

I heard a businessman talking about how he got an offer to sell his company for several million dollars when he was still getting it off the ground. He told his wife about it, and she said, "Don't you trust yourself to keep growing your business? I certainly trust you." He decided to hold on to his company, and later he was able to sell it for more than twenty times that first offer. Her confidence in him resulted in a lot of prosperity for their family.

I also read about a football player with a long career in the NFL who said he avoided getting injured because he knew his wife trusted him out on the field. He was sure that her belief in him actually kept him safe during the game.

That's a remarkable thing to say, but I think I know what he means. The people we surround ourselves with contribute greatly to our perception of ourselves. Everyone around us is a mirror in some way. That football player's wife was mirroring her confidence in his ability to keep himself safe, and so he did.

If you're not feeling confident that your husband is smart, capable, and competent right now, it's okay to fake it until you make it. Just be sure to act as if he is all those things while you're gathering your evidence. Gathering evidence can be a very powerful way to bring that vision into reality, and it will lead to enjoying the connection you crave.

CHAPTER 11

Pretend You Love Your Husband More Than Your Children

Do You Parent Your Husband and Honor Your Children?

I don't have kids, but my sisters, girlfriends, and students talk about how, when their kids came into the world, they were so vulnerable and utterly dependent. They say that caring for them is unspeakably gratifying because it's purposeful and important. They speak about how those little people need them for their very survival and how that need contributed even more to the deep bond they felt. They tell me how completely smitten they were with their babies from the moment they arrived.

Heather told me she felt that, after the birth of her first son, her husband didn't really need her attention, at least not like her son did. She felt that she could focus all her energies on her son and that her husband would be fine. "He wasn't vulnerable and dependent like my baby, so I just let him fend for himself." Heather's baby was giving her much more of a high right then, so this behavior felt natural.

She also found herself unwittingly ordering her husband around. She'd say "Hand me that bottle" or "Go get the diaper bag." She was on a mission to care for her son, and it was an overwhelming amount of work. In the course of getting everything done, she inadvertently started honoring her child and parenting her husband.

Another husband told me that since the arrival of their new baby, he can't seem to do anything right for his wife. "Only she can wash the bottles the right way," he said. "Then she complains that she's so overwhelmed and tired. It's hard to know what to do for her other than just staying out of the way." So to keep the peace, he backed off and let his wife run the show. She may have noticed him playing on his phone while she was starting a load of laundry and decided he was unbelievably lazy or selfish. She probably resented that he was relaxing while she did all the work and wondered if she'd had a child with a child. From her point of view, he was certainly acting like one.

You Are Your Husband's Spokesperson

It's normal for mothers to fall madly, deeply in love with their children. But one of the best gifts you can give yourself and them is to at least pretend that you love your husband more. After all, those kids are half him, and they want nothing more than to have the home-court advantage of happy, united parents.

If you're trying to give your kids that happy home but finding it a struggle to keep the peace, here's a quick way to see if you are unwittingly pouring gasoline on the fire. Ask yourself these questions: What are the first three things that come to mind about your husband? How would you describe him?

Would you say he's grumpy a lot, loses his temper easily, and is obsessed with his phone? That he's forgetful, impatient, and insensitive? Or would you say he's hardworking, smart, and generous? Maybe you'd say he's dependable, thoughtful, and successful?

Whenever I meet a wife whose first few words about her husband are negative, I know right away that their marriage is a struggle. The surest indicator of a happy relationship is a wife who speaks highly of her husband. And the surest indicator of a marriage with big problems is a wife who automatically brings up her husband's faults.

You might think that's because a happy wife has married a good guy and an unhappy wife has not been so lucky. But there's more to it than that.

When a wife naturally speaks highly of her husband, she's demonstrating that she respects him. And when she respects him, that brings out his natural desire to make her happy, which makes her feel cherished. So when I hear respectful comments coming out of her mouth, I know that things are going pretty well at her home.

If, however, a woman naturally speaks critically or negatively about her husband, it tells me that she doesn't respect him and lets me know there's plenty of tension at home. He's sure to be defensive a lot, and therefore probably appears cranky, grumpy, or short-tempered. And she probably has no idea why.

Even worse, she most likely has a negative PR campaign going with the kids about their dad. If Mom is constantly complaining that Dad is a lazy slob, the kids are most likely going to take on that view, even though she's talking about their hero. Husbands get very defensive about that and start to seem hostile or distant but rarely say why.

It doesn't have to be that way.

When I've asked women to consider taking a different approach when they talk about their husbands in front of their kids, they'll sometimes say things like "I would, but it's true that he really is a slob" or "But he really is late all the time."

I get that they have plenty of evidence that their husbands have these negative qualities. But the "truth" is subjective in these cases. Yes, you may have years of evidence that your husband arrives late, but chances are he has also arrived on time on occasion. Perhaps that's the minority of the time, but it still calls into question the idea that he's *always* late.

Instead of constantly complaining about your husband's lateness, you could decide to say nothing about it or you could wait until he's on time and then mention how much you appreciate it. Your kids will get a completely different impression about their dad when you decide to focus on the positive.

Even if you believe you're speaking the absolute truth about your husband, when you criticize him in front of or directly to your kids, there's not much upside. But I have seen lots of distant, cranky, hostile husbands change overnight when they start to feel respected again.

You Can't Criticize Your Husband Without Hurting Your Kids

Another downside when you criticize your husband in front of your kids is that you're also criticizing them by extension. They came from that guy, so in a way you're putting them down when you put him down. You're also creating a vicious cycle where you reinforce the criticism of your husband, because your kids will parrot what you say and remind you what's wrong with their dad in the future.

Until she learned the Six Intimacy Skills, Evelyn believed her husband was cranky from working a lot, so she was always saying to the kids, "Dad's just being grumpy." She didn't think she was being disrespectful—just the opposite. She thought she was cutting the guy some slack, even though he'd been in a bad mood for the last decade. But when she changed her attitude, she was surprised to find out how much she had been contributing to that bad mood. Like when her husband said he'd gotten a bad deal on their new car because he paid for half of it and she got to drive it to work every day, her first thought was, "What about the years you were out of work and I paid for everything for you?" But instead she made a decision to be respectful. She said, "Yes, I did get a good deal on that. Thanks for being so generous." He beamed and was in a great mood after that.

In line at the hardware store later that day, Evelyn picked up a pink gardening hat and said, "I want this!" Then she put it back.

Her husband said, "Do you want it?"

Evelyn shrugged and said, "No, that's okay."

But her husband said, "I think you do because you said you do." He handed it to the cashier and said, "We'll take this."

She even noticed that her kids were getting along better and everybody seemed happier. Perhaps her husband wasn't as naturally grumpy as she'd thought. Perhaps he had just been living up to his bad PR.

One powerful way you can start honoring your husband is to be respectful of him in front of the kids. You could decide to always tell a positive story about him, even if it's hard for you to think about him that way. Your kids are likely buying into whatever you say, so you have a lot of power to represent their dad as capable and wise, or at least as the guy who keeps everybody in the family in mobile phones.

Growing up, my mom's PR about my dad was that he wasn't working up to his potential. She would tell us kids that he was a really smart guy and he could be making a lot more money and doing something he enjoyed a lot more than taking X-rays at a hospital. She actually brought people to the house to talk to my dad about various career opportunities she thought he should pursue. She would say what a shame it was that he didn't try to move up in the world and insist that he worked the graveyard shift because he couldn't get along with people. As a result, I grew up believing that my dad never achieved his potential and had poor people skills to boot.

My parents split up for the last time when I was seventeen. They were both at their worst during that split, which tore up the whole family. I could see for myself that my dad had serious anger issues, and I didn't have any relationship with him at all for years.

Then I learned the Six Intimacy Skills. Not only did I gain a completely different perspective on my husband, I saw my dad through new eyes as well.

Looking back, I now see that my dad worked two jobs to support a wife and four kids so that my mom never had to go to work. He worked the graveyard shift because he could make a little more money to bring home to his family. I also remember him helping me with my homework and taking us to Disneyland and to the beach for cookouts. I remember him sharing his love of reading, teaching me to use power tools, and helping me plant a strawberry patch.

The headline of that story could have been: "Man works really hard, provides a house, food, clothes, toys, and family vacations for six people." *That* guy deserves a medal. But, because of the way mom portrayed it, we grew up thinking of dad as a tragic, angry underachiever.

When I thought about all that I had gotten from my dad, I became a lot more grateful to and respectful of him. When I finally spoke to him again, one of the first things he said to me was, "Whatever I did in the past to upset you, I'm really sorry. You've always meant the world to me, and I've always wanted the world for you."

Only a Man Can Be a Good Dad

Another problem with criticizing your husband in front of your children is that you are undermining his authority and power. When you think about all the things that only a father can provide for a child, that's really a big loss.

I got a taste of how helpful a father can be when my husband and I were babysitting my six-year-old nephew Nate. I got him into the tub for a much-needed bath after a day at the fair, but I wasn't making much progress getting him washed. He told me I wasn't allowed into the bathroom, so I would just crack the door a bit every so often and say, "Nate, it's time to start washing off now. How about using some soap?" But he kept ignoring me in favor of playing with his toys.

I told my husband, "Nate's refusing to clean himself off."

John immediately marched into the bathroom and said, very authoritatively, "Nate! Wash yourself!" Nate grabbed the soap and immediately started using it vigorously.

John's authoritative approach was very different than my friendly suggestions, but it was really effective. A few minutes later I said, "Nate, it's time to get out of the tub and get ready for bed."

He ignored me.

I turned to John again, who walked in and said, "Nate! Out of the tub!"

Nate jumped out and started toweling himself off.

What a difference! Just like Matthew's dad Mike, John knew exactly what to do. It's as though men come with special talents for child-rearing that seem rather irreplaceable—and so helpful if we're willing to respect them.

I'm an amateur in the child-rearing department, so maybe I was doing it all wrong to begin with, but it was enormously helpful to me as an aunt to have my husband's help getting Nate to cooperate. I can only imagine what a big role fathers must play in keeping harmony at home.

Marcia couldn't understand why her husband would let her boys get rowdy when they were at a restaurant. She felt like he didn't notice them shrieking or jumping up and down, and then it was up to her to settle them down, which they didn't do easily. She resented having to be the bad guy while her husband just powered through his meal.

After some coaching around this issue, Marcia tried a different approach. When the boys were getting out of hand at a wedding, she turned to her husband and said, "I wish they would settle down. I would love to fool everyone into thinking we have well-behaved children." Her husband smiled, then immediately went over to the boys and put his head next to theirs. He was out of Marcia's earshot, but whatever he said, the two boys instantly changed their demeanor, sitting up straight in their chairs and quieting down.

Her husband not only did the heavy lifting, he got a better result than Marcia usually did in that situation.

"I realize that I hadn't left much room for him to do that kind of thing before," Marcia told me later. "I was the expert on these things, or so I thought, so he would hang back. But it's such a relief to have his help."

Your husband might also be happy to help more if he knew how pleased it would make you—and how much you wanted his help.

CHAPTER 12

Dishonesty Is the Best Policy

"Respect" Is an Action Word

When Gladys first started implementing the Six Intimacy Skills, she found herself apologizing to her husband quite a bit for being disrespectful. One day he turned to her and said, "You don't have to apologize for every little thing you say that's disrespectful."

Gladys paused and then said, "Actually, it's no longer acceptable to me to treat you disrespectfully, and therefore it's important for me to remind myself when I do. I feel you deserve my respect. You're my husband."

Today Gladys' husband brags (in an endearing way) to anyone who will listen about how wonderful his wife is. It's not hard to see why. Her decision to become a respectful wife not only makes him feel loved, it makes Gladys very attractive.

Still, deciding to become respectful is not always easy. When Lily and I discussed treating her husband respectfully, she told me "I just don't feel that I can respect him. He's put on so much weight, and he doesn't really have a relationship with our kids. He's on his computer all the time. I simply don't respect that."

Her husband's faults seemed really glaring right then, but there was more to it than that. He was also supporting the whole family, made Lily laugh a lot, was an accomplished musician, and took care of their cars.

In other words, he had good qualities too. The pieces Lily said she couldn't respect were only part of the story. If she opened her eyes a little wider, there was plenty to respect about her husband.

Your husband is the same way—he has some negative qualities, and you may be distracted by them right now. But focusing on those negative qualities is expensive: It's costing you the connection you could be enjoying. Maybe you feel like you have no choice but to focus on those things because they're so painful for you—but you do have a choice.

You've probably heard the expression "Love is not a feeling; it's a decision." Respect is the same way. You can decide to be respectful to your husband the same way you would be respectful to a stranger in a waiting room. Somehow, it can become more challenging to do it with our husbands when we are feeling hurt, disappointed, or lonely. But it can be done.

I'm not saying you will always agree with your husband when you decide to be respectful to him. That would be oppressive. Respect just means *honoring* his choices. It means you don't tell him what to eat, what to do at work, how to drive, how to be neater, or how to be more romantic. That would be controlling, and control is disrespectful. Respect means you refrain from rolling your eyes at him, dismissing what he says, or speaking for him.

Instead, remind yourself that you married a capable man and act accordingly. Treat him as though you trust him and expect him to make good decisions.

It's Okay to Fake It

It might feel false at first. It might feel like the biggest lie you ever told to act like you respect your husband. But just hang in there—it's totally okay to pretend. You don't have to *feel* like it to make this transformation. That's what I mean when I say "Dishonesty is the best policy."

Are you feeling disgusted with your husband's football-watching habits? Pretend you respect him and go do some self-care. Do you want to strangle him for trampling muddy boots all over the house? Lie to maintain that cool respectful exterior and then express your desire for a clean floor. Are you at your wit's end because he overdrew the account again? Instead of letting him have it, act like you trust him by letting him handle the fallout.

Why? Because it's better for you. When you act respectful, two things will happen: First, your husband will respond to you with more tenderness and generosity because he feels safe. He'll finally be getting what he's always craved—and so will you. Second, you'll actually start to *feel* more respectful of your husband. You'll hear yourself saying those respectful things in a calm voice, and it will start to affect your subconscious, like an affirmation. You'll also notice that as you're being more respectful, your husband becomes more thoughtful, attentive, and helpful. Suddenly he seems like a better guy. It's a virtuous cycle: The more you respect him, the more he acts like the man you fell in love with, which is a guy who's not so hard to respect.

Just making this one choice—to treat him with respect whether it seems like he deserves it or not—is going to have a far-reaching impact on how you and he interact every day. The level of respect you bring to the relationship determines whether you spend your time smiling and laughing together and enjoying each other's company or sleeping in separate beds with a thick layer of hostility throughout the house.

If you doubt that there is anything more important to your husband than having your respect, consider Dana's experience when she and her husband went to marriage counseling. The counselor asked them each to make a list of all the things that made them feel loved. Dana began writing furiously, but she noticed that her husband wasn't writing anything. That made her upset because she figured he wasn't even doing the assignment—more proof that he just didn't care about the relationship.

But after she read her list of a dozen things that made her feel loved, her husband shared what he had written. It was just one word: "Respect."

Don't Confuse Criticism and Honesty

One of the things I often hear is how important it is to be honest in a romantic relationship, but I know I used to be confused about that. I thought that meant that if I didn't like my husband's old, ratty U2 shirt from the last millennium, I should tell him, "That shirt is disgusting, and you should throw it out."

But that's really criticism, which has nothing to do with honesty. It's very easy to criticize; it doesn't take any responsibility or maturity. But being honest about how you're feeling and what you want takes both maturity and vulnerability.

If I'm so out of sorts that I find it necessary to criticize my husband's shirt—as though him changing his shirt is actually going to impact my happiness—chances are I am a little frazzled and depleted. If I were honest, I would probably have to say, "I'm so tired I can't see straight, which is making me cranky." What other explanation can there be for being so focused on what someone else is wearing?

How can you tell if you're being critical or honest?

Criticism is about the other person: something they are doing wrong, should improve, or that's just bugging you.

Honesty is when you speak about yourself. That's how you can tell the difference.

For example:

"You're wasting a lot of time playing video games" is a criticism and a complaint. There's nothing honest in that statement.

"I miss you" is about you and therefore is completely honest.

"I feel like you're never emotionally available for me" is an insult and a complaint that's trying to pretend it's an honest feeling. There are no feeling words (guilty, sad, afraid, etc.) here to make it honest.

"My sister really hurt my feelings, and I'm so sad about it" is a tender truth.

"You're such a slob" is hurtful and critical.

"I would love to wake up to a clean kitchen in the morning" is an honest desire.

The first thing you'll notice about the honest statements is that they're a lot scarier to say than complaints and criticisms. It's a lot riskier to put yourself out there that way. But it's also much more likely to bring you the response and connection you're craving.

Before I knew this, I ran around saying critical, hurtful things and calling it honesty. I told myself I was just voicing hard truths that had to be said. In reality, I was an unpleasant toothache of a person. I was constantly complaining. There is nothing heroic about that.

Now, if I revert back to my old unfortunate ways and say something snide, I know I have the tools to restore the intimacy quickly by apologizing for being disrespectful, just like Gladys.

I use those very words: "I apologize for being disrespectful when I complained about your U2 T-shirt." And I leave it alone after that. Because sometimes, if I'm really out of sorts, it's tempting to go on to say, "It's just that it's got that stain on the front and it's so ratty." But if I say that, I've just been disrespectful again, and now I owe my husband another apology. Better to just quit while I'm ahead—which is right after I've apologized.

The wonderful thing about having the ability to apologize is that it can restore intimacy fast. I've seen the wall of tension fall down instantly when I've said those powerful words: "I apologize for being disrespectful."

If there's a lot of tension and distance at your house, you might ask yourself if there's something you've done that's disrespectful. If so, you have the opportunity to apologize and restore the intimacy. When the intimacy in your relationship is gone, it's almost always an indication that the respect is missing too. You might be surprised at how quickly you can get both back with a simple apology.

A Tale of Two Retired Husbands

Kathy had a high-paying job as a CFO of a private school, and while she liked the security and status of the position, she knew accounting wasn't her true calling. So when she accepted an offer to work at an even more prestigious school, she knew within days that she'd made a big mistake. She continued to slog it out for several weeks, but a month later, things had come to a head. She could barely get herself to go to work in the morning. Something had to give, but her husband was retired and they depended on her income to live.

Kathy didn't know what to do, but she had been practicing the Six Intimacy Skills for years, so she decided to trust that her husband would step up to relieve the pressure during her personal crisis. Her message to him was: "I can't continue to work in this career. I've reached my limit." She didn't tell him what he needed to do or that she was tired of being the sole breadwinner. There was no blame or shame. She just spoke for herself.

Sure enough, her husband saw an opportunity to help his wife and he jumped at it. He said, "I'll get a job, and that way you won't have to worry so much." Kathy was so relieved and happy to hear those words. Within weeks her husband was working selling cars. He was so happy and proud to have the job because it allowed his wife to change to a career she absolutely loved: working as a certified relationship coach with me.

Every morning her husband would get up inspired to go to work. He'd say, "I am going to sell some cars today!" He even said, "Honey, I am so happy that you get to do what you love while I'm out earning a living for us. I'm just so happy this is all working out." He was really motivated to be providing for his wife so she could have what she desired. That risky decision paid off for Kathy and Doug: Today Kathy is one of the most successful relationship coaches in the world and has been instrumental in helping thousands of women make their marriages last and thrive. But she never would have gotten there without expressing her desires and triggering Doug's hero gene.

Around that time, I read an advice column about another couple in a similar situation. The husband said that he had decided to retire four years early. His wife hadn't wanted him to do that, but he did it anyway. To show how unhappy she was about it, she stopped speaking to him. The husband complained that they were now sleeping in separate bedrooms, and his wife had started locking her door so he wouldn't try to sleep with her.

In this case, the wife tried to control her husband, but it didn't work—he retired anyway. So she punished him. Of course the intimacy in their relationship was destroyed in the process. Too bad she didn't know the Six Intimacy Skills. That couple could have been enjoying affection and intimacy like Kathy and her husband.

Being honest and respectful is much more effective in both getting the desired outcome and keeping the connection you enjoy with your husband. When you trust your man, he feels a fierce sense of responsibility. I see this over and over.

In this abridged excerpt from *The Empowered Wife Podcast* episode 96, I interviewed Darla, whose marriage was full of tension and conflict. The lack of intimacy was excruciating, and she didn't know how to break out of it.

DARLA: My marriage was just cold war after cold war. We couldn't make up, and it was just a pattern.

I didn't understand how this could happen because my husband and I met at church. He was from another country. He came on a fiancé visa to marry me, and we had to prove our love to the US government so that he could come in. So, of course, this is a marriage made in heaven! And things are good for about the first two to three years.

Then things started taking a turn. And at the worst part, I would think, "I hate you!" I would even say it under my breath sometimes. It's so painful.

I used to park in the garage, and I didn't want to go in the house. He would leave on a trip, maybe to see his family overseas for like a week, or two weeks, and I wouldn't miss him. Things were not going smoothly, but it just started out so well—I didn't know what happened.

Now I know I was disrespectful. We would argue, and I would raise my voice, and then he would get mad at me for raising my voice. I didn't realize that was disrespectful, and then the cold war could last days, two weeks, and it would spiral. I didn't know how to pull out of it.

LAURA: Then during the cold war, was there no talking, or was there arguing?

DARLA: A lot of times, it was no talking. Just him avoiding me.

Our daughter was young, and I didn't know about self-care then, so I felt overwhelmed with that. I was the breadwinner at the time—financial breadwinner—and I felt responsible for the home *and* the financial side of it. I felt overwhelmed and felt like I was in a hole.

LAURA: Were you thinking, "Why do I even need this guy?" Did it ever cross your mind to maybe end your marriage?

DARLA: I had so much faith that God brought us together. I knew I had a covenant. I made a covenant before all these people, before God. I'd heard that marriage morphs into something where you're not in love, and love is a choice. I knew these things we hear over the years, and [I thought] I made this choice, and it's my fault. And I'm just going to have to get through it, even if there's not a lot of love. I didn't know that things could be better.

LAURA: Wow, but you were so unhappy and sad! And you were willing to continue on like that, for the rest of your life, it sounds like.

DARLA: Yes; I have other things that bring me joy. But I would hope that, since my marriage is just that important, it could have been something that brought me joy on a daily basis. But I was stuck.

LAURA: Was there ever a moment where you thought, "Okay, we just can't go on like this, something's really got to give"?

DARLA: Yes, and I made that decision to stay with him. I just took it day by day. But the thought of saying "I hate you!" in my mind really showed me how unhealthy it was.

LAURA: And how painful it was, for you to get to that point. So what happened?

DARLA: I was looking through Amazon recommendations for books. I came across your book one day, and I started reading some of the testimonials, and most of them sounded good—but I've read several marriage books, and they all seem the same, and they all say, "respect your husband and give up yourself for him," basically. But this was so different.

I saw the book and I was like, I'm not going to spend money on this book. I'm gonna see if the library has it—so I checked my local library, and they had it. I picked up your first book and started reading it, and I started experimenting with everything. All of the skills that you talked about. Everything worked within two weeks, like my marriage was completely different, and it was like a miracle, Laura.

LAURA: Wait, what did you try? What kinds of things did you do?

DARLA: Yes, so in your first book, you talk about maybe starting in the car. So I started in the car with duct tape [keeping my mouth shut]. And I decided it's really hard not to tell someone when the light turns green to go, or where to park or slow down. So it was perfect practice for me. I was sitting in the car, and I wouldn't tell him where to go or how to get there. And I could ease my way into these skills. It worked really well.

One day I had a vase of flowers on my lap, and I was thinking, "What if he has to slam on his brakes?" And it ended up happening! He slammed on the brakes, and I didn't say anything. And my daughter's in the backseat, and she's like, "Mom, you didn't say anything!" Then my husband turned back to her, touched my head, and said, "You see? Your mother trusts me."

I have so many little stories about things that worked just out of the blue. Things he would say to show me he was responding to what I was doing.

LAURA: Beautiful! So within two weeks, you felt like you had a new marriage! You started by relinquishing control in the car. What else did you do that was different?

DARLA: I stopped telling him what to wear.

Every Sunday morning, he would ask me what to wear for church. We would always get in an argument—like, almost every Sunday! He would have, like, two things out, and I would pick the wrong thing, and he would start disrespecting me or insulting me, but *I* was starting it.

To this day, sometimes he still asks me what he should wear, but I just don't tell him anymore—and that was actually the first time I used "Ouch!" I shouldn't be telling him what to wear in the first place, but he insulted me, and I said "Ouch!" And the argument stopped, and I was like, "This is magic!" Usually it would go on and on, and we'd be in a cold war on the way to church. It just stopped, and I was like, "Oh my goodness! These skills work!"

LAURA: Wow, that is so cool—and he still asks you. What do you say now when he asks you?

DARLA: Most of the time he doesn't, but every once in a while he does. But I just duct tape about it and kind of laugh, and he kind of laughs about it too.

I stopped reminding him to take out the trash. And I gave him gratitude for the things he deserved. For so many years, I didn't. I always thought, if I thank him for something, it may become optional to him to do it. And I learned that's not the truth. I started getting all this thanks back. I was stingy giving him gratitude. So that works beautifully—he showered it back on me.

I didn't criticize his gifts. I became a better receiver. I stayed out of his business. That was big for me, Laura. He was kind of starting a company around that time that I was reading the books and wanting to change. And he would ask me all the time, "What do you think about this? On the website?"

I was maybe a little more on the fear side, so I would've said, "Take a step back," and tell him to not be so gung ho into building this business. But I decided, because I had just read your book, that I was going to duct tape about it instead of giving him my fears and my opinions.

Well, now this business is our major source of income, and I would have stifled that by sharing my fears. I get to stay home part-time with my babies, and I would have stopped that process from happening because of my fear, so I just had to duct tape.

Like you say in your books, why would I know what's better for my husband's business than my husband? That makes so much sense to me. Now I just let him talk and duct tape, and it works beautifully.

LAURA: He wants to be seen, heard, and respected, and you're giving them that. I'm totally impressed that you did that. Did that bring up some fear for you, not asking him about the business and thinking, "This is not going to go well!"?

DARLA: Of course! And I still think that sometimes.

I treat it like an experiment, and almost 100 percent of the time, it works out. He is right in the first place, and he really does not want my opinion. He just wants to talk it out and know that he makes good decisions. So that's probably one of the things that has changed our marriage, is me not being helpful. You're the first person that told me

I didn't have to be helpful. I didn't have to emasculate him by helping him so much with his business. Once he made his own decisions, he could feel the weight of those decisions. And there was such a weight taken off me that I didn't have to be responsible for his decisions. It made me a lighter person.

LAURA: So he looks into his wife-mirror and he sees reflected back to him, "I trust you. I think you make good decisions."

DARLA: I used the spouse-fulfilling prophecy. I said, "You make great decisions." I said that one morning. And I said, "You have great ideas!" And then later that day, he said, "I have a great idea!" Now he'll come to me and my daughter and be like, "I have an idea!" and he wants us to say, "You have the best ideas! What is it?" And he does! He has great ideas.

LAURA: When you first said, "You make the best decisions! You have great ideas!"—did it feel like a stretch? Did you feel like, "I'm not so sure about this, but I'm going to say it anyway"?

DARLA: A little bit. I mean, this has been fairly recent, so I know the skills to be true, and I do trust his decisions. But yeah, back in the day, I would have to say things like, "Whatever you think!" and leave the room. Because it was weighing on me so much, like I couldn't say anything else. I just had to leave the room. I didn't know what the right decision was.

LAURA: This is a very conscious effort on your part. Does it take focus?

DARLA: It takes a lot of focus. It's still a process that I'm changing the way I'm speaking and thinking, but it's gotten a lot easier, and it's totally worth it. It's totally worth it for the intimacy. It's a choice to choose intimacy.

LAURA: Yeah, it's a choice, and you know how to choose it now. You didn't know how to choose it previously, but now you do, and it's a price you're willing to pay. It sounds like a great marriage.

DARLA: That's how I feel, yes.

LAURA: Now, he also came to you with bad news at one point about an affair.

DARLA: Right, yes. So life is good, and we had our baby boy. I had self-care this time. It was so much better because with my daughter I didn't have self-care, and I was just worn out.

At seven weeks the baby had an appointment, and my husband was acting kind of withdrawn and distant. I knew something was coming. I tried to stay on my paper. So he sat me down when the baby was seven weeks old. He was bawling. He could hardly get the words out, and he told me that he had an affair. It had been years earlier. My heart was broken. It was with a friend of mine.

And it's kind of like when you don't have words. You're just quiet. Like you don't even know what to say. But he had just been with me through this intense delivery. It was short, but no epidural, and he was there. He was my partner. And he was taking good care of our family. I decided that there was one thing that was on my paper, and that was to forgive him. Forgiveness is on my paper.

I know now that forgiveness is more for me than for the people that we forgive. So I did forgive him, and we just started to heal together. And I tried to not talk about it with him. Of course, things came up in awkwardness, even between the other couple and us.

But I tried to smother it. I didn't give it oxygen. And I realized that I was responsible for healing myself. He wasn't responsible for that. So I really started digging deep and reading certain books on healing and being a loving person and forgiving, and I really realized that was on my paper.

It's been about two and a half years since I found out, and we are so good now. But that was really, really hard to go through. But I had the Skills. Thank you so much, I had those Skills, because the affair happened pre-Skills. Before, I didn't know anything. Now, I had your Skills to help me through it.

And I knew not to go to marriage counseling. I think, just by default, we would have gone to marriage counseling before, but I knew that it would just be speaking badly of my husband during the sessions. And he proved himself to me that he was an excellent father and husband, and it wasn't necessary. That was a hard time, but we made it. And things are better than ever.

LAURA: Oh, wow! Impressive! I love that you saw that forgiving him was on your paper, and I want to have you walk us through that process a little bit. Because I think this is very challenging for a lot of women, to find that forgiveness. I'm wondering what your process was for that.

DARLA: Well, I wanted to keep my side of the street clean, so if that meant forgiving him and the girl, my friend that did that to me, then I was going to do that, so I did tell him I forgave him. I even texted the girl, before she texted me, that I forgave her, and that I didn't think she was the same person that did that to me so many years before. So I think my main theme in my mind was that I wanted to keep my side of the street clean, and how could I hold so much against other people if I had forgiven myself for my past?

LAURA: Amazing, so this really affects the way you show up in the world to everyone: to this friend that betrayed you, to your husband. How would you say that you've changed personally?

DARLA: Well, I love having gone through it, so that I can help other people. I feel like it's a test that I passed and I feel like I know how to have grace with people. And to not expect perfection, to be more empathetic with people. I have gone through a little bit of pain and have shown people that there's definitely hope.

LAURA: I hear this feels like an accomplishment, first of all, and I agree. This is a huge accomplishment. You've created a wonderful family where there could have been a lot of heartbreak and a lot more conflict, and there's just so much dignity and such a good clean feeling, being able to text somebody and say, "I forgive you" before she even talked to you.

DARLA: I like that word, "dignity." I felt good about it, good about myself for doing it. That's a perfect world, just showing up as my best self, like your book says.

LAURA: What is your marriage like now?

DARLA: Whereas before I wouldn't miss him if he'd gone on a one-week journey somewhere, [now] I miss him if he's gone thirty minutes! We text several times a day, saying we love each other; "I love you," and "thanks for working."

I'm just a more pleaseable person, more laid back. I don't have to get my way all the time. I don't have to be a know-it-all. That's such a relief.

He flirts with me. He takes my daughter to and from school most days so I can sleep in the morning with the baby. That's so nice of him—and he'll tell me to come closer to him on the couch.

Not long after I'd started the Skills, he kissed me and said, "I feel butterflies!" I was thinking that takes me back to even pre-marriage, engagement, falling in love—those same feelings. So renting that book from the library was so worth it—and now, of course, I own every book you've written.

Relinquish Control of Your Man

All control is based in fear. If you're not afraid, you don't need to try to control what your husband says on the phone, what he eats for lunch, or how much money he spends.

If you've ever corrected your husband's driving or told him what to wear or when to mow the lawn, you were suffering from the illusion that you could control him.

I know this sounds extreme—I once thought so too. But over time I came to see that knowing where I end and my husband begins, and behaving accordingly, was absolutely critical to having a great relationship. It improved the rest of my life in big ways too.

PRESCRIPTION

If you have a hard time refraining from commenting on something that is your husband's responsibility or decision, ask yourself:

1. What am I afraid of?
2. Is my fear realistic?
3. Can I actually control the situation?
4. Is it worth the intimacy it would cost me to try to control?

When you feel the urge to control, try asking yourself these
questions first to empower yourself to make a choice
about whether to say what's on the tip of your tongue or
to focus on your own happiness and self-care instead.

CHAPTER 13

Stay on Your Own Paper

"A true soul mate is a mirror, the person who shows you
everything that is holding you back, the person who brings you
to your own attention so you can change your life."

—Elizabeth Gilbert, Author

I Can't Get Away with Anything Anymore

John was driving me to a radio interview recently. He got into the left-hand turn lane and I said, "Why are you turning here? Shouldn't we be going straight?"

That's right—I was telling him how to drive to a familiar destination, in an urgent "do as I say" tone. It wasn't pretty. And I was on my way to a show where I would tell other women how to stop controlling their husbands and boyfriends!

In the old days, John might have snapped at me, accepted my invitation to have an argument, or just sighed heavily and then acquiesced to my demands. But these days he responds to me differently, knowing that my standard for myself is to focus on my own responsibilities instead of commenting on how he's handling his.

John just looked at me, one eyebrow slightly raised as if to say "Really?"

I was busted.

"It's stuffy in here," I said. "I'm going to roll down the window and let some of the hypocrisy out of the car."

But what's wrong with offering a navigational tip, you might argue? What if my way is faster or better? Shouldn't I be able to say so?

Of course! I can say whatever I want. We all can. But there are definite downsides to micromanaging my husband's driving. It's annoying, for one thing, so it hurts the intimacy and connection between us. In addition, there isn't much upside to backseat driving. Going straight instead of turning left and then arriving at the same place at around the same time isn't exactly a big payoff.

Not saying anything about the way he drives and taking the opportunity to laugh and talk together on the way instead has a huge upside. Doing that every day for years and years makes our time in the car together sweet and fun.

The Best Self-Improvement Project

Getting married was the best self-improvement project I've ever undertaken. I can say without a doubt that I'm a better sister, friend, daughter, and coworker now than I was before I started practicing the Six Intimacy Skills with my husband. My happy marriage is my greatest accomplishment because in learning to nurture intimacy, I also gained humility, discipline, dignity, respect, self-care, gentleness, and acceptance. Where those virtues were once a list of words that I didn't fully comprehend, I now enjoy the astonishing benefits of having some degree of each of those qualities—all because I desperately wanted to feel loved and desired.

The reason being married has been such an effective teacher is that every day I'm faced with my spouse-mirror. I get an immediate and accurate reflection of my energy from my husband. When I'm happy and playful, he's typically attentive and affectionate. When I'm controlling, he's reliably distant and defensive. When I'm vulnerable, he's quick to respond with tenderness and protection. When I'm grateful, he looks for even more ways to delight me. When I treat him respectfully, it engenders passion and adoration. When I'm anxious, he tries to comfort me, unless I'm anxious about him or something he's responsible for—then we're back to distant and defensive.

In other words, he's a reliable barometer of my attitude, which I have complete control over.

Granted, he's also a separate person who has complete control over his own attitude, and he may have an unpleasant demeanor from time to time. He's only human, after all. But when I embarked on this journey, the most shocking part of all was finding out that, most of the time, my husband was reflecting back to me what I was bringing to the party. In other words, I recognized that I had a lot of power—much more than I realized.

Confusing Courage with Controlling

Practicing the Six Intimacy Skills is a lot like applying the Serenity Prayer to my marriage.

God, grant me the serenity to accept the things I cannot change, the courage to change the things I can, and the wisdom to know the difference.

Who can argue with the universal truths in this prayer? Well, I did, for years. Before I discovered the Six Intimacy Skills, I was pretty unclear on which things I could change and which I couldn't. For example, if we were going out to a party, I figured I had a say over what "we" were wearing. That meant I could criticize John's shirt or tell him to change his shoes, and I believed I was still squarely in the part where you change the things you can. I figured I was just being courageous. So I couldn't understand the hostile response I was getting from simply trying to *help* him dress better. Granted, I wanted him to dress *my* way, but my way was clearly better.

In actuality, my attempts to help John dress better were far from courageous. That was me acting out an irrational fear that people would think my husband didn't dress very well if he didn't wear what I thought he should wear. I was afraid people were going to judge *me* for how he was dressed. Maybe some people do, but that's not something I can control, so I don't try anymore. My husband and I have a mutual agreement to alert each other about unseemly nose hairs, but other than that, I don't see it as my responsibility to make sure he's presentable. He was perfectly capable of dressing himself before I was born, and since I thought he was so attractive when we fell in love (and I still do!), he must have been doing just fine with his threads. Now I rarely say anything about what he wears except "That's a great shirt on you—it really brings out your eyes," or other similar compliments. And guess what? He dresses himself very well.

Here's a metaphor I've come to rely on for deciding if I should comment on something: I ask myself if this is something that's "on my paper." As a kid at school, it was very tempting to look at someone else's paper, to see if she was doing the homework right. But ultimately my grade was a reflection of what was on *my* paper when I turned it in, not hers. I was responsible for—and only responsible for—my own work.

Today when I ask myself if something's "on my paper," I think about everything I'm responsible for and in control of, such as how I dress, what I say, what tone of voice I use, my attitude, which websites I visit, who I talk to, where I go, what I eat, how much I sleep, and whether or not I floss. Everything that I don't have direct control over, responsibility for, and choice about is *not* on my paper, and therefore I don't need to worry about it. That would take energy away from what's on my paper.

My version of the serenity prayer is more like a flow chart:

God, whose paper is this on?

Answer A (which comes up way more than you might think):
    Not mine.

Then help me be respectful and *grateful* for it.

Answer B: Mine.

Then help me be brave enough to honor my desire about it.

It turns out that my husband's clothes are not anywhere on my paper. That means his choice of attire is something to be respectful of and grateful for. After all, I'm not the expert on his life—he is. I haven't been dressing a guy for decades, but he has. And I'm not exactly a fashionista anyway, so I'm not sure how I got started being so authoritative about his clothes to begin with.

One of the unintended consequences of applying my version of the serenity prayer in my marriage has been that whenever I find myself thinking that my husband should change in some way, it's actually a sign that there's something going on with me that I'm not paying attention to. Whenever I'm obsessing about what's on his paper—what he's written, why it's not right, why I think he should change it—it means my own paper is in some kind of trouble. I'm oblivious to the questions I haven't answered for myself, the blogs I haven't written, and the lesson I'm not taking in or practicing—and, therefore, the peace and joy on the other side.

I also see this with our coaching students all the time.

For instance, Jenna was very focused on how her husband's schedule didn't sync with hers and how they didn't get to see each other very often. When she was going to bed, he was often staying up late. When she was up and ready to start her day, he needed to keep sleeping. She asked, pleaded, begged, and cajoled him to change his schedule to be more like hers—more like what she thought the schedule of a normal person should be. But the more she insisted, the more he resisted. She took that as a personal rejection. "If he really wanted to spend more time with me, he could do his work earlier and get up earlier, and then we'd be on a similar schedule," she told me. Her plaintive tone told me that Jenna believed her husband really needed to change for her to be happy.

She seemed confused when I asked about her self-care. "How are you doing with your oil painting?" I asked her, knowing that was something she enjoyed very much. She was quiet for a moment and then admitted she hadn't painted a thing in months. "How's the rest of your self-care?" I pressed. The longer we talked, the clearer it became that Jenna's husband's schedule was a clever distraction from her real problem: the inner critic who had moved into her head and was preventing her from painting anything because it wouldn't be "good enough."

It's a lot easier to find fault with someone else than to find the courage to face our own fears and faults. There were plenty of interesting things happening on Jenna's paper, but she was missing them. When she put herself on a regular painting regimen, her concerns about her husband's schedule melted away.

When Papers Collide

Everything in your world—your decisions, your responsibilities, your relationships, what you wear and eat—that's on your paper. Everything in your husband's world—his decisions, his responsibilities, his relationships, what he wears and eats—that's on his paper. Know the difference, and your marriage will be a cakewalk. Get them mixed up and it becomes a forced march.

But what about things in the middle, things you're both responsible for or that impact you both, like your children, your finances, and the household chores? What if what's on his paper impacts you? How can you know whether to weigh in on the things that you share or keep silent?

Tiffany felt she understood the concept of staying on her own paper, but she wanted to know what she should do if her husband's paper overlapped with hers or if her daughter's paper overlapped with both of theirs. Tiffany had been feeling resentful about picking up dirty clothes her daughter Anna was throwing on the floor instead of in the hamper. She made a new policy: When her daughter put things in the hamper, she would wash them for her. Anything *not* in the hamper wouldn't get washed.

Her daughter didn't pay much attention to the new policy and continued to leave clothes on the floor. Tiffany was prepared to follow through and let the consequences be what they may, but her husband came in and gathered up all the dirty clothes—even the ones on the floor—and washed them. Tiffany was hurt and angry that her husband was undermining her efforts. She asked him to stop, explaining that she was trying to teach their daughter the consequences of not using the hamper, but her husband was more interested in getting the chores done than worrying about where the dirty clothes belonged. Frustrated, Tiffany wanted to know how she could get her husband to stop washing her daughter's clothes and help Anna understand that actions have consequences.

I asked Tiffany to think carefully about just what was on her paper, what she really had control over. She thought for a moment and said, "I don't pick up socks from the floor. I only wash what's in the hamper." Those were clear limits, which were perfectly on her paper.

Her next question was, "How can I teach my daughter to use the hamper if my husband keeps indulging her?" Now she was back on her husband's and daughter's papers.

I asked Tiffany what the benefit would be to her if her husband did stop picking up the clothes off the floor. "I would get my daughter to start picking up her clothes," she answered. I asked her how it would benefit her if her daughter started picking up her clothes, since she was not planning to pick them up herself. Tiffany thought hard and said, "Well, her room wouldn't be such a mess all the time."

"How does it affect you if her room is a mess?" I asked.

"I don't like to see the mess in there!" she said. "In fact, I'm sick of it."

"Is it within your control to have her room be tidy?" I asked.

"Well, so far it doesn't seem like it is," she said. "I guess you're right. I would love to have it be tidy, but I can't make her clean it and I don't want to clean it myself. I can always close the door and walk away," she admitted. "That might be the best thing."

It's reasonable to want to have order in your home, and it's reasonable to want to teach your daughter to be tidy. But as much as Tiffany felt that her husband was undermining her efforts to mother her daughter, it would have been just as interfering for Tiffany to insist that her husband do things her way. After all, dads often do things differently than moms. By staying focused on her own limits (not being willing to pick up dirty clothes from the floor), Tiffany was able to untangle her paper from her husband's and her daughter's papers—two distinctly sovereign individuals whom she can either accept or reject, but not control. This also allowed them to have their own father-daughter relationship without interference from Tiffany.

She could have easily gone down the path of trying to convince everyone that her way was right—that the daughter needed to put clothes in the hamper—but it probably wouldn't have worked. Tiffany would have also created plenty of tension and stress in her home by doing that. Instead, she looked at her own feelings and desires and responded accordingly.

Tiffany knew that she could continue to express her pure desire to have a tidy room. By detaching from the outcome, she was choosing harmony and intimacy with her husband over a few dirty socks that she no longer has to pick up. She even took a playful approach by saying to her daughter, "You're so lucky your dad did the laundry! Otherwise you'd have had to go barefoot today."

In a light way, she acknowledged the different policies between her and her husband, and let her daughter know she was taking her chances with her socks.

CHAPTER 14

Communication Is Overrated

"In every marriage more than a week old, there are grounds for divorce. The trick is to find, and continue to find, grounds for marriage."

—Sir Robert Anderson, Author

One Word That Says It All

Before I learned the Six Intimacy Skills, I didn't think of myself as a nag. Looking back, though, I often said the same things over and over—which is the very definition of nagging. So yeah, I was a nag.

I felt justified in doing this because I didn't think my husband was *listening* to me. I believed that if I delivered my message in a slightly different way, if I got him to really understand the urgency or the importance, he would do what I wanted. Naturally, that never worked. That's because what I was really doing was trying to control his actions.

Now, communicating with my husband means chatting about the movie we saw together or making plans for the weekend—not the dreaded "we have to talk" conversations I used to rope him into. This is always astonishing to my coaching students at first, because they're also in the habit of trying to talk their way into having their husbands see their perspective.

These days, I'm confident that I can say what I mean in one sentence or sometimes just a single word, and I no longer repeat myself like a trained parrot. In some ways, I say much less than I did before, and that has helped a lot. Saying less has led to greater communication, in that my husband understands me much better.

I had heard about communication being the key to a good marriage so often that I was constantly trying to get John to talk more. And I talked more too—I figured I just needed to talk until he saw things my way. I used the "have good communication" advice as a license to keep talking until John was a beaten-down pulp who didn't dare disagree with me. That wasn't exactly bringing us closer together.

But today, I know that talking less and choosing among my real thoughts—the ones that pertain to me and all that concerns me—will be what gets me the connection and passion I crave.

Your Minimum Drama Requirement

I recently asked one of my coaches if she and her husband would be willing to participate in a TV show. The producers wanted to film the interactions in a home where the wife was practicing the Six Intimacy Skills. My coach agreed to be on the show, but she said, "Wow, they're going to really think this is boring because there is very little conflict in our house anymore."

That's my experience too. There's just not much to argue about once you learn these skills and give up the need to control everything. Once you know how to advocate for your desires and your feelings, and you're doing it in a respectful way to a man who loves you and wants you to be happy, the drama vanishes.

Most of the time our marriage is really peaceful, so I have to find my drama somewhere else, like on the volleyball court. Sometimes I suggest that my students take acting lessons as a drama outlet. We all have our minimum drama requirements, so if you don't want that drama to manifest in your marriage, consider providing it for yourself somewhere else.

The End of Compromising

Your husband really wants you to be happy. When you're happy, he feels successful as a husband and as a man.

No matter how bad things are in the relationship, your husband's desire to make you happy is alive and well. If it doesn't seem like that right now, that's because when you're in conflict or a cold war, your husband's need to defend himself will supersede his drive to please you. But as soon as he feels respected again, he'll be looking for any chance to delight you.

The more he knows about what will make you happy, the easier it will be for him to feel successful as a husband. That's why it's so important for you to know your desires and express them clearly. If your husband knows how to make you happy, he can do something about it—and then you're both happy.

That's why it's important to take your own happiness seriously. If mama's not happy, nobody's happy.

My job in my relationship, therefore, is to know what I want. My feelings help point the way to what I desire, so I'm always asking myself, "How do I feel? What do I want?" Once I know the answers to those questions, I express them as clearly as I can, without attaching an expectation. If John sees a chance to make me happy, he takes it, which is a win-win. I don't need to control anything, because John's got my back.

In addition to everyone being happier this way, it has completely changed the way we negotiate. As long as I'm focused on my own emotions and yearnings and I'm respecting his thinking, we can negotiate practically anything together without compromising.

Here's what I mean: We bought our home in Southern California in 2007, just before the financial collapse. Suddenly our house was worth less than we owed on it, and the payments felt high because our income and investments went down at the same time.

My husband was very concerned. He said, "Looking at the numbers, I think we should sell the house and downsize so we can save money."

My first reaction was to feel sad. I said, "I hear you, and if that's what you think is best, I'm willing to do that. And I would really like to stay in this house. I love it here."

I said "and" instead of "but" because I wanted to honor both his thinking and my feelings at the same time.

He took in what I said and went to think it over. When he brought it up again, he said, "I think we can stay for a while longer. Let's see how things go."

I didn't compromise, but neither did he: My desire influenced what he thought. After hearing what I wanted, he thought we should wait and see what unfolded. If he had come back and said "I think we should move," I would have gotten behind that, because I knew he'd taken my happiness into consideration. That would have influenced what I thought about moving and made it seem like a better option to me.

If I had said, "I think it's best that we stay here because the market will go back up again and then we'll wish we had," we would have had a completely different conversation. And by conversation, I mean argument. It would have been all about who was right and who was wrong. Instead, I didn't question his thinking or try to insist that mine was better. I just went with my authentic desire, which is in a different realm altogether from thoughts.

If I had said, "Can't we figure something out so we can stay here?" I would have been implying that he wasn't handling the finances in the most efficient way. Then we would have argued about how to best spend our resources, and that's not much fun.

In my answer, I focused on two things: letting him know I respected his thinking and expressing my pure desire without manipulation or expectation.

We had that conversation a few times over the following year. Each time his message was the same, and each time my message was the same. In the end, we stayed put, the economy rebounded, and we never stopped holding hands and snuggling.

Not long after that, I told John that I wanted a new car. His response was, "I don't think it's a good time. I'd like to wait until we have more cash on hand." While I was taking that in, he asked, "Why do you want a new car?"

I told him that the leather on our car's seat had started cracking and was chafing the backs of my legs. That was my motivation for wanting a new car.

"Would seat covers fix that?" he asked.

"Yes, that would do it," I agreed. At that moment, my desire for a new car diminished. He didn't think it was a good idea to get one, and he presented a perfectly good solution to my problem.

That time, what he thought really influenced what I wanted. I didn't even want a new car anymore. I wanted seat covers.

That's how we negotiate everything now. I never feel like we're compromising. I often hear that compromise is a big part of marriage, but that's just not my experience. I find that what he thinks colors what I want and what I want colors what he thinks. When we each represent our own areas of strength, a solution emerges that we're both on board with.

When John tells me what he thinks, I know he's taking my happiness into consideration because that's a big part of what makes him feel successful. If I'm clear on my desires and I let him know what they are, they serve as our North Star. He knows I trust what he thinks, so he can operate from the confidence of knowing that I have faith in him. In this way, we're both at our best.

Communicating this way would have seemed like mystical sorcery to me before I learned the Six Intimacy Skills. It took me quite a while to figure out that I could negotiate like this in my relationship and not have any drama. But after all these years of enjoying the intimacy and peace we get from this approach, I can't imagine it any other way.

How Not to Communicate

I watched a TV show that featured a couple seeking investment funding for their product called "The Elephant in the Room." The idea was that a woman could use a little stuffed elephant to let her husband know she was mad at him without saying anything. She could just put the elephant out, and when he got home, he would know she wanted to talk.

What a terrible idea! Just uttering the words "We need to talk" is an intimacy killer because it's the same as saying "You're in trouble."

Your husband hears that as, "I'm about to tell you everything that's wrong with you," and immediately he's on the defensive. Forget about connection and intimacy—they have no chance of thriving when you make that kind of overture.

No wife ever got happier from starting a conversation with "We need to talk." Seeing someone trying to create an entire product that would wordlessly destroy intimacy drove me batty. Fortunately, none of the investors on the show thought the product was a good idea either. One even said, "I think if I saw that elephant when I walked in, I would turn around and go hang out at the local bar until I thought the thing had blown over."

The moral of the story? Saying "We need to talk" is communication you're better off without.

Do This Before You "Communicate"

Helen and her husband, Paul, were on opposite work schedules while Helen was a Relationship Coach Training student. One day they agreed to meet in the parking lot of a restaurant that was on his way to work and on her way home so they could see each other for a few minutes.

Helen arrived first, and when she saw Paul driving up, she struck a sexy pose and waited for him to come over and give her a passionate kiss.

Instead, Paul pecked her on the cheek.

She encouraged him by saying, "Come on, kiss me like you mean it." But he still didn't. He just pecked her again and said, "I don't want anyone to think you're having an affair. Let's just go inside."

Helen was shocked. "How can we be having an affair? We're married!"

Her husband said, "But people don't know that. They might see you meeting a man in a parking lot and giving him a big passionate kiss and think something fishy is going on. This is a small town, and I don't want anyone to think that about you."

Helen was hurt. She wanted to enjoy that brief moment together, and she thought it was silly to worry about what other people might think—especially because she and Paul weren't doing anything wrong.

They went inside, and she let it go so they could enjoy their time together, making a deal with herself that if she was still upset later, she could bring it up then.

When she got home, she relayed the story to the other women in her Relationship Coach Training class, explaining how weird and hurtful she thought Paul's behavior had been.

One by one, fellow students, who were her friends by this time, weighed in with their support and thoughts. They acknowledged her disappointment: "Sounds like you didn't feel desired." They brought in Paul's perspective: "It seems like he's trying to protect you." They asked, "Did you have a certain expectation you were attached to?" They also reassured her: "Maybe he's a little more prudish about a public display of affection, but clearly the man is crazy about you and loves you to the ends of the earth. Is this incident worth bringing back to him if it will cost you intimacy?"

By the next day, Helen had a totally new perspective. She told me, "I can see now that Paul was just looking out for me. I was so fixated on wanting him to give me a big kiss and show me how attracted he is to me that I missed that piece and got my feelings hurt. But now I can see that he just wants to protect me, and that feels like love too."

By delaying a conversation about the incident until she'd communicated with other like-minded women, Helen completely avoided NET (Needless Emotional Turmoil). Twenty-four hours later, there wasn't much to say. Once she fortified herself with the perspective of women who support her happiness and her marriage, she felt complete.

Where Can I Get Girlfriends Like That?

As Helen's story illustrates, it's normal to feel a sense of urgency when there's a breakdown in your relationship. It takes some self-restraint to put an upset aside until you can get another perspective.

When you have other women to lean on, who are standing for your marriage, being able to turn to them instead of your husband can bring just as much relief and better perspective, with fewer potential pitfalls for your romance.

I've found it invaluable to talk to like-minded women early and often in support of my marriage. They hold me accountable for my part of what might seem like a conflict, and they can also serve as listeners if I just need to be heard. My husband can't be the be-all and end-all because that is just too much pressure for one mere mortal man, especially with all the talking I like to do.

Another reason my husband can't be the only person I talk to about my relationship is that sometimes he's going to appear to be the problem. In that case, I need someone else to talk me down or help me clarify my messge so that it's about how I feel and what I want instead of what's wrong with him. It takes more than one person to support a great relationship, and girlfriends are wonderful for that.

But you'll want to be judicious about which girlfriends you discuss your relationship concerns with. You want to pick women who won't laugh at you when you say, "I want to feel desired, cherished, and adored every day." Some women will think that's not possible.

We've all had girlfriends who are quick to say "Divorce him!" or "You deserve better!" when we mention anything wrong with the relationship. They probably mean well and want to protect you, but they may not be thinking through how much heartbreak a divorce would cause for everyone concerned. That kind of comment can deflate your hope and optimism, which are critical to having a marriage that lasts and thrives. If what you want is to smooth out those rough spots and get to a more passionate and playful place, you'll want to avoid sharing too much with those particular friends.

If asking yourself "Are they standing for my marriage?" before you share with your girlfriends, sisters, or mom about the challenges in your relationship leaves you with a very short list of people to confide in, you're not alone.

Practicing the Six Intimacy Skills is critical to a happy marriage, but it can be tricky to practice them by yourself. Some women try to do it alone and feel like the Skills don't work for them, when really, they just needed a little encouragement and support.

That's one important reason I created programs where you can not only train in the Six Intimacy Skills but also join a community of women who support you in the process while they do the same thing.

Remember my story where I started out feeling elated that I had the Six Intimacy Skills and then found myself having a big blowup in the car again? My marriage was up! Then it was down. It was a roller coaster.

It wasn't until I had a like-minded community that I was able to step off that roller coaster, and to this day, I rely on my coaches and the courageous community of women who practice the Intimacy Skills to keep my marriage shiny.

CHAPTER 15

Top 10 Ways to Control Your Husband (None of These Work)

Why Trying to Control Everything Sometimes Seems Reasonable

For a long time I didn't even *realize* I was controlling. I thought I was just smarter and more honest than my husband. Little did I know that I was shooting holes in the bucket of our intimacy for no good reason. It wasn't until I learned to recognize my controlling behavior and make a different choice that the romance returned.

On the road to giving up my controlling ways, one thing I tried was to control "politely." I thought I could package the control so that it didn't *seem* like control—sort of like switching to "healthier" cigarettes. It seemed like progress to me, but let's face it, I was still controlling.

My goal was to control him without him even knowing it. This seemed like an improvement to me, but his response was as hostile as ever. All of it got me to the same lonely spot: wondering why my husband was withdrawn, distant, and defensive.

I'm not an irrational person looking to ruin my marriage. So why did I (and millions of other women) think trying to control things I can't control seemed so irresistible?

The answer is that I was afraid. All control is based in fear. If you're not afraid, you don't have to try to control anybody or anything else.

There's no reason to control people unless you think you're going to have to wait longer, pay more, lose sleep, gain weight, be embarrassed, drive further, go without, or work harder if you don't.

If you identify with being controlling, that means you're afraid of something. Fear comes up for lots of different reasons. For the record, here are many of the embarrassing ways—none very effective—that I tried to control my husband, followed by the sometimes irrational and often ridiculous fears that were underneath my actions.

1. Making helpful suggestions

I've said things like "If you put things in file drawers, you'd be able to find them more easily" and "If you didn't fall asleep with the radio on, you'd sleep better and be more rested."

Fear: His office (and therefore our house) would be messy. John would be tired and grumpy.

2. Speaking on his behalf

People would ask him questions—doctors, waitresses, delivery people—and I would answer for him to make sure that everyone got the right information and impression of our family.

Fear: He would leave out important information and embarrass me.

3. Making decisions for him

I told him how much to contribute to his 401(k), which clothes to get rid of in the closet, and which phone he should buy. Since I believed I was smarter than him, it was only logical for me to make those decisions.

Fear: He would make the wrong decision—i.e., not the exact one I would have made.

4. Shooting him disapproving looks

I frowned at the lettuce he bought (too wilted), grimaced when he talked about buying a new car (too expensive), and rolled my eyes at the shows he enjoyed (too lowbrow). I was quieter but just as bossy.

Fear: Our food would go bad too quickly, he'd spend too much money, and he'd embarrass me by liking *The Three Stooges*.

5. Asking leading questions

I'd say things like "Is that what you're going to eat for lunch?" "Do you have to leave so early to get there?" and "Does that shirt go with those pants?" (Does this line of questioning make you want to smack me?)

Fear: He wouldn't be healthy, we'd have to be apart longer than we need to, and people would think I dressed him funny.

6. Announcing that "we" need to go to counseling

The underlying message, no matter how you look at it, is that he's a failure as a husband. In my experience, this wins hands down for the most expensive way to try to control your husband.

Fear: I married the wrong guy and was never going to have the life I craved unless he changed.

7. Telling him how *I* would do things

This would be something like "I usually go slower on this road because it's so narrow" or "I would take my car in for service if it was making that noise." It's amazing just how much I knew about practically everything back then.

Fear: We would crash, or we'd end up with a big unnecessary car repair bill that would put us in debt and I'd have to skip my pedicure.

8. Criticizing him

Saying things like "Don't you see you're being passive-aggressive?" or "It's just that you're such a slob." As if my insights would help him finally understand the error of his ways and he would correct them right on the spot. Isn't that how human nature works?

Fear: I wouldn't get a tender, thoughtful, attentive husband until he changed. And I'd have to clean up his messes.

9. Making demands

I told him, "You need to call your mom" or "You have to diversify your portfolio." I felt this was okay because clearly I was right.

Fear: I would be embarrassed in front of his family and we'd be broke when we grew old.

10. Undoing and redoing things he'd just done and then showing him how _I_ did them

I'm talking about important, earth-shattering things like emptying the lint filter or making the bed. If I didn't constantly show him, how would he ever learn? Poor thing!

Fear: I would have linty clothes and a lumpy bed or have to do everything myself.

Just by reading this book, you're cultivating a new awareness. The next time you try to control your husband, you're going to realize what you're doing. You might decide, as I sometimes do, to pretend that you're not, but you'll know that you are. It's actually pretty uncomfortable at first. Okay, it's excruciating when you first realize you're doing it. But here's the deal: You're making progress because you're aware. From there it's just a small hop to empowerment, where you can make a conscious choice instead of being stuck in a lousy rut.

Ask Yourself Four Questions

If you find yourself tempted to say something controlling, frown at the produce he bought, or refold the laundry he just folded, just telling yourself to stop is not very effective. So what should you do instead?

Ask yourself some questions. Even better, get a girlfriend to ask you. The answers will help you figure out what you really want to do in that moment and then do it. This way you won't end up thinking, _Hmmm, maybe I should have kept my mouth shut._

These are the four magical questions to help you decide whether you'd rather act on your fear or choose your faith.

1. What am I afraid of?
2. Is my fear realistic?
3. Can I actually control the situation?
4. Is it worth the intimacy it would cost me to try to control?

Let's say I'm tempted (as I still am from time to time) to tell my husband that he should call his slow-paying clients to collect from them. Here's the conversation I have with myself before I go down that old road:

1. What am I afraid of?

I'm afraid that if he doesn't collect from those clients, it will hurt his cash flow.

That's not a great response, because I still have to ask, "So what if his cash flow suffers? How does that impact *me*?" So I rephrase the question using my first answer as a setup: *"If his cash flow suffers, I'm afraid...."*

My answer: *I'm afraid that he'll go out of business and we'll go broke.*

Now we're getting somewhere. The fear that's pushing me to want to control my husband is that we're going to run out of money and have to go without.

Could I have come up with that answer on the first try? Sure, if I was really in good form. But it's human nature to try to distance myself from my vulnerability at first. I got there eventually and that's what counts, but sometimes I spend a little time trying to pretend it's about someone else first. It's not. It's always about me. So I keep examining the question until I show up in the answer.

In this case, since our finances are combined, if my husband's income goes down, it could affect me for sure. I might have to cut back on things I like to spend money on, like volleyball league fees, lunches out, and fresh flowers. That would be uncomfortable and I would rather avoid it, and since our financial fates are intertwined, it seems only logical that I would do my best to make sure his finances stay strong.

But let's go through the rest of the questions and see what happens before I march in to tell him to make his clients pay right away.

2. Is my fear realistic?

Is it really true that I would have to cut back on volleyball, lunches, and orchids if my husband doesn't collect from his clients promptly? It's certainly possible, but when I consider the facts, it's probably not likely. My husband has had his business for more than a decade, and he does pretty well. He's had very few accounts that he never collected on. Most of his clients have worked with him for many years, so it's the same bunch of companies that have been paying him on the same schedule for a long time.

So is my fear that my husband's cash flow will suffer and I'll have to make sacrifices because of it realistic? Nope. It's more like a monster under the bed that turns out to be a sock when I put on the light. And asking this question "Is my fear realistic?" is a great way to turn on the light.

Often when I ask myself this question, the answer seems pretty ridiculous. Like, "No, it's not realistic that if he wears the wrong socks to the party it will ruin our night."

Usually it makes me laugh, because it's obvious I'm being controlling. My fears tend to seem a little silly in light of this question.

One of my certified coaches, Tatianna, taught a workshop where she brought these questions to the participants. One woman in the workshop was trying to get her husband to drink lots of water because she was afraid he would get a urinary tract infection (UTI). When Tatianna asked her whether this fear was realistic, the woman had to admit that her husband had never had a UTI before. Suddenly something that had seemed so serious a minute ago became hilarious in light of this question.

So the control urge might die right here at question #2, because your fears aren't always realistic, and when you realize that, you feel silly and back off. Suddenly you're free to make a different choice—one that makes you much less controlling. In that case, you're done. No need to ask yourself anymore questions.

But that's not *always* the case, which is why we still have two more questions.

Sometimes you might be trying to control something because it already happened once and you're afraid it's going to happen again. Maybe your husband has already had a fender bender. Maybe he already forgot to pick up one of the kids at school one time. Maybe he already paid a bill late. So your fear is *not* unrealistic.

What do you do then?

Move ahead to question #3.

3. Can I actually control the situation?

In the past I have tried to tell John that he should call his clients to collect from them, but that never worked. I can't *make* him collect from his clients, and it's just as well—maybe some of them choose him because he gives them lenient payment terms. How do I know? It's not my business.

Kenda was frustrated because she felt her husband Jack was over-indulging his grown son. She had asked him in every possible way to stop giving his son money, but that only resulted in Jack giving him money on the sly. Terrified that she was going to have to go without something because of this financial drain on them, Kenda wanted me to coach her on how to express her desire to get her husband to stop sending money to his kid.

She was trying to disguise her fear and urge to control as a desire.

I totally relate to that, because I used to think I wasn't being controlling if I was just asking a question—even if the question was, "Don't you think you should clean the garage today?"

Kenda felt her fear was realistic, but when it came to the question "Can you actually control it?" the answer seemed to be no.

The problem is, I don't know a way to *actually* control husbands. They usually resist mightily. In fact, the more you complain, remind them, encourage them, leave little notes, and politely follow up, the more likely they are to resist—even though you think you're being perfectly logical and they are not.

No matter how logical you feel and no matter how much you tell yourself that you're on the side of right, you can't control your husband. It just doesn't work. I've tried and tried and have never been successful.

Kenda had already tried to get her husband to change dozens of times, so there was nothing more to do.

"But he's not setting any limits with his son," she told me. "He's making him financially dependent and spending money that I want him to keep in his bank account!"

"I hear you," I told her. "But is it something you can control?"

It wasn't. The only option we could come up with was for her to accept that he was going to make his own decisions about his financial relationship with his son. Forcing him to do what she wanted was not an option, which meant it was time to move on to question #4.

4. Is it worth losing the intimacy it's costing me to try to control?

Since Kenda couldn't get her husband to budge on subsidizing his grown son, the only realistic outcome of continuing to try would be to cause tension in her marriage. Trying to control was going to cost her intimacy and peace, and it wasn't going to make her feel any safer.

When I asked her if it was worth the intimacy it was going to cost her to try to control this issue, especially since she had agreed that she couldn't control it, Kenda admitted that continuing to insist he stop giving his son money was a lose-lose proposition.

Here's the twist: That acknowledgment turned into empowerment when she realized that by not trying to control his contributions to his son, she would free herself from NET (Needless Emotional Turmoil). It was the best option available to her. Instead of being a victim, she was making a thoughtful choice.

There was one more benefit of Kenda leaving the topic of her husband's financial relationship with his son alone: Soon after she had apologized for being controlling, her husband said, "That kid is costing me too much money. I'm going to let him know he needs to start paying his own way. I'm not doing this anymore."

It's not right and it's not fair, but it is human nature that when people feel controlled, they sometimes dig in their heels and do the opposite. By stopping her controlling behavior, Kenda gave her husband the best chance of being able to make his own thoughtful decision.

By the time you answer the four questions, the urge to control has typically subsided. In the beginning, you may forget to ask yourself these questions, particularly if you're in the habit of controlling your husband. But if you do it a few times, it really changes your perspective. It's not so hard to resist going down a dark alley once you've thought it through.

What If I Still Want to Control?

Sometimes you'll ask yourself all four questions and the desire to control will not have abated.

Sometimes I can't get myself to go through the questions. Sometimes I just blurt out, "Hey, you're overcooking the *carne asada!*" and I cause a loss of intimacy in my relationship.

In those moments, I guess you could say the answer to question #4 is "It's more important to me to pretend that I'm in control than it is to preserve intimacy."

Fortunately, I don't do that very much anymore, so even though I'm not perfect, the intimacy is really good around here. Now that it's easy and fun most of the time, there is grace in my relationship.

Natalia noticed the same thing when she and her husband were getting ready to go on a camping trip. She had a certain time in her head when she wanted to leave. Unfortunately her husband had more to do to get ready than she thought. As Natalia's pre-determined time approached and they still weren't on the road, she started to get testy with him...and then she realized she was being controlling. How much was the "best time to leave" she had in her head really worth to her? So Natalia apologized. She told her husband, "I would rather feel close to you and leave when the time is right than be angry with each other and leave when I wanted." It was a win for her to be able to choose connection over control.

Your Life Is Waiting

The really great part about relinquishing inappropriate control of your husband is that your life gets a lot more exciting.

It can also get terrifying.

In fact, one of the hidden benefits of controlling someone else, I've discovered, is that it's less scary than focusing on your own life. Even though I felt like I had made a huge leap when I stopped controlling my husband, it was really just the warm-up for the scary stuff that was ahead.

Michelle felt the same way. After nearly divorcing her husband, she discovered the Six Intimacy Skills, which she found frightening. But she practiced them anyway, and her life was so transformed, she decided to train to become a coach with me. During training, she was scared about passing certification. It really meant a lot to her. She studied hard, and…she passed. Suddenly facing and paying attention to her own purpose instead of being lost in what her husband was doing was a whole lot scarier.

In fact, one of her first coaching students, Gina, was pretty hostile. She kept saying, "I don't think this is going to work for me. I'm sure glad there's a money-back guarantee," which was completely nerve-wracking for Michelle. While she and I were talking about how to best support Gina, I admitted that I'm scared all the time too.

I started running my coaching company without really having any idea how that's done or having the kind of business experience many people start companies with. It was pretty terrifying, especially at first. I was making things up every day, having no idea if they would work. But my purpose, my mission to end world divorce, is so inspiring and motivating that I keep going in spite of my fear.

Writing this book was scary too; I knew it was going to make some people mad. It still often seems much easier to focus on my husband's business than my own purpose in the world.

That's been my experience with the Six Intimacy Skills: They opened the door to a scary but very exciting world—and that's the one I really want to live in.

When you find yourself tempted to control someone else, another question to ask yourself is, "What am I trying to avoid in my own life?" or "What am I afraid to face?" Chances are there's something scary in front of you, and your urge to control someone else is just a distraction that seems less threatening.

CHAPTER 16

*Get Him to Do More
by Doing Less*

"Women who seek equality with men lack ambition."

—Marilyn Monroe

What People See When They Come to My House

I very rarely wash dishes—John typically does them. That's been our routine for years: I cook and he washes the dishes. It started when I said, "I want to make dinner, but I don't want to do the dishes." John immediately offered to do them and I responded with, "Great! Thanks."

That doesn't mean the dishes always get done right after a meal. To be honest, there are dishes in the sink right now. And if people came over, they would see them. (Actually, people *did* come over today, so they *did* see them.)

Sometimes dishes stay in the sink longer than I'd like, and mostly I choose to leave them there rather than spending the time and energy doing them myself. Of course it would be nice if my kitchen was always perfectly clean, but what I value even more is that when people come over they see a relaxed, happy Laura instead of a stressed-out, exhausted Laura. I'm not a martyr or a victim, nor am I the kitchen elf.

Once in a while, if I really want to have a spotless kitchen right that minute, I wash dishes myself. But when I do, I know that's my choice. Realizing that I'm making a choice to wash the dishes is like living on a completely different planet than the one I used to live on, where I thought I *had* to do everything because John had left me no choice. Since he wasn't doing things when and how I wanted them done, I believed he was leaving me with the burden of cleaning up after both of us. I was so resentful that *he* did that to *me*.

Today I see many other options. One is to leave the dishes until John gets to them and keep minding my own business, even if my most pressing business only involves looking at pictures of beautiful gardens while sipping tea. Another option is to decide to do the dishes because I want a clean kitchen now—but to do them without being resentful or complaining under my breath.

If I'm being totally honest, I also have a couple of laundry baskets of clean clothes waiting to be folded in the bedroom. They've been there for two days. Folding clothes is one of my responsibilities, and John never mentions it or complains that the laundry isn't getting folded fast enough for him. In fact, in all the years we've been married, I've never seen him stomp over to the laundry baskets and sigh heavily while grimacing because he was so disgusted that I had taken so long to fold the clothes.

But that's what I used to do with the dishes when I thought they'd been in the sink too long. It wasn't very dignified, but I didn't realize I had any other choice. I thought it was vital to avoid the embarrassment of people seeing dishes in our sink. It turns out that that isn't as painful as I thought it would be.

Today the fear of embarrassment about unsightly dishes just isn't something I worry about. One of my friends actually thanked me for having dishes in the sink when she came over! When I asked her what she meant by that, she said, "It means I don't have to be perfect either."

My house isn't perfect, and my friend can see that I'm human too. That's an additional source of connection in our friendship, which helps us to be vulnerable and imperfect together in other ways.

The consequences of having my friends see that my house isn't perfectly tidy aren't painful or embarrassing. In fact, the loss of intimacy I experienced from trying to make my husband do things when I thought he should was far worse. And exhausting myself by doing everything to keep up appearances just didn't seem worthwhile.

Sometimes I'll express my desire by saying, "Kathy is coming over shortly and I would love it if the kitchen was clean when she got here." If John doesn't decide to do the dishes then, I can always jump up and do them myself if I really want them to be done. That option never goes away.

My job is to know what I want to do in each situation. What do I want to contribute? What is more important to me right now—taking a nap or having a spotless kitchen?

Now I know that it's all a choice—*my* choice.

You Can't Be Grateful and Resentful at the Same Time

When my husband does chores around the house but not the way I want them done, I'm still grateful. And I always make sure to express my appreciation.

I used to say things like "It's great that you did the dishes, but how about wiping off the countertops?" That was very demotivating, ungrateful, and controlling, so I don't do it anymore. Today I say, "Wow! Thanks for doing the dishes. I really appreciate it." And if the counters are still dirty, I can either wipe them off myself or I can leave them. Sometimes John comes back around and does them anyway.

Sometimes our students don't give their husbands a chance to do certain chores because they're in such a hurry to have them done *now*.

I've discovered that the less I jump on things to get them done, the more John picks up the slack. I've also noticed that by taking a more relaxed approach, John sees things that need to be done and volunteers to do them—just like I always wanted him to in the bad old days. That seems pretty miraculous. I didn't realize that by being so efficient and in such a rush to do everything, I was actually impeding him from making the contributions I wanted him to make and that he wants to make.

Stop Helping

Another way I was stressing myself out unnecessarily was by doing things for John that he could easily do for himself. I used to make his doctor and dentist appointments, wake him up so he wouldn't oversleep, and drop off his dry cleaning for him. When he misplaced his keys or his wallet, I would jump up and save the day by finding them.

I don't do any of that anymore because I know he can do it himself. And I have my own important things to do—like napping and working on my mission to end world divorce. The result is that John figures things out for himself, and he takes more initiative to do other things. But if I forget and start bossing him around, that initiative disappears.

Our students have had the same experience. Regina bought tickets for an out-of-town business conference that she thought would be perfect for her and her husband to attend since they were in business together. She came home and excitedly told him about it, but he didn't seem that excited. In fact, when she asked him to go with her, he flatly declined. "How can I express my desire so that he'll come to the conference?" she asked me.

I asked her why she wanted him to come, and she told me that she wanted them to both be on the same page in their business.

"Does he think the conference will be valuable?" I asked.

"I haven't asked him that," she admitted.

By committing to the conference without consulting her business partner and husband, the message she was sending was that she thought something should be done, and she'd figured out what that was and then unilaterally made the decision—and the purchase—for both of them. Her actions said, "Your thoughts about what's best won't be necessary." As a result, he was not showing much enthusiasm. What if he had a very different idea? There wasn't much room for him to express that, since she had already bought the tickets.

I asked Regina if there was a missed opportunity for her to say to him, "I want to increase the sales for our company, and I heard about this conference where we could learn to market better, so I thought it might be fun to go together. What do you think?" Or she could have simply expressed her desires by saying, "I want to increase our sales. What do you think we should do next?" That conversation could have opened up a lot of possibilities and elicited his best thinking about what to do. As it was, she really didn't know what he thought about the direction they should take their business.

Instead, she had tickets to a conference that he was resisting attending—probably because he didn't want to be told what to do. That's just human nature, and especially male nature. Her actions could certainly have been interpreted as saying, "I think we need to do something, so I did it. You should come along because this is the direction I'm taking the company." That sounds much more like a boss than a partner or wife.

Regina had a great opportunity to be curious about and respectful of her husband's ideas. She realized that she wanted to see what his contribution would have been, because she really didn't know.

If you're curious about and open to your husband's ideas, you'll be amazed at how often he comes up with something elegant you never would have thought of. Or he'll say "Let me handle it" and take care of the situation altogether.

Stop Vacuuming to Create a Vacuum

One way to lighten your load is to think about something in your life that you feel responsible for but that's appearing as a burden or a struggle. Maybe it's something tedious that you don't want to do. Then ask the man who loves you most in the world to help.

One powerful way to invite his help is to stop doing whatever it is that has you feeling resentful, exhausted, or burdened. You don't have to say anything—just don't do it.

For example, Elena was running low on energy just before dinner when she felt a headache coming on. It was her routine to make dinner, set the table, and get the kids settled down to eat while her husband unwound from work. But on this particular day, she just didn't feel well enough. She announced that she had a headache, and without saying anything more or asking her husband to do anything, she went to lie down on the couch. Her husband caught on immediately. He found ingredients for dinner and fed the kids and himself, as well as reminding the kids to let Mommy rest because she didn't feel well.

Elena didn't ask, demand, or plead for him to do that. He just did it in her absence. All she had to do was nothing.

What if you did the same thing? Maybe you'd give yourself a break from doing the laundry, for example. It's hard to say what would happen if you stopped washing the clothes until you actually try it.

When Jennifer came to one of my live events, she had a specific goal of getting help with what she considered the worst chore of all: mopping the floor. After getting some coaching, she went home and told her husband that she couldn't mop the floor anymore and wanted to hire some help. He looked surprised, but after a moment, he said, "That seems like an unnecessary expense. Why don't I do it instead?" She thanked him and resigned her job as the family mopper that very day. By saying she could no longer mop, Jennifer created a vacuum (no pun intended), and her husband filled it.

You might think that would never happen with your husband, but you really don't know until you experiment. I used to think I could predict my husband's actions in many situations too, but I really can't. Neither can you. We can speculate, but we don't really know for sure. That can be scary for those of us who like to feel like we're in control. It's also a great relief to be able to drop some of your burdens and let the man you married help lighten your load.

If something is becoming burdensome for you, consider letting it go for a while to see what happens. You might just end up with one less responsibility.

It's Not Disrespectful to Give Him More Information

Sometimes we have coaching students who get completely stressed out because they think that if their husband makes a suggestion, they have to go along with it or else they're being disrespectful. That's simply not the case. Your husband may come up with a suggestion that creates another conflict for you because he doesn't have all the information yet.

For example, Genevieve told her husband she wanted to bring her car to the mechanic to check out a strange noise. Her husband suggested that they take it the next day after work so he could meet her there and give her a ride home. Genevieve struggled with how to respond, knowing that she'd already made plans to see a friend after work the next day. Her husband saw the anxious look on her face and asked, "What's wrong?" So she told him about her scheduling conflict. Her husband said, "No problem. Let's do it the next day." That worked for Genevieve, so the problem was solved.

Without that piece of information, her husband wouldn't have been able to make her happy. Withholding your desires so you can go along with your husband's thinking is defeating for you and your relationship.

Genevieve wasn't being disrespectful by letting her husband know that she had other plans. Even if she didn't have firm plans, she could have said, "I wanted to go to yoga with Misty tomorrow after work." That's not disrespectful—it's a clear expression of desire. If she just said, "No, that's not a good idea," *that* would have been disrespectful. But giving your husband more information about what you want is not the same as arguing with what he thinks.

Say Yes to Yourself

Allison was enjoying some much-needed self-care by relaxing with a book on the couch when her husband asked her to come out to the garage and help him with his truck. He wanted her to put her hand into the gas tank and hold it steady while he screwed something else in.

Allison couldn't think of anything she wanted to do less. She groaned and sighed at the thought of leaving her pleasant perch, but because she wanted to be a "good" wife, she got up to help. Almost immediately she was making snippy remarks to her husband. After they finished working on the truck, they spent the evening bickering, and the kids followed suit. It was a miserable evening for the entire family.

I don't recommend that you say this, but just for a moment imagine if Allison's husband had asked her for help, and she had responded by saying, "I'll help you, but if I do I'll be cranky for the rest of the night. Or else I can stay right here and be happy and relaxed. Which would you prefer?" Which option do you think her husband would have chosen?

I promise he would have picked the latter option, but her husband didn't get that choice. Instead he got the help he was asking for as well as a cranky wife who didn't do a very good job of saying yes to herself that day. Her whole family suffered because of it.

A lot of wives I work with believe that pitching in to help anytime your husband asks is a critical part of being a "good" wife. But don't you think your husband would rather have a happy wife than your help every day of the week? If helping him is going to interfere with your self-care or your happiness, then it's probably too high a price to a pay.

Your husband might be irritated in the moment when you don't help him, but remember that even more than your help, your husband wants you to be happy. That's his priority. To be clear, I don't recommend that you give him the choice of helping him and being cranky or not helping him and being in a better mood. Instead, consider using the phrase "I can't." That's it—just those two powerful words. It could be shorthand for "I can't or I will miss my self-care and be irritable" or "I can't say 'yes' to you right now without saying 'no' to myself." He may say, "why not?"—especially the first time you say it. There's no need to go into detail. Just stick with your mantra: "I just can't."

"I can't" is a really effective phrase that was trained out of me at an early age. What I learned and practiced saying a lot was "I can do anything if I put my mind to it." Maybe you learned the same thing. But if I'm honest, I used that phrase to do anything for everyone else while I neglected myself for months at a time. I'm sure that wasn't the intent of the can-do slogan, but that's where I ended up. I see our students doing the same thing.

The problem is that I really *can't* do everything I want to do. In theory I want to learn Spanish and stand-up comedy and grow organic food in my garden that I then make into delicious meals for my family and friends. But I don't do any of that. I can't. Because what I *actually* want to do is write books, play volleyball, run an international relationship coaching organization, walk to the bookstore with my husband, and pick up my niece from school on Fridays. Those are my real priorities, and that's what I spend my time doing.

I still hate to acknowledge that there's anything I can't do, but it's true. There are many things I can't do if I want to also be relaxed and happy and have the energy for an intimate, passionate, peaceful marriage. The phrase "I can't" is enormously helpful for acknowledging the limits of my capacity. Perhaps you'll find it helpful too. Consider trying it out a few times to see how it sounds coming out of your mouth.

When Allison said yes to helping her husband with his truck, she was also saying "No, Allison, you can't relax and read a book right now." And there's something sad about saying no to yourself when what your soul needs most is yes.

CHAPTER 17

Your Husband Is Better with Money Than You Are

One Less Chore for You

Most women I know have a lot of responsibilities: husbands, homes, kids, and jobs, just to name a few.

One responsibility that you may be able to relinquish to your husband is the job of watching over the bills.

If that seems unimaginable to you, welcome to the club. I resisted this idea mightily. Most of our students do too, at first. We all felt that handing over the job of balancing the budget and paying the bills was giving up something that we needed to control. Especially if you make all or most of the money in the marriage, this idea can sound ridiculous.

Because of that, I consider relinquishing the chore of managing the finances the graduate work of the Six Intimacy Skills. First you need to get to the point where you're experiencing connection and ease because you've become more respectful, and he is responding to that by cherishing you. *Then* you can think about relinquishing the finances. That's why this chapter is near the end of the book.

So if this suggestion has you feeling uncomfortable, just skip it for now and return to it later, maybe in a few months. If your marriage is currently in crisis, switching up the handling of the finances is not the main priority. Practice the other intimacy skills first, then come back to this idea once you and your husband are feeling more connected, relaxed, and secure in your relationship.

If you are feeling brave enough to experiment with this suggestion, then let's get started. Or, if any of this seems scary to do on your own, you can get support from a Laura Doyle Certified Relationship Coach.

One of the obvious benefits of giving up managing the finances is that you can use your newfound time for more self-care. Even better, trusting your husband to handle the money for you both is going to take your intimacy to a whole new level. It may not seem obvious that by letting your husband handle the finances you're going to feel more cherished, but that's what happens. As our student Bethany said, "I didn't think there was anything wrong with the way we were doing our finances before, but things are a lot better now that I've relinquished that chore to my husband. Our relationship and finances have certainly improved since we did this."

It's No Fun to Be Mrs. No

Penny had managed the household finances for so many years, she couldn't imagine it any other way. As a military wife, she felt she had no choice but to handle bill-paying while her husband was deployed early in their marriage. More recently, his job and commute kept him away from home a lot. To Penny, it seemed impractical to ask him to do one more thing when she was a stay-at-home mom with more free time. Their family time was already so scarce, it just didn't make sense for her to put one more thing on his plate.

But there was a problem. Penny found herself in the unpleasant position of often having to be the one to say, "No, we can't afford that," to her husband. She didn't like being Mrs. No. She felt like a killjoy, squashing her husband's ideas whenever she said "We don't have the money."

On top of that, because she'd always controlled the money, neither Penny nor her husband thought he would be capable of doing it. He simply didn't know how, Penny told her coach. She said she tried to keep him apprised of the family finances, but it was hard because he didn't really seem that interested.

When her coach asked her if her husband managed money, budgets, or inventory at work, Penny hesitated before she answered. "He absolutely does," she acknowledged, sounding a little surprised herself. "He manages a really big budget and a good deal of inventory." In that moment it became obvious to her that her husband clearly had all the skills he needed to manage household finances. It was just that neither of them had been looking at it that way.

Penny's coach suggested that instead of making the decisions alone and reporting back to her husband, she could engage him by saying, "I don't know what to do. We can either save some money for the trip to Disneyworld or we can fix the garage door opener like you wanted. What do you think?"

Penny liked that idea immediately. "As a soldier, my husband is a guy who wants to find a way to solve the problem," she said. "If I come to him with that kind of question, he's going to want to get involved."

She wasn't handing over the responsibility for their finances completely, but she was taking an important first step. The immediate benefit would be that Penny wouldn't have to be the one to say, "We can't afford to go to Disneyworld, but look how nicely the garage door opens and closes." With her new approach, her husband would be contributing his best thinking to the family's financial decisions, and she would no longer be lonely Mrs. No, the family killjoy.

Did You Spend $37 on the Visa?

In the first episode of the series *Breaking Bad*, Walter White is a chemistry teacher moonlighting at a carwash to make ends meet. His wife asks him, "Did you spend thirty-seven dollars on the Visa at Staples?" He admits that he did, and without bothering to mask her frustration, she tells him, "We don't use that card, *remember*?"

Walter apologizes, and it's very clear that this man is completely emasculated. He has no autonomy to decide what to buy or how to pay for things, because his wife decides that for him and corrects him when he doesn't do things *her* way. No wonder he went bad.

I hate to admit that I used to do the same thing to my husband. I was calling all the shots, so there wasn't much for John to contribute to the conversation, which was actually just a monologue I wanted him to sit through.

I'm not the only one. This is something that commonly happens when we women are controlling the finances—just like Walter White's wife. We say things like "Don't hit the ATM because we're so low you'll overdraw the account" or "You can take out forty dollars this week, but no more than that."

It's totally understandable, in a way. If you're responsible for balancing the budget, then you want to control your husband's spending because that's a budget item. The problem is that you put yourself in a position no wife really wants to be in, which is being her husband's boss—or even worse, his mother. That's a lonely position.

What I want to be is my husband's lover. I want him to desire, adore, and cherish me. Men don't desire their mothers, so when I'm acting like my husband's mother, I'm pouring cold water on the embers of passion. So I don't want to be the person who tells my husband he can only take $40 out of the ATM. It's not fun, it's not sexy, and it doesn't feel very dignified either. I don't miss it at all.

Your Husband Is More Likely to Win If He Knows the Score

Besides not being good for our sex life, controlling my husband's spending was not very conducive to our family's prosperity. It was so emasculating that John's self-esteem suffered, which meant he didn't have as much success in his work life as he does now. I was also so busy worrying about trying to control his spending that I was distracted from my own purpose in the world. As a result, our income was stymied.

I was also depriving my husband of the sense of accomplishment that comes with providing for his family. That's his primary motivation when it comes to earning. It would be like asking him to play a game of basketball without knowing the score. Sure, he could go through the motions and make some baskets, but he wouldn't have much of a sense of urgency or pride because he would have no idea how well his team was doing. He wouldn't know how much effort to put into the game.

One of the things we commonly see when husbands take over the finances is that they begin to excel financially. It makes sense that when he sees a direct connection between what he earns and what his family gets as a result, his motivation and ingenuity increase. Once he knows the score—the amount of money in the coffers—it's game on. That's completely different than being the worker bee that hands the money over for someone else to divvy up. Now he has more connection to what he's getting for his efforts.

Feel Cherished While Getting What You Want

Laney had recently given up the family finances when she saw a pair of boots online that she loved. She told her husband about them but decided she wasn't going to buy them because they were too expensive. Her husband encouraged her to get the boots she loved.

Since Laney wasn't controlling the finances anymore, it wasn't on her shoulders to make the numbers balance, so why not? Her husband wanted her to be happy, and he liked the idea of his wife getting the boots she wanted.

"It was a great moment," Laney said. "I felt special and spoiled in a nice way, because I wasn't the one who had to balance the budget. I didn't have that old feeling of guilt that I would have to trim the grocery budget or not get something for the kids. I could just enjoy being the proud owner of these beautiful boots that my husband wanted me to have."

It's not unusual for husbands to be more generous with their wives than the wives would be with themselves, but that generosity is obscured when you're the one who's paying the bills. Let your husband take over that chore and you might be surprised how much he wants to spoil you.

That was Tia's experience when she gave up managing the finances.

Initially she was worried—especially when she saw her husband running up debt and putting them in a tight spot. She was tempted to use this as evidence that she was better with money, and take back the chore of paying the bills. Instead, she decided to wait and see how he would solve the problem.

A few months later, Tia was feeling particularly discouraged as she wondered how in the world she would afford an upcoming girls' trip, one that she'd planned long ago and had been looking forward to for ages.

The night before she was supposed to leave, her husband sold his fishing rod so she could go.

"This was the rod of his dreams! And it was only a week before the opening of fishing season," Tia told me. "Here's what he said: 'I can buy another fishing rod, but I can never buy your happiness in this moment again.'"

Needless to say, Tia's husband did eventually turn things around and get them back on solid financial ground. But the gains in trust and intimacy were worth far more than money.

"I was so controlling before and didn't even realize it. Now I can see that I was keeping him from treating me the way he wanted to," Tia said.

Your man wants to give you special treatment, too. Give him an opportunity and he'll show you.

Keep Dating Forever

Another benefit of relinquishing control of the finances is the miracle of perpetual dating. Now when my husband and I go out, I don't even bring my purse because I know he's going to treat me. He opens doors for me and we hold hands too. I never even think about having to pay for things when we're together. He always does.

Granted, he's taking the money out of our joint account, which I contribute to too, but so what? I don't have to figure out what the tip should be or think about how much we're spending. I just get to say "Thank you for taking me out to lunch." It's like when we first met and he was always treating me. It's a sweet continuation of those early days.

Sometimes our students will say, "But I'm the one making all the money. He's 'treating' me with my own money, which is not such a treat." But I love the *feeling* of being taken care of, which I get from this arrangement. What does who earns the money have to do with who manages it? The last thing I want to do when the working day is done is look at bank statements or bills.

Is He Up to the Task?

You might have some resistance to the idea of letting your husband handle the money. You might have concerns that he misses due dates, bounces checks, or spends too much. What you're really saying is that you're not sure your husband is responsible enough. I get it. I remember feeling that way too.

But when a wife is in control of the finances, that can contribute to her husband seeming irresponsible when he's actually perfectly capable. If you say to your husband, "Don't take more than forty dollars out of the ATM," for example, he may revert to being a teenager who thinks, *Just leave me alone, Mom*. Your husband's not being stubborn or irresponsible when he does that; he's just being human. There are times when you're triggering the exact response from your husband that you will later use as evidence that he's not up to the job of handling the finances. Worse still, most wives don't have any concept that they're contributing to the whole mess. All we know is that we're being responsible and frugal—and he's not.

This is yet another example of the helpful-hurt-hopeless cycle. You're trying to help him be more frugal, which he hears as control and criticism, so he gets hurts. He responds by rebelling or just ignoring you, which hurts you. Next thing you know, everyone feels hopeless.

Instead of trusting your husband and expecting him to rise to the occasion as a responsible adult, you're reinforcing that you're the "mom" who will take care of things if he screws up.

You don't want to be your husband's mother. You want him to find you irresistible to kiss and touch. It's hard to get there when you're telling him what to do with his money.

Chaya experienced this for herself when she turned over the finances to her husband only a few months before they decided to buy their first house. At the last minute, they needed an additional $10,000 to complete the purchase. Her husband asked Chaya if she had any idea how to come up with the extra money.

The old Chaya would have jumped into action to fix the problem, and filed this away as evidence that she just couldn't count on her husband to take responsibility. She would have felt pressured and resentful. There would have been plenty of tension and likely a fight.

This time, Chaya decided to stay on her own paper and trust her husband to come up with a solution, offering only what she could without becoming resentful. She shared that she had just received a tax return for her business that got them halfway to the number they needed and left the rest of the problem to him. Her husband rose to the occasion, finding the additional funds without any help from Chaya.

Chaya was proud and happy to discover that through the whole home-buying process—one that can be tense for even the strongest couple—she and her husband had never stopped feeling connected. As a result, the day they closed on their new home was a purely joyful celebration, with kisses and hand-holding where there might well have been tension and bickering.

"Before, I never thought he was capable. *I* was capable and responsible, and he was the irresponsible one—like I was the mom and he was the little boy. So I would bulldoze and make things happen my way," Chaya told me. "But that was lonely and stressful. I can see now that I was making things harder than they needed to be. I love being able to trust my husband like this, and I love how peaceful our new home feels!"

How to Set Up Your Experiment

One thing you can do if totally relinquishing the finances to your husband feels too scary is to consider it an experiment. After you try it, if you find that this really just doesn't work for your family, you can always go back to the way you've been doing things. I hope that knowing you're not locked in to this new division of labor will help you be brave and go forward boldly, because there is so much to be gained.

That said, I would not announce to your husband that this is an experiment when you start. I urge you to keep that part to yourself. If you say to your husband, "Let's just try this, and if it doesn't work, we'll go back to the way things are now," he's likely to give up before he starts.

My experience and the experience of thousands of our students is that once you relinquish control of the finances, it takes your intimacy to a whole new level—and you are not going to want to go back.

Consider presenting the finances as something you can no longer do. The phrase "I can't" is great to use in this situation, as in, "I can't manage the finances anymore." Pick your reason; at least one of these is bound to be true: "It's too stressful," "It's costing me too much," or "It's draining me."

What you're really saying is that it's draining to be your husband's mom while he acts like a bad little kid or even a good little kid. But you're not saying that *to* him, because that would be offensive and hurtful. Let "I can't" serve as shorthand for "I can't be your mom anymore and also have the kind of marriage I want to have" or "I can't manage the finances for both of us and still be as happy, relaxed, and playful as I want to be in our relationship."

Separate Accounts Separate You

If you and your husband have separate bank accounts, you might think you don't really need to change anything because you're not mothering him. As long as you're not controlling what he does, why change, right? Plus, it's nice knowing you can always put your hands on some money in case you need it. I still remember early in my marriage wanting to know I had the escape route that money provides.

But when you give up control of managing the money, you don't lose your spending power—that stays the same. You still have access to the money, just as you did before. What you give up by joining financially is separation. When you keep separate accounts, you lose the intimacy that comes from trusting each other. You can't have financial intimacy with separate accounts.

Sharing our money completely means I really have to rely on my husband. It's one more way we're connected. Our financial fates are tied together, and I wouldn't have it any other way.

It wasn't until we had joint accounts and he was managing them that I experienced this level of vulnerability, which is a key ingredient to intimacy. It brings us a level of connection and financial intimacy that I wouldn't ever want to give up.

How to Worry Less

When I say your husband is better with money than you are, what I mean is that he's less likely to worry about it than you are.

One of our gifts as women is that we're good at knowing how we feel and expressing it. We live in the realm of feelings, and because of that, we are also feelers around money. We feel fear that we're going to run out of it. We feel guilty when we spend it. We feel sad when we lose it.

For women, money is about security. We want to make sure there will be enough if there is an emergency, that there are savings for retirement and for the kids to go to college.

For men, money is more about accomplishment. They are likely to be less emotional about it, and that can be advantageous. Worrying about money means indulging your fear, and your husband is less likely to do that than you are. By letting your husband handle paying the day-to-day bills, you'll eliminate a source of energy drain on yourself.

Also, as you can imagine, people make better decisions about money when they're not worried. Because your husband is less likely to worry, this really gives him an advantage.

I'm not saying he is never going to get emotional or excited or fearful about money. He will. He will certainly take his cues from you and respond accordingly. I know I can freak my husband out by saying, "How are we ever going to retire with the real estate market going down so much?" My level of urgency and drama about it will set him off too.

I can certainly bring him down that road with me, but in general, he's calmer and more reflective around the ups and downs, which is another reason I'm so glad he's the one managing things.

How Good Do You Want Your Relationship to Be?

It's so good for my inner strength to know that I am loved every day, to hear that I'm beautiful, to hear that I'm wonderful. I really can't imagine it any other way than how I have it now. If I know something is going to make my relationship even better and bring more connection and passion, I want that. That's where I want to live.

For me, it's not enough to say, "At least we're not in a crisis because we don't want to kill each other or divorce anymore." I want to have the sweet tenderness of feeling cherished and taken care of every day for the rest of my life. I'm guessing you do too.

Relinquishing control of your family's finances is vital for getting to that level.

In this abridged excerpt from *The Empowered Wife Podcast* episode 107, I interviewed Matthew, the *husband* of a recently certified Laura Doyle Relationship Coach. I invited him to give a husband's perspective on the changes in his family as a result of his wife using the Six Intimacy Skills and the Connection Framework.

LAURA: Matthew, what was your experience in your marriage before?

MATTHEW: "Hostile" would probably be the best word to describe it. Now I can tell you that I'm more in love with my wife than I've ever been.

Through courtship, it was fantastic. We fell in love, we got married, and we decided to move back to Colorado in order to have children. Then, once my wife got pregnant, it seemed as though everything changed—and I don't know if everything changed because she was in this nesting phase, but it led to a control phase that did not end until a handful of years ago, when she met your group.

In that control phase was anything from something as little as "You don't know how to feed the baby properly, so I'm just going to do it" and "You don't know how to handle my finances" to "You can't handle the house"—where I just essentially tuned out. It just got progressively worse, and I had built up so much resentment, and from my view, there was so much disrespect. It was just putting me in the corner, which is difficult for a husband. Because once you have kids, you're no longer the primary. You're now the secondary. And I think any guy would be lying if they said it didn't hurt.

We found ourselves in a position where, candidly, we were at that point of breaking, and it just—the arguments got worse and worse, the nitpicking got worse and worse, and something had to change. And that was around the time when Melissa found you.

She heard about your book, and then, subsequently, I heard about it. It was passed along to her by a friend. She read the book, and I have to tell you, literally within a matter of weeks, our entire lives changed.

LAURA: Wow! That was quick.

MATTHEW: It was quick, but I will tell you my wife is a very determined person, and when she decides she's going to flip the switch, it's pretty remarkable.

LAURA: What was your reaction when, in a couple of weeks, you were noticing a big change? What's going through your mind at that point?

MATTHEW: I thought, maybe, she was going to divorce me. I thought, "Whoa, whoa, whoa, wait a minute. Things have changed, and they are for the better." I heard things like "I trust you." "I trust you to make decisions." "You are the man of the house." "You're our leader." It was definitely a new experience because I hadn't felt that since our courtship.

At first I couldn't believe it. I thought, "This is not going to last. This is phony. These are mind games. She's screwing with me somehow. This is going to backfire on me." So my defense mechanisms were still up. I was still very guarded. I was still very angry and very cantankerous with her. It took me a while to accept that this was the new reality.

LAURA: How did you start to believe it?

MATTHEW: I started believing it when she actually started to relinquish control. Things like the finances. She said, "Hey, look, I realized I was out of line. I realized I was disrespectful when I hired a financial adviser, when you're not only perfectly capable, but you run a very, very successful corporation, and I don't know why I ever doubted you."

Things like that. Those were things that gave me confidence in myself because I had been beaten down for so long that I had lost a lot of confidence in myself and as a husband and a dad.

LAURA: Did it scare you when she was asking you to lead?

MATTHEW: At first it was scary, but I had always been very vocal with my wife in saying that it's important to me that I take care of her. And that I provide for my family, that I provide for my children—and that stems back to my own personal background. That's the way it has been for generations in my family. Call it old fashioned, but the husband of the family provides for the family, leads the family, and is the rock. So for me it was liberating and it was exhilarating because I finally found my place.

She allowed that to happen, and I give her all the credit in the world because she really took in every single thing that you and your team had put forth and put it into action.

I can see a change in her that is just remarkable. She's become more calm, more patient, more understanding, and she listens now. Before, she never listened to me. Now she's taken that into the rest of her life, where she listens to me, she listens to our kids, she listens to my parents, which is a tricky thing to do. She listens to everybody and then kind of formulates a really good thought process and advice.

There was a time in our relationship where I thought, "This is doomed, this is not going to work, there's no freaking way we're going to make this work." I mean, I went so far as to start to look for apartments. I went so far as to start to get our finances in order on the off chance that there was a separation. It was bad! And now I give her all the credit in the world because, had this not happened, there is no way we'd be married today. No way!

LAURA: What changes did you experience personally?

MATTHEW: I experienced a kind of liberation. But I'm not gonna lie. I had not been in charge, the man of the house, in a very long time, so it was stressful because I own and run a company. And then, on top of that, now all of these things kind of fell into my lap, and I had to navigate how I was going to do that. But any guy who is given the opportunity to show their worth and show what they can do—especially when your biggest critics are your family and your biggest supporters are your family—if given the opportunity to show them what you can do, you find a way to do it quickly.

LAURA: How else did you change?

MATTHEW: I changed into a more understanding and loving person. When we were going through our difficult time, I was angry all the time. I would be angry at her. I'd be angry at the kids. I'd be angry at the toaster. I mean, it was just a perpetual cycle of anger and frustration, and so what has changed is that I am no longer that person.

I was no longer living for the moment. Now I live for the future, what's going to happen in the future, how we're going to grow as a family, how my wife and I are going to become even stronger. And those are the things that really have changed me. Like I mentioned earlier, I became in love with my wife again.

I always loved her, and I was in love with her once, but truthfully there was a part in our lives where we fell out of love with each other, and it was mutual. It wasn't just me. That needs to be clear. But I have absolutely fallen back in love with her, and this has been an absolute blessing in our lives.

During the time when we were having issues, my wife was also a very high-powered executive. She ran sales teams across the country, and she was a very powerful person and that bled over into our relationship. When we would argue, or when we would talk, or when I was vulnerable to my wife at that time—which was rare—I would instantly get the manager. I wouldn't get the loving wife; I would get "Well, you need to do this, this, and this in a certain timeframe," and I remember just being like, "Well, that's not what I'm looking for. I just need someone to give me a hug." It doesn't sound masculine, but I don't really care about that. I really just needed a hug and a kiss and [for her to] just say, "Hey, it's gonna be okay." And I never got that, and I think any guy would also be lying if they said that's not what they need. I know that's what I need. Sometimes you just need your wife to wrap their arms around you and just tell you they love you and give you a kiss, and that's it.

LAURA: How did you react to that [when you got the manager instead of the wife]?

MATTHEW: I would just point-blank tell her, "I'm not your employee. I don't work for you. Don't boss me around. I'm trying to be vulnerable, and I don't like it."

So what happens is I'm no longer vulnerable. No longer go to her with things that normal people would go to their spouses about. And it just becomes where I'm not going to tell you what's going on my life, and you're not going to tell me—so we were roommates. And roommates without the benefit of sex.

LAURA: So that wasn't happening either?

MATTHEW: Oh, if it was, it was very dull. It was clinical. It was just an operation—it didn't really mean much, and she was very quick at that time and used it candidly as a weapon against me. "If you don't do this, we're not going to do this. And you have to earn it"—and I just remember being like, "This is not what I signed up for."

LAURA: I heard, and you can confirm these rumors, that you have gone on a health kick recently?

MATTHEW: I have. I'm not ashamed to say that I'm a recovering alcoholic. I am sixteen months and ten days sober.

LAURA: Wow! Congratulations!

MATTHEW: Thank you. I realized I needed to make a huge change in my life from a health factor in terms of losing weight. I coach both of my sons in football and baseball, and I got to the point where I just couldn't run with them anymore, and I thought, "This is crazy—I mean, I might be forty-five, but I can beat a ten-year-old in a race, right? I should be able to." So I started this health kick.

I should say, with the drinking, it is certainly not anyone's fault but my own, but during that time period when my wife and I were in this hell, alcohol was my escape. It was something that was very easy for me to do because the more she nagged, the more she griped, the more I drank, and the more that kind of dulled everything.

Alcohol was my way of coping and dulling all of the criticisms and disrespect. It's not my wife's fault—it's my fault—but that was a contributor. And I am very proud to say that after my wife went through this transition, through your program, it turned my entire mindset around. And this goes back to living for the future. Whereas before, I wasn't living for the future. I was living day to day and thinking, "This is just going to implode. I don't know what's going to happen, but I'm going down this weird rabbit hole." It took me a little time, but then I just realized, "Hey! I can be vulnerable with my wife, and not only will she not criticize, but she's going to support me now."

And that was very difficult for me, incredibly difficult, to come out to her and say, "Hey listen, I have a problem, and I need your help." Not only was she supportive, but she has been supportive every day. She quit drinking herself. And it's that love and respect that I get from her that keeps me sober and that keeps me moving forward. I never thought that I would be this fulfilled. I truly never thought that I would be this healthy again, but I am! It really is because she and I are a unit. If I didn't have her, I would be in a ditch somewhere, and I absolutely say that without any hesitation.

LAURA: Wow, that is astounding! I'm so impressed! Would you say that she had tried to get you to stop drinking previously?

MATTHEW: Oh, sure. The more she pushed me, the more I drank. The more she would criticize me, the more she would tell me, "You have a drinking problem," or "You have an anger issue, you have a mental issue"—I mean, it got to the point where she was blaming me for everything, and every time she would say, "You do this, you do that," I would do the opposite. She'd say, "Don't eat so much." Okay, well, I'm going to go get a double cheeseburger. "Don't drink so much"—I tell you what, I'm going to have a bottle of wine and a six-pack tonight.

LAURA: Yeah, so she had her foot on the accelerator when she thought she was putting it on the brake. But it was quite the opposite.

MATTHEW: Absolutely.

LAURA: You've lost some weight as well as getting sober, is that right?

MATTHEW: I've lost almost eighty pounds.

LAURA: Eighty pounds! So you're sixteen months and ten days sober, and you've had an eighty-pound weight loss. And you attribute all of this to the great connection you have with your wife?

MATTHEW: Without a shadow of a doubt. Her change has impacted not only me, but all of us. It's something that has let me love myself again. Not just me loving her again, but I have this insatiable appetite to love myself. I fully contribute to our close connection now, and it has everything to do with me falling back in love with her.

LAURA: Wow, I am so impressed! I mean, those are really impressive changes that you made, and it's just so helpful to hear you describe the way your wife used her influence instead of control and criticism and got such an incredibly different response. I love this insatiable self-love you're describing. How is your confidence now?

MATTHEW: Colossal! It's huge! Not only am I falling back in love with my wife, but our intimacy and our love life has never been better.

And for any guy to have not only routine intimacy with your wife, but new and creative intimacy with your wife also, gives you a huge boost in confidence. We talked about vulnerability, but my wife's ability to be vulnerable with me in the bedroom gives me the confidence to be vulnerable with her. Not just in the bedroom, but outside of that and in all aspects. So whatever you've done, keep it up, because this is a part that I absolutely love, and again, from a man's perspective: Sex is like water. Sex is like food. It has to happen. And the more you have, the more you love, the more you're willing to do things, at least from my perspective. And I don't know if I'm going too deep into this or divulging too much, but for me, for any guy, sex is something that's as necessary as breathing.

LAURA: I love that you went into that. I don't think I would have been brave enough to ask about it directly, so thank you for volunteering because this is a big part, and it's something we do talk a lot about. I love that you brought that forth and what a difference that's made for you. It sounds like part of your inner strength is knowing you have this great sex life with your wife.

MATTHEW: For me, it's better than before we got married when we first met because we know each other now. We love each other and respect each other, and we have that ability to be vulnerable and intimate in a way that we never could before.

LAURA: What tips do you have for women who are currently struggling in their marriage? What should they do?

MATTHEW: I think the biggest tip would be to back off. To slow down, and if you could make just one adjustment, that would be relinquishing some of the control.

There's likely some level of control that has emasculated a husband and that has probably put them in a position that I was in, which is "[If] you're not gonna respect me, I'm certainly not going to respect you." If there is a beginning, what you should likely start at would be, try—as tough as it might be—to show some respect and relinquish control, and [whether] that's a rapid thing or a slow thing, I can guarantee your husband is going to react in a positive way because the more love, respect, and empowerment, the more men respond.

LAURA: It just occurred to me that your wife was relinquishing that control and showing that respect, and it sounds like you were still drinking at that time.

MATTHEW: I was.

LAURA: And you had given up hope, so you didn't really care. So she was showing this respect and giving you this trust kind of in the face of some things that people could have said, "Well, this isn't going to work because he's drinking and he doesn't care."

MATTHEW: Right.

LAURA: Wow!

MATTHEW: The other thing that I would mention to any woman who's having an issue in their marriage is don't give up. Continue with it. You can't do it for two weeks and think that everything's going to change. I will tell you this—and I firmly believe this because one of the reasons why [at first] I kept drinking, one of the reasons why I was very defensive and angry, was because I was waiting for the other shoe to drop. I thought, "There is no freaking way this is going to last, this is some mind trick, this is her trying to manipulate me in some weird way." And there was kind of a persistence on my wife's part, and then it just snowballed into "Okay, this is real, this is not a joke, this is not a mind trick, this is—this is real life." So the suggestion that I would make is don't give up.

SKILL
#4

Receive, Receive, Receive!

Receptivity is the essence of femininity. The more you're willing to receive gifts, compliments, and help from your husband, the more feminine and attractive you'll be to him and the more special treatment you'll get.

Being a good receiver means that you smile and say thanks when he tries to buy you something, tells you you're beautiful, or offers to carry something for you. If you have been unreceptive in the past because the gifts, compliments, or help were not what you had in mind, your husband may have gotten the message that you don't want special treatment from him. Receiving is the ultimate act of giving up control.

The more receptive you are, even if you feel uncomfortable in the moment, the more confident you'll become.

PRESCRIPTION

Make a point of graciously receiving everything you're offered, whether it's a stranger holding the door for you, a bagger at the grocery store offering to help you out to your car, a friend paying for lunch, or your husband putting up a curtain rod. Say "Thank you" and nothing more. No explanation is necessary, so you don't have to offer one.

Even if you're afraid you'll owe a debt to someone (you won't—by definition, gifts are free), receive

each gift with open arms and gratitude. Respond to
compliments by saying only "Thank you," even if you
don't believe the compliment. Let others lighten your
load by helping you move chairs or carry boxes.

If your husband offers a gift that isn't quite right for you, keep
in mind that if you reject a gift, you're also rejecting the giver.

Make "Receive, receive, receive!" your mantra.

CHAPTER 18

How to Get More Gifts, Compliments, and Help

Are You a Good Receiver?

Have you ever had someone say "I love that outfit" and responded by saying something like "I got it on sale"?

Or maybe a friend has offered to buy your lunch but you insisted on paying your share. Or a party guest has offered to stay to help you clean up and you said, "Don't worry about it—I've got it." Or someone has apologized for being late to meet you and instead of thanking her for the acknowledgment, you've said, "Oh, that's all right."

Do you identify? Me too. I've done all those things. For years I had no idea how to receive compliments, gifts, help, or apologies, so I rejected them. Of course I didn't know I was rejecting the person also—that wasn't what I wanted to do. I didn't realize I was dismissing my own femininity and rebuffing the people who wanted to be kind to me.

Great receiving habits make you appear more attractive and confident, and they'll help you create better intimacy and connection in your relationship. Receptivity also inspires your husband to cherish you.

The reason receiving is such an important skill for intimacy is that you and your husband bring different gifts to the relationship, like the yin and yang of Eastern philosophy. Yin is the feminine energy and yang is the masculine energy. The feminine is receptive, and the masculine response to receptivity is the inspiration to cherish that receptive person. That gives him purpose and meaning. But if you don't receive from him, then the cycle is broken. He doesn't get to feel proud, and you don't get to feel taken care of, and so the intimacy is lost.

Without someone to receive and benefit from his efforts, the masculine doesn't have much purpose. Men who have no one to receive from them aren't as motivated and inspired as men who do.

One of the ways we see this show up is that married men make more money than single men. Several studies, including a Virginia Commonwealth University study, found that married men earn 22 percent more than their similarly experienced but single colleagues. Married guys are more ambitious, more inspired, and more purposeful. They have someone to please.

Receiving graciously means that when someone else makes an effort to do or say something for your enjoyment or to ease your responsibilities, you accept it without dismissing, joking, or diverting attention. You don't turn it away. For instance, if you think you're having a bad hair day and someone says "Your hair looks great," instead of brushing their compliment away, just smile and say "Thank you!"

When your husband gets you a present that isn't quite what you had in mind, you can receive it by saying, "Thank you for thinking of me!" If he says "I'll do the laundry" and you suspect he's going to wrinkle the clothes by folding them like origami, accept his help instead of saying, "No, I'll just do it myself."

If someone apologizes to you, you might be tempted to let him or her off the hook quickly by saying "That's okay." Instead, receive the apology by saying "Thank you" or "I appreciate that." Let the other person finish talking, instead of interrupting to say "No, no, no—don't worry about it." Let others apologize to you when they've done something inconsiderate or thoughtless, even if it's a small transgression. Be gracious enough to give them the space to apologize, and honor yourself by receiving it instead of dismissing it. You can put them at ease by letting them know you've accepted the apology rather than acting as though no apology was necessary.

Practicing the skill of receiving will attract more gifts, compliments, help, and apologies—and that's not all.

Good Receivers Are More Self-Confident

You may be wondering, why is it so important to always receive graciously? There are seven reasons.

1. Being a good receiver makes you more attractive because you appear more feminine.
2. Being a good receiver gives you more intimacy and a better emotional connection. In a way, when you receive, you also give. Doesn't it feel good when you give someone a present and they are genuinely happy to get it? If you reject a gift, you also reject the giver and the emotional connection you could have had with that person.
3. Being a good receiver makes you more confident. Contradicting someone who compliments you is the same as putting yourself down. That reveals that you feel undeserving. If you take in what he's saying and adopt his positive perspective, that makes you feel good about yourself. Nobody has to know that you don't feel deserving yet.
4. Being a good receiver increases your tolerance for good things. If you're not in the habit of accepting compliments, gifts, and help, then you probably aren't comfortable having them. Things won't get better until you increase your tolerance. One way to do that is to just hang in there with the receiving until you get used to it.

The day after a play date with a friend and her kids, Renee's friend texted her to say, "That was fun yesterday. Your kids are so cute!"

Renee's impulse was to respond immediately and say "So are yours!" Instead, she stopped herself.

Renee was just learning the feminine art of receiving, and she was keenly aware of her urge to "even the score," which is a common way of relieving the discomfort that we sometimes feel when we receive a compliment. As an experiment, Renee decided to just thank her friend without reciprocating. She texted her only "Thank you!" and nothing more. It was not as awkward as she imagined, because Renee knew that when she gave someone else a compliment, she didn't expect one back. As a result, Renee got to really enjoy this compliment about how adorable her children were, which, like any proud mother, she loved hearing.

5. Being a good receiver attracts more gifts to you, because people love to give to good receivers. One woman told me that when she was learning about the feminine art of receiving graciously, she got to observe her child's teacher modeling good receiving. When the kids got her end-of-the-year presents, she *ooh*ed and *ahh*ed about each gift, making each child feel special. Her ability to receive graciously was itself a gift to those children, who got to feel connected to their beloved teacher. We can do the same thing in all of our relationships.
6. Being a good receiver gives you more free time because you have more help, including emotional support, advice about your challenges, and help with chores or other responsibilities.
7. Being a good receiver feels great. You are the princess while you're receiving. Why shouldn't you enjoy that moment?

Good Receivers Are More Attractive

Since men are naturally very attracted to the feminine, the better you are at receiving, the more attractive you'll be. When we take a feminine approach, there's nothing a man won't do to please us. That starts with acknowledging that we're different—and really celebrating that.

If you're feeling cold and your husband offers you his jacket, thank him and luxuriate in that jacket. That's being receptive and allowing him to be masculine with you, which feels good all around. If he tells you that you're beautiful, accept the compliment graciously. If he offers to help you carry the boxes you were about to move, let him. There's no downside. Just smile and say "thank you."

I find now that I've been taking a feminine approach with my husband for so long, I have it with me wherever I go. On a plane recently, a man sitting in my aisle asked if he could get my bag from the overhead compartment. I didn't have a bag in the overhead compartment, but I kind of wished I did because it would have been nice to let him get it. I would have felt feminine, he would have felt masculine, and we'd both have felt good. These days I accept those kinds of offers out of habit. I've gotten used to getting special treatment.

A few minutes later, on our way to baggage claim, we came to a long staircase. Another man who had been seated next to a businesswoman offered to carry her rolling suitcase down the stairs for her, but she said, "No thanks, I've got it." He ran off ahead very quickly, probably feeling rejected, and she muttered, "Well, this is scary," as she tried to navigate the stairs and her bags by herself. Then she turned to me and said, "I'd have to be able to do this myself if he wasn't there!"

She missed a chance to get help with her luggage, which it seemed like she could have used. And she missed the chance to feel feminine because she thought she *had* to be independent. She didn't.

Consider too that you can't give and receive at the same time. The more you're doing things for a man, the less you're in a position to receive. And your doing the giving is less appealing to him because it's less feminine. Your husband doesn't want you to schedule his doctor's appointments or buy his underwear, because he would rather be doing things to delight you. If you spend time taking care of yourself instead of him, you're more likely to be receptive, grateful, and happy when he puts gas in your car or weeds the garden. Seeing you satisfied from his efforts is a big part of what makes him feel successful as a husband.

What to Do When You Receive Gifts You Hate

When we reject gifts and compliments, we squash intimacy, insult the giver, and miss out on having something delightful.

Before they were married, Tara's husband got her a bottle of perfume for Valentine's Day. It wasn't one she particularly liked, and she let him know that and discarded the gift. He hadn't bought her a present since, and they'd been married for fifteen years.

When Tara learned the Six Intimacy Skills, she had the painful realization that she'd taught her husband never to buy her anything all those years ago. So she decided to concentrate on practicing the skill of receiving to see what emerged in the gift-giving department.

Sure enough, for Christmas her husband bought her the first gift of their entire married life: an unusual, beautiful, name-brand sweater. Tara was delighted and astonished. She gratefully thanked him and put it on to show him how well he had chosen for her. She found she didn't want to take it off, both because it made her feel beautiful and desired, and because it symbolized a new, gratifying connection between them.

I had one woman ask how she was supposed to pretend she liked a gift her husband got her even though she didn't. "That's dishonest!" she complained. Maybe. But maybe bringing manners into the relationship will help preserve the intimacy, and maybe that's more important. Only you know what fits for you. I know that for me there was a time when I was critical of everything my husband picked out for me if it wasn't what I would have picked out for myself—so he stopped buying me anything. I should have saved us both a lot of time and married myself.

You can always find something truthful and polite to say when a friend gets you something. You might say "What a pretty color" or "I've never seen anything like it—thanks!" Extend the same courtesy to your husband. Do this because you want to nurture the relationship and show you're open to being showered with gifts. The gifts won't all be exactly what you would have picked out, but for that you can go to the store and buy things yourself.

Sometimes we reject gifts without even realizing it. One woman told me, "I would never reject my husband's gifts." Her husband overheard her and said, "What about the juicer I gave you? You sure complained about that." She'd rejected that because it didn't match her agenda, which was that he should get her something more romantic. Granted, a juicer isn't the most romantic present in the world, but it was something he thought she would like.

If you have also gotten that kind of gift—a battery recharger for Valentine's Day, say, or a Swiss army knife for your birthday—you are not alone. At a live event, I asked who had received a gift from her man that was a bit of a head-scratcher, and almost every hand went up. Your husband has a different perspective than you do, and he may see something about you that you don't see about yourself or be thinking about your safety or comfort. Instead of getting stuck on that, consider the thought behind the gift. The woman who got the Swiss army knife for her birthday said she ended up really appreciating that gift over time.

You deserve to have practical, functional things as well as sweet, luxurious things, and your man deserves the pleasure of giving you all of them. So start receiving graciously and the gifts will multiply and come with greater enthusiasm almost immediately. It takes more courage—for me, at least—to receive compliments, gifts, and help graciously than it does to retreat to false modesty.

Even if you feel guilty, uncomfortable, undeserving, immodest, or out of control, just say thank you. Adopting the habit of a gracious receiver will help you draw things to you with minimal effort, instead of having to pull them toward you by force or manipulation.

Sometimes accepting a gift graciously is the greatest gift of all. It shows that you understand that others, especially the man in your life, feel pleasure when you allow them to give you something.

So how do you do that? When you're given something, do what your mother taught you to do. Smile and say thank you.

Receiving Is Harder Than It Looks

It sounds deceptively easy to receive graciously, but we don't always do it. Why is that? There are six reasons.

1. Receiving can make you feel out of control.

You can't predict what the other person will say. Everybody else may be looking at you, putting you unexpectedly in the spotlight. You might think, *Everybody is looking at my hair now, and I don't feel that good about how it looks.*

2. Receiving graciously can make you feel as though you're being arrogant.

What did we all learn in junior high? Don't be stuck up! You may still be thinking, like you did back then, *People will think I'm conceited if I say thanks when they compliment me.*

3. Receiving graciously can bring up feelings of distrust.

You may wonder if the compliment is insincere or meant as a manipulation. Let's say a salesperson gives you a compliment. You might think, *He's just trying to butter me up so I'll buy something.*

4. Receiving graciously can make you feel undeserving.

You don't want to impose on anyone, so you'll refuse help. You might think, *I can't expect other people to help me with my work. Everybody has to pull their own weight.*

I used to think other people were keeping score, because I was always keeping score. That's what part of me believed was appropriate for gift-giving: tit for tat. Instead of simply accepting things that were offered for my enjoyment, I calculated whether I could afford to reciprocate or not, and then responded accordingly. Gift giving and gift receiving made up a giant scorecard, and it seemed like I could never get ahead. I constantly felt bad for not keeping up or cheated if I felt I'd gotten less than I'd given.

5. Receiving graciously can pose a threat to your independence—or so you think.

As columnist Connie Shultz wrote, "My husband had to convince me that letting him make me coffee in the morning did not mean I was giving up my right to vote and own property."

When I was newly married, I would have been hard-pressed to admit that I needed help from anyone. I once carried a heavy box of books from our car up the stairs to the apartment, even though my husband would have happily carried them for me. I was proud because this showed I could take care of myself. And I can. But everyone needs help from time to time, and accepting help doesn't make you weak—it makes you more feminine. I missed a lot of chances to be intimate with a man who only wanted to make me happy, make my life easier, and please me.

Now it's no longer my goal to be independent. What I want is to be *inter*dependent with my husband. I don't *need* his help, but I *want* it.

6. Finally, receiving graciously can be difficult because sometimes you have an agenda.

For instance, let's say your husband wants to take you to dinner and to a movie and you're afraid it will cost too much. Your agenda is to save money, so you say, "We can't afford it. Let's just watch something at home instead." Seems practical and harmless, right?

Nope. You just rejected his gift. Refusing to go out for the evening or implying that your husband is being financially irresponsible calls his judgment into question. That will make him less enthusiastic about taking you out on a date in the future. And whether you know it or not, consciously or unconsciously, *you are always teaching people how to treat you.* You felt as though you had a valid reason for rejecting his offer to take you out, but with that decision, you made saving money more important than having a night of fun and the intimacy with your husband.

Receptivity Is the Essence of Femininity

The reason you deserve special treatment is because you're a woman; it's your birthright. So start acting like you deserve it by receiving graciously. You'll appear more self-confident, and over time, you'll feel more deserving too.

When *So You Think You Can Dance* host Cat Deeley was nominated for an Emmy, the judges started congratulating her as soon as she came onto the stage. They also told her how beautiful she looked. Cat graciously received the compliments and the congratulations. She didn't divert attention from herself—she just took it all in, smiling radiantly and looking the part.

The judges had also been nominated for an Emmy, but Cat didn't let that distract her from basking in the spotlight of being noticed and complimented. She demonstrated gracious receiving perfectly, which is part of what makes her so successful, attractive, and confident.

The ability to either receive or reject is part of your power as a woman. You don't have to receive everything that's offered to you, but deciding whether to receive or reject certainly impacts your relationship with the giver.

Diane complained that her husband Kurt was not romantic. She said he did all the wrong things when he took her to Las Vegas for her birthday. "We agreed that we would meet at the hotel since he had to work late," she explained. "While I was in the room waiting for him, there was a knock on the door and a man was standing there with a huge birthday cake. At first I said, 'You have the wrong room,' but then I saw that it said 'Happy Birthday Diane.' I couldn't believe Kurt sent an entire cake! It cost over a hundred dollars, and we only ate one piece! They had cupcakes right in the hotel lobby at the gift shop, which would have been cheaper and I would have been just as happy."

But rather than a story about a husband who is not romantic, Diane's is a story about a wife who was too concerned about money and criticized the present her husband chose because it wasn't what she would have chosen herself. She overlooked how sweet and thoughtful he had been in favor of sticking to her practical agenda of spending money only on the things *she* wanted to spend money on. The romance-killer wasn't Kurt, it was Diane, because she was unwilling to receive a gift that wasn't exactly what she had in mind.

I've behaved the same way. I've let my husband know that the flowers he bought weren't the kind I would have really liked. I've told him that the jewelry he bought me wasn't my style, and that the restaurant where he made us reservations on Valentine's Day wasn't very healthy. I'm sorry to say that in the past I've completely dismissed, and unwittingly discouraged, my husband's gifts and thoughtful gestures because they didn't meet my specific ideas of romance, cleanliness, thriftiness, or nutrition. I wanted him to do exactly what *I* thought he should do, and when he didn't, I tried to instruct him on how to do better next time.

As you can imagine, my approach squashed my husband's motivation to do anything nice for me at all, because he rarely felt successful making me happy. People need positive reinforcement, and John rarely got it from me. I didn't realize that I was cheating us both—me out of feeling surprised and cherished when he did something thoughtful, and him out of feeling proud and successful when he pleased his wife.

If you're in the habit of rejecting your husband's gifts or if your response to his last offering was "Why did you get me this?" then you've trained your husband that he can't please you and discouraged him from trying. So one of the things I invite you to do to have the kind of relationship you're dreaming of is to become pleaseable by receiving graciously.

Maybe you've had the experience of getting a battery charger for Valentine's Day too, but you're not the only one who got an unromantic or unwanted gift from your husband. That has happened to every woman on the planet who's lucky enough to have a man buy her a present. When it happens, you have a choice: Will you choose good manners and intimacy? Or will you be critical and reject your husband in the name of "honesty"?

You can be polite and authentic at the same time by concentrating on the gesture. Even if you don't love the gift, make sure he knows you like that he was thinking about you, and that you appreciate his thoughtfulness. You won't feel cherished until you learn to receive graciously.

In this abridged excerpt from *The Empowered Wife Podcast* episode 69, I interviewed Catherine, who was overwhelmed and exhausted just counting the number of mistakes that her husband was making with their children. He had retreated into his work, but when he was there, the tension and conflict were high.

LAURA: What were things like in the bad old days?

CATHERINE: The hallmark for me was feeling resentful. It almost became like my standard operating system, just feeling frustrated and resentful. After my third child was born, it became apparent to me that this was a big problem.

I really love family life and raising my kids. I really threw myself into it. I love reading research and thinking carefully about how to raise my children, and I really wanted to get it right.

So I read books, listened to podcasts, and read research and found it really fascinating and enjoyable! This led me to be an expert on parenting: what the kids should eat, how we should talk to them, how we should help them manage their emotions, how we should discipline them, [and] how they should play.

The more I learned, the more I could see that there were big problems in the way that my husband was parenting, and I really wanted us to be on the same page and for us to be a real team and a partnership.

My natural inclination was to try to educate him and coach him. So I kept this running list in my head about everything that he had done that could be improved. I thought I was being really helpful! And it was really important, obviously, because our children are our most important thing to both of us. So I'm doing everyone a favor by really dedicating myself to getting this right.

We would have conversations in the evenings, and I'd go over what had transpired, and maybe some leading questions about where he thought that might have come from in his own childhood. I'd become his psychotherapist and parenting coach.

He would tolerate it, but he would often go quiet, and the quietness got longer and longer.

I would think, "Doesn't he take me seriously? He's not committed to this and doesn't want to change." I would fill in the silence with all the stories that I would tell myself. He would be quick to say he needed to go do some work.

He loves his work and is very dedicated, always has been, but it became more and more, even during evenings and weekends. He was also traveling a lot for work at that time, and I felt really alone. We don't live near my family, and raising kids, I felt quite unsupported. I got really accustomed to doing everything myself. I had this pressure on myself that I had to do everything right.

My husband and I weren't spending as much quality time together as I would have liked. My time was filled with kids from the moment I woke up. I'd be balancing lunch boxes, dinners, washing, the folding, tidying up toys all night. I just remember so clearly walking through the house picking things up, putting things away, thinking, "I have to do everything, this is my life now."

I was constantly thinking about how this was my husband's fault. Blaming things on my husband that couldn't possibly be his fault. Something went wrong with the washing, and I would feel this rage and blame, just all this resentment, and then think, "Hang on! This can't be his fault."

I started to get those little sprinkles of awareness that maybe there's something not completely rational about how I'm thinking, and I'm very logical. I just had this awareness start to emerge that maybe I am not being completely fair or that this isn't completely objective. I might have something to do with what's happening inside my own head and in my own heart. I was just desperate for my life not to feel like that.

There was also a lot of good we've always had. He's just a delightful person and an incredible father, always wanting to help others. So we still had a great bond. We weren't heading towards a divorce or anything like that, but sometimes I would daydream about parenting with somebody that saw everything the way I saw it. And I'd think, "I'm stuck here now, but wouldn't it be great if I could change it?"

So many other people would see him and see how amazing he is, and I would be able to see what they were saying, but I couldn't feel it. I would hear them commenting he was such a great dad, "he's so involved," or "he's always wanting to help you, he's such a nice guy"—and I would say, "Yeah, he is." But I didn't see it.

I really wanted to enjoy family life, and I really love being with my kids. I love parenting, I love family life. But I wasn't enjoying it the way that I wanted to. I couldn't even relax when we were all together because I would be so triggered by everything that my husband did. Like, it would only be five minutes, and he would give the kids something to eat that I didn't want him to give them, or create competition where there didn't need to be, or something that I would react to. Family time, holiday time, wasn't the sanctuary of togetherness that I wanted it to be.

[Then a] new baby, trying to help the older child, and the elder was starting school, and doing all the drop-offs and all the pickups, and sleepless nights and appointments all the time—it definitely exacerbated how I viewed my husband and what I viewed as his parenting mistakes. The stakes were really high, and this added a lot of pressure and tension to what had already been there.

I would think, "How can we ever get anywhere with this if you're making all these mistakes?" And deep down I thought it was because of him. It became very emotionally charged. We were really trying, having date nights and spending lots of time together, and I would bring my laptop on the date night, and I could see his face falling. I kept on thinking that he was avoiding having these conversations, [about] things like money or the kids or therapy, all the things that we couldn't talk about because he was so busy with work. I thought, "We can relax and have fun together once we've sorted all this out," so it was like we could never escape the magnitude of all the things we had to resolve and work through, and I kept thinking, like, "I'll be respectful, I'll be happy and joyful when there's something to be happy and joyful about."

LAURA: Just as soon as that happens.

CATHERINE: Yeah.

I downloaded your audio book *The Empowered Wife.* I went through it very quickly. I [saw myself in] every single bad example that you said in the book. I did everything: I commented on what he was wearing, I gave him helpful feedback all the time, I wanted him to do his help the way I did, and if he didn't do it the way I did, I'd gently tell him all the reasons why we do it this way, why this is better. There wasn't an example that you brought forward in your book that I hadn't done. I thought, "Oh, my goodness"—like, my stomach really dropped off. I had been doing so much to try and change how my husband showed up, to get him to hear me, to get him to change, and I hadn't even thought for a second that the only person that I can change is me, and if I change, he'll change, or that if I change, I might not need him to change. I could just love him the way he is.

I remember I actually went downstairs because I had been quite open with my husband about doing these courses and trying to find the solutions and he was very supportive because he's always very supportive. So I came downstairs and said, "I just listened to this book, and she outlined everything that can go wrong, and I have done everything."

He said, "Have you done everything right or everything wrong?" not wanting to presume or get into trouble.

I said, "Everything wrong!" and he said "Oh, I just wanted to hear you say that!"

LAURA: Whoa! Such a humbling moment.

CATHERINE: It *was* a humbling moment. I enjoyed it! I actually felt like I needed to hear this. There was just an immediate energetic shift for me from having to defend my territory, having to stand up for what was important to me, to "What do I need to learn here?"

It felt foreign to me, but it also felt good because, finally, there's a way forward that I can influence. I can always have control over how I show up. There's always something I could do, and that feeling is so empowering. I could transform any situation by showing up differently and by looking at it differently.

Instead of saying, "He's choosing his work over me, he's always going to work all the time, he works all weekend, he doesn't see how much I do or what impact it has on me"—instead, when he would go and work in the evenings, I would go and do something for myself. I'd go and read a book, read your book or another book, or have a bath, and I started meditating before bed, which is something I had been dabbling in and found really helpful. I actually looked forward to having time to myself when my husband was working.

Another thing I stopped doing was doing everything. I put boundaries around how much domestic work I would do in a day. The state of things didn't matter. If I was feeling exhausted, I even actually said, "Eight o'clock! That's it! Tools down." And then I'd go and have an hour, an hour and a half to myself before I go to sleep. Because I need time to be happy. I started to realize how important it is for my whole family to have a mom that is showing up as her best self and that is happy and joyful and can see the light of things and not be weighed down by all of this pressure and responsibility.

I used to call myself the primary parent because I did more of the care, and I would think, "I've done so many more hours than you, and you're playing catch up because you don't have as much time with the kids."

Now I really feel in many ways *he* is often the primary parent. On a weekend, I'll be spending time for myself. It's not even primarily—we're a team, and it's not how one person's doing it better than the other person or anything like that.

LAURA: How would you describe your relationship now?

CATHERINE: It's really connected, and I have a lot of faith in him, and I really respect him. I respect him as a father, I respect him as a parent, even if there's some things that I do differently, and I think he could probably do them slightly differently too. But I don't dwell—that doesn't define him as a parent anymore, and so there's just a lot of respect, and we have each other's backs. We're both working on ourselves. I've been doing all of this work on myself and trying to show up as my best self and making time for myself and my own growth.

My husband's been really inspired by that too, and he's doing heaps. He's reading books and getting motivated and doing more exercise. He's really ambitious and making plans and dreaming big. I feel like our relationship is us both watching each other grow in our own independence, in our own lives.

I'm not all over what he's doing, and he is totally supportive and respectful of what I'm doing, and we admire each other. There's just so much playfulness and tenderness. He plans dates—the date nights of the past were all orchestrated by me. Now I just say, "I'd love to go out."

Sometimes I don't even say that, and he surprises me! He's arranged a babysitter, and we're going to see a movie. We hadn't seen a movie for four or five years because I couldn't come to terms with using the two hours that we had together that week watching a movie when we needed to talk about so many things. I thought that if we just relaxed and had fun and enjoyed each other's company, that would be a waste of time because we had so much to resolve.

Now we're seeing movies again, and he's taking me on dates and picking the restaurant, and it feels just like when we were first dating, it's bringing this romance back.

Everything changed for me, just not having any expectations and being delighted with whatever he's doing.

He brings me breakfast in bed on a Sunday. He'll take the kids out and go to the bakery that's got my favorite things. It's a drive, but they go and choose Mommy's favorite things, and they bring them back and I get it in bed, and I just feel really doted on. He always wanted to do that, and I would sometimes receive a cup of tea, and I would say a simple "Thank you!" But now I really praise him and say, "Thank you, I love this! I love having tea in bed."

I feel like a goddess luxuriating. I never really let myself have that experience because there was so much resentment, I couldn't feel like a luxuriating goddess. And now, when I do, I can see my kids love it, my husband loves it, I love it.

There's also so much sharing of the load. My husband was taking my youngest to his childcare. He had taken on the drop-offs and pick-ups. He said that he wasn't sure about this daycare. "I really think we need to look somewhere else." I felt resistance but said, "Okay, I hear you. You want to see what other options are around, and let me know what you think?"

I had already toured lots in the area. He found one that was really close by and thought that would suit my son really well. I had some reservations about it, but I said, "Okay, I trust your judgment. Let's give it a go." He did the tour and arranged the enrollment. And he became the main point of contact with the childcare center. He loves solving problems and getting it done.

My son had his first day yesterday at this daycare, and my husband was so right: It was so much better. After his first day, my son was so happy and exploring the different areas—so much happier than he had been at the previous place, so I was able to text [my husband] and say, "You were so right, this is the perfect place for our son." He loved hearing that.

Just being able to receive his influence is amazing, and that builds respect for me. When you first start, it can feel like you're not being your genuine self, you know, that you're withholding what you really think or what you really feel, and that you might be betraying yourself, or something. The more I practice it, and have your exact cheat phrases, and retraining your brain and retraining your body as well, like these physical responses of fear or stress, it becomes your new normal, and it elevates your view of yourself, your partner, the world. It really is a personal transformational journey.

Instead of focusing on the negatives, like I did for most of my life, I'm really practicing these new muscles of focusing on the positives, and the more you do, the more I receive. I really have to stretch myself sometimes because my husband does so much now, I can feel like I'm not doing all the things that a mom should do. I can have these sneaky thoughts in my head of "Maybe I'm being lazy" or "That's really something I should be doing." Those were very disempowering beliefs. Now it's like stretching myself to receive, and my life doesn't have to look like other people's overwhelmed and exhausted life.

I've previously refused to spend any money on babysitting or help around the house if I wasn't working, only get help when I'm making money. I had this rule for myself, and I was very controlling about the money, the budget, and savings, and paying off a mortgage.

My husband was saying, "Maybe you need more free time, maybe you need some time to do the things that make you happy, or maybe we could have some help and that would elevate our lives." I would say, "Well, once we earn well, then we'll do it," always finding a reason.

We started getting some help from a babysitter, and she's an amazing cook. My husband realized that, for less than the price of takeaway each week, we can have her come and just do some cooking, some meal planning, so you don't have to spend half the day on the weekend cooking. It is the best money you could ever spend.

It's this creative solution that I would never allow myself to receive or even contemplate. In Australia, help in the home is something that only the rich and fancy people have. We don't really have nannies. It's really something that you can't have, that only the super wealthy have. But it's not, actually. Now I have it too.

LAURA: What would you say to a woman who is stuck where you were? She's that woman walking through the house picking things up by herself, she's full of resentment and wants to have a beautiful family life. Where should she start?

CATHERINE: I think the first place to start, for me, was honoring how I was feeling. I'm feeling like my head was full of resentment, but my body was tired. I was depleted, and it's very hard—even today it's very hard to avoid those tracks of thinking when you're exhausted.

I think it's realizing that the best thing that you can do for everyone in your life is to tend to yourself first and put some boundaries on how much of your energy you can give out and what you need to do to restore yourself.

It can be really hard saying that to someone that's got a newborn or little kids. This was me! I discovered these skills with a little baby, and it is possible to put yourself first.

I never used to put myself first, even when eating food. I would find myself angry at three o'clock in the afternoon and realize that I hadn't really eaten much and probably hadn't eaten properly that day. And now I always have fresh food in the fridge and snacks that are healthy, and I really prepare my food the way that I would prepare my children's food. Because I need to be cared for. I always used to put myself last and felt that it was my obligation, and it's not. The best thing that you can do for your kids is to look after yourself really well.

LAURA: I loved how you describe it as a service to your family.

CATHERINE: Yes. With the Skills, you've got some stores of energy, or, at least, there's things that you can do that will help you to feel more like yourself again. For me, it was experimentation, and sometimes I would do self-care and get my nails done with a friend, or something that's not really my thing that doesn't fill me up. For me, it was just like pouring water through a colander or a sieve. It was press pause on my life and then return and press play again, and I didn't feel any better. But self-care is not these prescribed activities. It's taking time to do the things that make you feel good again that make you feel like you again.

For me, it was experimenting and exploring and reading books and even this personal development work that I love. It makes me feel excited and energized, and that's what I need, but I also love going for walks and running and doing yoga, and it makes me feel good.

I love having cups of tea and really sitting with them and saying, "I'm nourishing myself, this is for me," and I think that definitely has to be the first place that you start when you feel resentful.

And then from there a big thing for me was expressing gratitude for everything. Finding the things that my partner was doing, all the ways that I was being supported, and really focusing on those and receiving those, and then relinquishing control of those very high standards that we can put on ourselves that can make life really challenging. Not only relinquishing control of how my husband did things, but also relinquishing control of these really high standards or high expectations that I had to get things just perfect every time, and it's just not achievable, and it's really not healthy either. It doesn't lead to a good place. And really letting go of those "shoulds" and just being right where we are, and sometimes things have to fall by the wayside.

LAURA: What would you say if you could go back in time and talk to Catherine, knowing what you know now?

CATHERINE: Knowing my personality, I would say to myself, "This starts with you, and you can have everything that you want. It can be the way that you want, but not how you think—you can't control your way to the outcome that you want. You can't make this happen by controlling everyone, but you do have the power, you do have influence, but it all starts with you. The only person that you have control over is you. Just start with looking after yourself, and go within and get curious about how you are showing up." Obviously, if I could, whisper, "Go and find Laura's book."

LAURA: Yeah, it's just time traveling.

CATHERINE: It's a very big shortcut, and you pieced it all together. Sometimes I look back at my journaling before I discovered you, and I read back and think I was getting there. I was finding things that were helping, and there was insight there. The Intimacy Skills are such an amazing shortcut—you don't have to figure it out on your own.

Sometimes you hear, like, "the surrendered wife," and you can recoil and think, like, "Oh, submissive, or like doormats, or something," and it's just not that at all. The people that are drawn to you are people who maybe have a controlling streak, very impressive people. They're people that are just a joy to be around and call me on to a higher standard to a more dignified life, to a joyful, happy, playful kind of life, and having those people as friends and [a] support group, and being exposed to coaches, who are further down the road—it just really embeds the change and gives you that support.

If I can give hope to someone that was where I was, I'd love to be able to do that because it's not a nice place to be in, and there is such a joyful option to take.

Reveal Your Heart with Vulnerability

If what you want is intimacy, you must be vulnerable. It feels risky, and it is.

You'll know when you're being vulnerable because part of you will resist. Maybe you'll want to hold back your tears or pretend you weren't disappointed or that you don't need help. Memorize that feeling and bravely walk into it as much as you can, because that's where the magic is.

Vulnerability is not only attractive, it's where you get that incredible, indescribable feeling of being loved just the way you are by someone who knows you well. There's nothing quite like it, and it really is worth risking everything to have it.

Vulnerability is not the same as weakness—it actually takes much more strength and courage to risk emotionally than it does to stay defended. Sometimes we don't even know we're defended—we just know that it would feel uncomfortable to admit we don't know what someone is talking about or to say we're lonely.

That's because it would make us vulnerable.

PRESCRIPTION

To practice being vulnerable, start by admitting
that you're hurt instead of defending yourself.

Instead of saying "You hurt my feelings,"
try saying nothing but "Ouch!"

Instead of saying "You're never home," say "I miss you."

Instead of trying to do it all, when you're
overwhelmed, say "I can't" or "I need help."

Instead of trying to figure everything out yourself,
ask for advice when you're not sure what to do.

CHAPTER 19

What Made Your Man Fall for You (and Still Melts Him Every Time)

"Vulnerability sounds like truth and feels like courage. Truth and courage aren't always comfortable, but they're never weakness."

—Brené Brown, Author, Columnist, and Speaker

Intimacy Requires Courage

My experience has been that to have the intimacy I crave, I need to relax into situations that I find terrifying, where everything in me wants to fight or run. I used to think that someday I wouldn't be vulnerable at all, but just the opposite has proven to be true. The comfort I've found around being vulnerable is that it feels more familiar now than it used to. I've also acquired a taste for the intimacy, connection, and love that's on the other side of giving up my defenses. So today, I strive to be vulnerable as much as I can.

Recently I was watching the movie *The King's Speech* at home by myself. Colin Firth was so courageous as the stuttering King George, it made me cry. John came home right in the middle of a very dramatic scene, and my first instinct was to try to compose myself so he wouldn't know I was a big pile of mush. I was fumbling to pause the movie when he came over and said, "How are you, cutie?" I knew if I responded I would lose it, so I tried to compose myself silently, but that wasn't working. It was pretty obvious that I was just a melty snowman on the couch. I didn't want him to know that, but he already knows that about me anyway. He smiled and gave me a tender kiss, because he loves my soft side.

I know that's how it is with vulnerability—I teach it all the time. But still my instinct is to not let anybody see that part of me. But then again, it feels so wonderful to be loved even when I'm in pieces.

When someone sees me—really sees the messy part, the part I don't want them to see—and they respond with tenderness, that's an amazing, indescribable feeling. It's one I want to have as much as I can.

You may think, as I once did, that vulnerability is unattractive. I thought it was a weakness, and since I'm a strong-minded, able-bodied woman, I didn't ever want to appear vulnerable. But I was completely wrong.

Home Is Where the Humans Are

One of the great common denominators of being human is that we're all vulnerable sometimes. We all experience joy and loss. We all cry and need approval. We all feel embarrassed and long for reassurance. We all judge ourselves and have dark thoughts. Every one of us wants to be loved. When we let those tender parts show, others connect with us because they recognize their own humanity in us and feel at home.

Today I consider my ability to go to that tender place one of my best qualities. When I'm there, I can feel how much affection John has for me and how much he wants to protect me. It's given me a fuller appreciation for the depth of his love. In my better moments, I recognize that my vulnerability is attractive. My husband responds in such a masculine way and I feel so feminine in return.

I now realize that I can enjoy intimacy with my husband *only* to the degree that I can be vulnerable with him. That means letting my tears come instead of masking my hurt with anger. It means that even when I feel attacked, I put my defenses down and let him see that I am fragile. It means holding steady even when I realize I could be rejected or abandoned when I'm least prepared for it.

When you let down your guard, the truth comes out in an endearing way. You feel the incomparable pleasure and joy of being loved just as you are, not for who you think you should be.

Intimacy and closeness spring from the relief of admitting you're not at all perfect and finding out that you're still lovable. Intimacy thrives when you know you're safe. That's when you can relax in your own skin and reveal yourself.

In fact, your vulnerability is what made your man fall for you above everyone else. He saw how delicate you are and felt that he could make a contribution by caring for you, comforting you, and protecting you. That's what made him want to commit to you forever.

I promise you, it still melts him every time he sees your vulnerability. It reminds him of his purpose and the connection he feels. That's a gift you bring to the relationship: the vulnerability that creates your bond.

A week before they were scheduled to move, Rachel experienced the magic of triggering her husband's hero gene by being vulnerable.

Feeling stressed about how much was still to be done, she told her husband that he needed to hurry up and finish packing his things and then disassemble some furniture in preparation for moving day. But instead of springing into action, her husband seemed distant and irritated. He even suggested she needed some self-care—a nice way of telling her to relax.

Exhausted and frustrated, Rachel decided the most urgent and vital thing to do next was to take a bath, which she did. Feeling refreshed afterward, she apologized for snapping orders at him, and leaned back into being vulnerable. She told him how much she was struggling and asked if she could borrow his brain.

"I'm over my head with this move. I would love to be all packed," she admitted.

Jacob immediately came to her rescue.

He packed for nine hours the next day and said he would arrange for the movers to give her whatever extra help she needed, even if it meant paying more. He was warm and encouraging, which made her feel calmer and less frazzled.

"Wow! What a difference," Rachel told me. "When I'm honest and vulnerable, it's like he can't help me fast enough. If I give him orders, it never gets me what I want."

Stop Fights with a Single Word

Another important aspect of expressing your feelings is letting people around you—especially your husband—know when you're hurt.

As wonderful as my marriage has been since I discovered the Six Intimacy Skills, sometimes my husband still hurts my feelings, and sometimes I hurt his too. He's a great guy and he loves me like crazy, but because we're so close, sometimes I still get hurt. Think of little kids playing together and bruising or scratching each other. From what I hear from thousands of students, including my team of coaches, that's just part of any intimate relationship. Sometimes you accidentally cause each other pain.

If we ever get to be perfect, I'll be sure to have a press conference and let you know what that's like. Until then, I'm glad I have the option of saying "Ouch!" when I'm hurt.

One of the ways I know that I'm hurt is that I'm mad at that person who hurt me. I start to think my husband is a jerk, and I want to make him wrong. But underneath that feeling, 100 percent of the time I find that I'm hurt. I feel rejected, abandoned, disappointed, insulted, or embarrassed. The hurt is always there underneath my anger. But anger is not great for creating connection and intimacy, so when I've got the wherewithal and the courage, I express my hurt instead of the anger. I choose the hurt because it's vulnerable, and I like my chances of snuggling and laughing together whenever I'm vulnerable. When I express my anger, that's an invitation to an argument that could inflict damage and distance to my relationship. That's not where I want to live.

When I first decided to respond with my hurt instead of lashing back at my husband in anger and defense, I had a pretty hard time remembering to say "Ouch!" in the moment. I kept seeing my opportunities in the rearview mirror, once the moment had already passed. That wasn't great, but it was still progress. Eventually I remembered to say it at the time, and finally it has become habit. It wasn't easy, but it's worth it because the connection is so much better afterward.

If I can remind myself that my husband loves me and didn't mean to hurt me, then I have a better chance of responding with vulnerability by saying "Ouch!" or maybe with silence or even tears if they naturally well up. That reminds him that we're on the same team but lets him know that I feel hurt. It also helps me avoid saying something I might have to apologize for later.

I'm *not* suggesting tears as manipulation here. I'm saying if you're genuinely hurt and are tempted to respond in anger, tears are a better way to be both authentic and vulnerable. When you cry, you're choosing to preserve intimacy and teach your husband how to treat you.

You might think, *I don't feel hurt when my husband says something mean. I feel angry!* Believe me, I know what you mean. But here's what I've discovered: Whenever I'm angry with my husband—or anybody else I'm intimate with—I'm also hurt. If I can go to the hurt beneath the anger, I have a better chance of preserving intimacy. Anger is easier because it feels safer, but hurt is more vulnerable, and that's what you're striving for.

When to Say "Ouch!" for Best Results

Let's say my husband says something that hurts my feelings. That doesn't happen very often anymore, but it does occasionally, because that's just how it is when you're so close to someone. When my feelings are hurt, I just say "Ouch." That's all that's needed. He gets it. I don't have to go into a lengthy explanation about how that comment touches a sore spot for me because my mother used to say things like that and I wish he would be more sensitive and on and on.

I get the job done with one impactful word.

Sometimes when our students use the word "ouch," they report back that it didn't work. Bonny said that when she said it, her husband looked at her oddly and said, "Ouch? What's ouch?" That's not an uncommon reaction when you first try this out.

Since even a toddler understands the word "ouch," we can be fairly certain that Bonny's husband understood it too. So his reaction wasn't about not *getting* it, but about not *liking* it. That makes sense, because it was the first time Bonny had said that, which means she was introducing a new way of conversing into the relationship. Part of her husband's reaction was to say, "What are the steps of this new dance? Usually this is the part where you say something mean, like what a jerk I am, and we bicker. I know *those* steps perfectly."

Even though the old dance wasn't much fun for either Bonny or her husband, they both knew how it went. So part of his reaction was in response to her changing it up. He may have also felt guilty or mad at himself for hurting Bonny's feelings, but since she didn't blame or shame him, there was nothing to defend himself against. The conversation at that point was only between him and his conscience, which may have been needling him for hurting her.

"Ouch" is great because it lets your husband know that you're hurt, but it doesn't say "it's your fault" or "you did something wrong." And since nobody's yelling at him or trying to control him, he has some freedom to think about if he maybe did say something unkind. Whether he did or not, you're teaching him how to treat you.

I used to talk for hours trying to get the same kind of reaction that I now get from a single "ouch." I used to tell John exactly how he should say things to me—that's how controlling I was. His response would be to ignore me or tune me out or turn up the TV, none of which were what I wanted, of course. Now I almost always get a quick heartfelt apology, like "I'm sorry, I didn't mean to hurt you" or some other acknowledgment that I'm unhappy—which is all I ever wanted.

Some women struggle with the vulnerability of "ouch." Kristen said she didn't want to say "Ouch!" because it would let her husband know that he'd hit a tender spot, and she didn't want to let on that he'd found her Achilles' heel. She worried that letting him know she was hurt would give valuable information to what seemed like the enemy, and that it could be used against her. That's the danger of vulnerability: you're undefended and open.

Once you say "Ouch!" you're choosing to be vulnerable. And by choosing vulnerability, you're invoking a sacred trust. Nobody who loves you wants to violate that trust. They want to hold it in safe hands.

But to invoke that sacred trust, you'll need to say "Ouch!" *before* the argument gets started.

For instance, let's say your husband punches you verbally by saying "I don't understand why you're so tired all the time. All you do is stay home with the kids all day." That's when you would want to say "Ouch!"

If you forget and respond instead by saying, "Maybe I wouldn't be tired all the time if you would lift a finger to help me out once in a while instead of playing video games all the time," you have now engaged in a battle. Insults are about to start flying back and forth.

Suddenly you remember to say "Ouch!" but instead of apologizing or calming down, he comes right back at you and verbally punches you again. Then you might think, *It's no use trying to be vulnerable with my husband. He'll keep right on attacking me, and I have to fight back to protect myself.*

The problem with this scenario is that you didn't say "Ouch!' until *after* you said something disrespectful and hurtful. So now his defenses are up too, and it's hard for him to see your vulnerability because he's peering out from behind his own fortress wall, thinking he's under attack. The path back to peace in your marriage now involves you making an apology. Ideally you say "Ouch!" *before* you engage in a fight with him, so you preserve the peace, the intimacy, and your own dignity.

If you engage in a verbal brawl, you're saying, "I don't need you to protect me." If you respond with authentic hurt and sadness first, the message is "I'm fragile and I need your protection."

If you feel like your husband is controlling, this is a great way to teach him that you don't like being told what to do. If he tells you how to drive or how to cut the birthday cake, you can say "Ouch!" to let him know that doesn't feel good.

You won't always remember to say "Ouch!" when you're hurt. As with saying "I miss you," it's vulnerable, and it may not always occur to you to say it in the moment. Fortunately, you don't have to do this perfectly. In fact, if you find yourself replaying a conversation you've had with your husband and thinking *I should have said "Ouch!"* that's progress. Next time, you probably will.

"Ouch!" is also a good way to communicate with friends, family, and even coworkers. I said "Ouch!" to an old friend once when we were having a heated conversation about a business deal. He accused me of being vindictive; I said "Ouch!" and nothing more.

His response was, "Why are you calling me a jerk?"

I said, "I didn't call you a jerk."

He said, "You just said I attacked you."

I said, "All I said was, 'Ouch!'"

He said, "Well, why are you saying 'Ouch!' if you're *not* saying I attacked you? I don't see anybody else around here."

At that point, I was feeling very dignified because I was staying on my side of the street. I felt clean. I said how I felt, but I didn't attack him. Moments later, he apologized for saying I was vindictive. Peace was restored and we both recovered quickly.

One of my coaches says that when she started saying "Ouch!" in her marriage, her husband followed suit and started saying "Ouch!" too. It changed the whole culture in their home to truncate arguments with that one powerful word.

Saying "Ouch!" Always Works

Jill told me that saying "Ouch" to her husband when he said something hurtful didn't work because when she said it, he didn't say he was sorry.

As with all of the Six Intimacy Skills, saying "Ouch!" is about taking care of yourself and keeping your side of the street clean. You can't control the outcome. But you can avoid further conflict, keep your dignity, and feel better about yourself if you respond to a perceived attack without striking back. That's the big benefit of saying "Ouch!"

You may also get an apology, which is great, but that's a bonus. Remember, you can't control what your husband does—only what you do. Saying "Ouch!" certainly puts the odds in your favor that you will get an apology or some other tender reaction from the man who wants to make you happy and protect you, but you can't *make* him apologize. It wouldn't be all that meaningful if you could. But no matter what, you'll still get all the fringe benefits—harmony, peace, and intimacy— that go along with expressing your feelings by saying "Ouch!"

Phone a Friend When It Hurts

What if the moment has passed and you didn't say "Ouch!"? You're replaying the incident over and over in your head because he was just so mean, but he doesn't even know what a jerk he was because you didn't react at the time. It's too late to say "Ouch!" because it's been hours or days or weeks. Now what? How do you let your husband know he hurt you?

Instead of rehashing an old conversation (even if it was just yesterday), try letting the previous conversation go but redoubling your efforts to say "Ouch!' in the moment going forward. Saying "You know the other day when you said I was always dropping things? That hurt my feelings" is not going to enhance your connection with your husband, so what's the point? Instead, vent to a girlfriend, sister, or relationship coach. Having someone other than your husband listen to you can go a long way toward soothing your pain, and it won't put any strain on your marriage or make your husband defensive.

That said, not every girlfriend is a great option for this kind of conversation. Your single girlfriends won't have the perspective you're looking for, and anyone who's going through or recently went through a breakup might find it tempting to pile on about how irresponsible men are, or how selfish, or how cruel. You don't want this to turn into a male-bashing session!

Instead, you want to talk to someone who respects your husband and can listen without complaining about what a jerk he is. Your best bet for someone who will be able to listen without fanning the flames is a friend who has a similar mind-set. I realize that's not always easy to find, which is one of the reasons I've helped bring together a worldwide community of women who are committed to practicing the Six Intimacy Skills and supporting other women in doing the same. We can vent to each other and still hold one another accountable for being the respectful and vulnerable wives we'd like to be. That like-minded community is one of the four pillars of my Connection Framework (I'll share all about this in Chapter 26), which I've found invaluable in my own journey of becoming a happy wife.

It's not helpful for your connection with your husband to discuss with him your hurt or scared feelings about him, but your feelings do deserve airtime. So I invite you to honor and express those feelings somewhere else. The more you preserve the intimacy in your marriage by avoiding comments that are disrespectful to or critical of your husband, the less you're going to have those hurtful moments. You'll be too busy laughing together and holding hands.

That said, whenever I coach a woman on how to become more desired, cherished, and adored, we often start with talking about what isn't working, why she's not happy, and what she thinks needs to change (usually her husband). Some women start off talking about what losers their husbands are, or how rude, or how stubborn. It's okay in that context. Start with your pain points and work from there. You won't stay there, but you get to begin wherever you are.

Jenna wanted my help on how not to overreact to her husband. She felt that she was too sensitive and wanted to figure out a way to not be so easily hurt. But I don't know of a way to not feel what you feel. Even if I did, I don't think I'd be eager to recommend it. I don't see being sensitive as such a problem. I think it's a gift. We women are often very sensitive. Feeling hurt is not an overreaction—it's your reaction.

When I'm hurt from an interaction with my husband and I forget to say "Ouch!" I take my process somewhere else instead of to him, like to my sisters, girlfriends, or my tribe of coaches. But at no point am I trying to just suck it up that I'm upset. That never works.

There's nothing in the Six Intimacy Skills that says to pretend you don't feel what you feel. I definitely don't want you to ignore your feelings. That's not what we do around here. When things come up, we talk about them.

However, I do find that as time goes on and you get better and better at the Six Intimacy Skills, there just isn't that much to complain about anymore, because your perspective and your reality have changed. As you progress with practicing the Six Intimacy Skills, you'll typically forget what you used to be so unhappy about.

Why Your Mother-in-Law Gets Better Treatment Than You

If you've ever felt like you were in competition with your mother-in-law for your husband's help and attention, perhaps it's because his mom appears more vulnerable than you.

If you're working, running the house like a tight ship, parenting the kids, and generally have everything under control, you may not appear to *need* any help. Complaining that you're tired, overworked, or resentful is not the same as being vulnerable—quite the opposite.

Letting him know you're having trouble keeping up and asking for help is vulnerable, but most of us hate to admit that.

His mom, however, may be expressing just those sentiments. He feels needed and purposeful when she wants him to install new bookshelves. When he runs over to help her, she probably expresses how very grateful she is. She makes him feel like a hero for coming to her aid. Every man likes to feel like a hero.

If your husband is very attentive to his mother, it's a sign that he's loyal and loving, and those are wonderful qualities. It shouldn't mean you get less help or attention because he devotes so much to her. It may just mean that he feels more needed and more appreciated when he helps her. Chances are good he'd be happy to do the same for you if the invitation was extended with the same vulnerability and appreciation.

CHAPTER 20

The Myth of Verbal Abuse

"You don't have to show up to every argument you're invited to."

—Mandy Hale, Author

Getting Rid of Godzilla

In the early days of my marriage, I'm not proud to say I used to rage at my husband. I would unload some really nasty words meant to tear him down and hurt him to the core. Nothing was off-limits in those out-of-control incidents where the toxic combination of fear, hurt, and anger would overtake me. It was terrible, and it left me with an awful hangover of remorse, as well as even more fear that I would eventually drive my husband away and be abandoned.

Amy was also a rageaholic. The resentment would build until she'd reached her limit, and then, she said, Godzilla would come out and wreak havoc throughout the land. Like me, she would say every hurtful thing that came to mind to demean her husband, even adding, "This is when the truth comes out!"

But after practicing the Six Intimacy Skills for just a few months, things changed. Amy found that she was no longer compelled to rage at her husband. Instead of sacrificing her own desires to please her family and employer, making herself happy every day and being grateful left her completely free of the urge to unload verbally.

She especially noticed her new freedom from her compulsion one day when her husband said, "I was thinking maybe you should plan and write out our meals for the week in advance and make a shopping list so we don't waste so much food."

Amy listened to her husband and thought about how adding a chore like that would crowd out her self-care. She said, "Oh, I can't! Sorry."

While that might sound pretty flip, Amy was just staying squarely on her own paper and being honest that this task was beyond her capacity. Her husband was still getting used to the new Amy and seemed surprised at her response, but a moment later he said, "You know, you're right—I should do it."

She smiled at him and said, "That would be great! Thank you." She felt so good because Godzilla was not getting strong. She knew there would be no ugly outbursts in the future because she had honored herself in that moment, preserved her time for self-care, and maintained her dignity. She was better able to meet her own needs and not find herself in that desperate place where the only way she could get relief was by hurting the man she loved.

I've had the same experience. I don't know where that mean-spirited, angry woman I used to be went, but she doesn't live here anymore, and I don't miss her. So it's not a stretch to say that the Six Intimacy Skills are a powerful form of anger management.

But what if you're not the one who's angry? What if it's your husband who does most of the yelling and saying mean things at your house?

The Cure for Verbal Abuse

If your husband is the rageaholic in your marriage, you might wonder if saying "Ouch!" when you're hurt will work. You might think he'll never change, no matter what you say or how you react. Maybe you've tried saying nothing to him when he's raging and he still continues to do it, even when you're not engaged in the conversation. It can be devastating to have to endure that kind of treatment. But there's hope for putting an end to verbal abuse in your marriage.

In my experience, verbal abuse is a symptom that the wife hasn't learned the Six Intimacy Skills yet. This does not mean that his temper is your fault; it just means you haven't yet discovered how to express yourself while preserving the emotional safety. So if your husband is saying some very harsh things to you on an ongoing basis, I have good news: You have the power to change the entire culture of your relationship by practicing the Six Intimacy Skills so that verbal abuse is no longer a part of it. It simply melts away.

Your husband could be an exception, but you won't know unless you experiment with the skills.

Chances Are You Either Started It or Piled On

Wanda was fantasizing about leaving her husband when she first heard about the Six Intimacy Skills. She told me he was constantly verbally abusing her. When I asked her for an example, she said, "Just yesterday, we were trying to get out of the complex where we live and there's a security arm that comes down after each car. But it was broken and we couldn't get out. My husband drives a very nice car, and he decides that he's going to try to squeeze around this broken security arm. So I told him, 'That's the stupidest idea I ever heard.' And he started yelling and swearing and calling me names I can't even repeat. He's just so angry! I don't think he's ever going to change."

As you likely noticed, Wanda was not exactly an innocent victim, even in her own telling of the story. From her point of view, her husband's anger was unprovoked, and therefore qualified as verbal abuse. But it's not hard to imagine that her comment made him feel disrespected and defensive. Wanda really had no idea that her words were just as biting and detrimental as her husband's mean comments to her. She felt that she was saying what needed to be said, not that she was undermining the self-worth of the man she chose to marry.

When Wanda started treating her husband more respectfully, she got a completely different response from him. He didn't even seem like the same guy who had yelled at her in the car that day. "I thought he was such a hostile person, but he's really not," she said. "I hate to think that I was the one causing him to be so hostile, but now I can see that I was part of the problem. He's like a different man now."

When I asked her if she would still describe her husband as verbally abusive, Wanda said no way. And she's not the only one. I hear similar stories from many students. Before she starts practicing the skills, often a student will tell me that her husband is verbally abusive, but as she describes the "abusive" situations, she also reveals the names she called him and the insults she threw at him. Once the specifics emerge, it's hard to see it as a clear-cut case of victim and abuser—more like a melee where a marriage should be. It's a culture of verbal abuse that they both cosign.

If most incidents of verbal abuse are actually two-way streets, perhaps saying your husband is verbally abusive is really about feeling like you're getting beat up during fights, even though your husband is likely also feeling beat up during those same fights. It's human nature to want to defend yourself and make the other person wrong for mistreating you—which is what is happening when you feel verbally abused. But in my experience with thousands of women, cleaning up your own side of the street goes a long way toward eradicating verbal abuse in your home.

You might be shocked that I would minimize verbal abuse by lumping it in with regular old bickering. Verbal abuse conjures a really angry, hostile, threatening person saying very degrading things and a victim who suffers through this horrible treatment. That's a terrible experience, and I'm not dismissing that.

Hearing those mean, ugly things said to you is certainly painful and degrading. That's something nobody should have to live with. But I've yet to hear about a case of verbal abuse that didn't go away when a woman learned and practiced the Six Intimacy Skills with another one of the four pillars of the Connection Framework, which is the support system that helps her put the Intimacy Skills into practice.

In my experience with tens of thousands of students, verbal abuse is a temporary, curable condition. Any wife can learn how to create a peaceful, emotionally safe relationship. In other words, you can put an end to verbal abuse in your home. It all starts with treating your man with respect and teaching him how to treat you by saying "Ouch!" when you're hurt.

If you find any of this overwhelming or feel like your relationship is an exception and that this just isn't going to work for you, that's usually a sign that you need more support.

You may have had an experience similar to that of Erica, who both learned the Six Intimacy Skills and got support from coaches and our community in practicing them: "I wanted a passionate and loving relationship with my husband, but I just didn't know how to make it happen. We fought often and hurt each other all the time. I told myself I was justified in my arguments and complaints. Learning the Six Intimacy Skills was one of the most valuable self-improvement projects I've ever taken on. When I learned to stop controlling the way my husband did things, practiced gratitude, and focused on self-care, the atmosphere at home became so peaceful. Suddenly we were laughing and holding hands like newlyweds. And my marriage became the one I dreamed of as a little girl."

Andrea said, "Each time I applied Laura's principals in my relationship, something amazing would happen in my marriage. Soon I found myself enjoying the peaceful, intimate relationship I had been longing for. It was an eye-opening, humbling, and life-changing—or should I say marriage-changing—experience."

CHAPTER 21

How to Get off the Fence and Be Happy About It

"You learn to speak by speaking, to study by studying, to run by running, to work by working; in just the same way, you learn to love by loving."

—Anatole France, Poet, Journalist, and Novelist

Sitting on the Fence Hurts Your Butt

Sometimes I'll have a student who doesn't hesitate to say that her husband seems deficient in so many ways that she can't see herself spending the rest of her life with him. She thinks about leaving often, yet she hasn't made a move. She is on the fence about her marriage, leaning heavily toward a breakup.

Other times, a student will tell me that her relationship is fine and her husband is a great guy, but she's not satisfied or she feels she's outgrown him. She thinks she *should* stay married, but she describes the relationship as unfulfilling and boring. She suspects there might be someone else out there who is better for her, someone who would make her happier than her husband does. This is a less overt but equally dangerous example of sitting on the fence.

Sitting on the fence hurts your butt. You can't get comfortable there. That's true when you feel ambivalent about anything—a job, a car, a friend. But when you sit on the fence in a romance, you pay an especially

215

high price for that uncomfortable seat, because you can't possibly be intimate with a guy you're only tolerating. You have a lot of power in this situation, and a choice: either accept him just as he is—quirks and all—or reject him and end the relationship. Merely tolerating your husband is a surefire way to make both of you miserable.

Hannah was firmly planted on the fence when I started coaching her. She had been working on making her nine-year marriage intimate, and she described it as solid. But she was still upset about an incident from two years ago.

After years of encouragement—or nagging, depending on who's telling the story—Hannah's husband finally quit smoking. Hannah was very pleased about this, but a short time later he came home smelling of smoke—more than once. She questioned him, letting him know that she would rather know the truth, even if it were that he was smoking again, than to have him lie to her. Each time he assured her he wasn't smoking.

Then one afternoon, Hannah came home unexpectedly and found her husband puffing away in the backyard with two butts in the ashtray. She had caught him red-handed, and she told him she was incredibly hurt by his betrayal. He apologized repeatedly, but for Hannah, the hurt ran deep and wasn't easy to get over.

Hannah insisted that they go to couples counseling to address his dishonesty. "That's where I learned firsthand that couples counseling doesn't improve your relationship," she told me. "He would nod his head and agree with the counselor and say everything he was supposed to in the sessions, but I realized he was just humoring us both. I finally decided to drop counseling altogether. But I still feel hurt! So what do I do now?"

Armed with "evidence" that her husband was untrustworthy, Hannah spent her days waiting and watching for him to betray her again. And though their marriage seemed fine on the outside, she found herself fantasizing about having a man she could *really* trust and be fully emotionally intimate with. After all, this one had lied in a big way. And since she was sure she had done nothing wrong, she felt justified in thinking that perhaps he just wasn't a guy she could stay with forever.

She was clearly planted on the fence.

You Can't Hug with Nuclear Arms

That kind of fence-sitting does plenty of harm to the person you're tolerating. Whether you've said so or not, your husband knows when you're on the fence, which means he knows you're thinking of leaving him. He may not admit it, but he's terrified—just like you'd be terrified if someone you loved and built your life around was letting you know in subtle ways that he might just go away for good.

And when people are scared, they get defensive. When they're defensive, they're much harder to connect with because they're feeling an overwhelming urge to either fight or flee. If your fence-sitting has gone on for years, your husband may have been bracing for the day you pack your bags for a long time. His response to living with the constant threat of heartbreak could be depression, cynicism, hostility, mistrust, or rage.

I'm not saying it's your fault if your guy exhibits some of these qualities, since he always gets to choose how he will react. But I *am* saying that you're definitely contributing to him feeling hurt, angry, and afraid. Given that he hasn't been able to persuade you to get off that fence, the power to restore the safety in your relationship lies with you. Without safety, there can be no emotional honesty and no vulnerability—two key ingredients for feeling connected and close. Even if you haven't said so out loud, threatening to leave a relationship is one of the most severe threats you can make. It's the emotional equivalent of threatening to drop a nuclear bomb.

Of course, you could argue that you wouldn't be on the fence if your husband behaved better. You might point out that's *he's* making *you* hurt, angry, and afraid too. You might wonder why *he* can't do something to improve the safety at your house. But if you're the one on the fence, he really can't do anything, because the threat of nuclear devastation—ending the relationship—is coming from you. You're the only one who can decide to stand down.

I'm not excusing him for having said or done hurtful things, for lobbing some grenades in the past. But that kind of damage is repairable. Your relationship can heal from that, and you can minimize further damage, but not while you're flirting with the idea of pushing the big red button that launches the warhead called "divorce."

The person who is willing to walk away from a negotiation always has the most power. Since that's you in this case, the responsibility for restoring the safety of the marriage lies with you.

Should You Stay or Should You Go?

There's plenty that's not perfect in your relationship, but you wouldn't have stayed in it if there weren't some very good parts as well, or at least some shared assets or kids. That's why you've had trouble deciding what to do and have come to rest somewhere in the purgatory between commitment and calling it quits. After all, if it were so easy to know what to do, you'd have done it by now.

There is a simple way to know if you should invest your energy in this relationship in the hopes that things will improve. There's just one question to ask yourself, and it's an easy one. The question is: Are you leaving him *today*?

That's not the same as thinking of leaving him next week or next month. To tell the difference, ask yourself, are your bags already packed? Are you walking out the door right now?

No?

I didn't think so. After all, why would you pick up this book if you really wanted to leave? You still have *hope*. There are many more cynical books you could be reading if you wanted permission to go. But you picked a book that is going to help you feel empowered as a wife, and one that shows you how to attract your husband's time, attention, and affection. That tells me that you're tired of being on the fence and that you want to jump off on the marriage side and figure out a way to make your relationship special and wonderful. See how I'm on to you?

I admire your courage and persistence. I respect your willingness to be accountable and your desire to improve your life. You're going to need some courage to get your relationship out of the ditch. But I know you can do it because I see women just like you doing it every day.

You may think my reasoning is oversimplified, that I don't understand your situation, that if I knew what horrors you were enduring in your relationship, I would change my opinion and tell you it's okay to just limp along until you leave him next month or next year. Perhaps you feel that even if you don't leave until next month, it makes no sense to waste your energy on a relationship that has never been good enough.

Complaining about someone is a symptom that you're tolerating, not accepting or rejecting him. If you decide to abstain from tolerating your husband, the only choices left are to accept him or reject him. Rejecting him means you leave. So if you're not leaving him today, you can stop wasting your energy complaining and tolerating by practicing the Six Intimacy Skills. This doesn't take away your option to leave in the future if you decide that's what's best for you. Just making the decision to accept him, however, is going to make you feel more dignified, calm, and secure. And you just might end up becoming a ridiculously happy wife and no longer wanting to leave.

Nurture Your Faith instead of Indulging Your Fear

If you've decided you're going to invest yourself emotionally in this relationship again (right? Didn't I hear you say that?), your connection will improve almost immediately as long as you go all-in. In poker, you go all-in by pushing all your chips into the pot, risking everything. In a marriage, going all-in means that you open your heart by being vulnerable, risking everything. You're choosing faith instead of indulging your fear. It means that when you find yourself getting annoyed with your husband's faults, you push yourself to make a list of his virtues so you remember why you chose him and why you continue to choose him. It means that you do everything in your power to accept him, quirks and all. It means you stop indulging in fantasies that someday you'll find a better man. You make a decision to see the good qualities in the man you married. It means you put your wedding ring back on even if he's not wearing his. It means saying to yourself, "I'm going to pin all my hopes on this working out."

That's entirely different from thinking, *I'll see how it goes for the next month.* Until you jump off the fence, you won't be able to create a lasting, gratifying love. But once you do jump, you'll be amazed at how quickly things improve. That's because everyone can relax when there's no immediate crisis or drama, no fear-based adrenaline shooting through the house. There's no tension, no waiting for the other shoe to drop. Your butt stops hurting.

You may feel a different kind of fear, though. Although you have to go all-in to make your relationship safe, doing so won't *feel* safe to you. It will likely feel risky—because it *is* risky. What if you put all your effort and energy into creating lasting love with your man and it doesn't work? You'll be terribly disappointed. Whenever we love someone, we also risk losing that love.

However, in my experience, the risk of getting hurt by going all-in is actually smaller than the risk of staying on the fence. You're taking a reasonable risk for the chance of a great payoff: the passionate, peaceful, intimate relationship you crave. You've got a good guy, an imperfect man who is *committed to you even when you waver in your commitment to him*. Chances are excellent that if you make yourself vulnerable, things will go well. The odds are good that you'll come out ahead on this risk because it's pretty safe to bet on a man who's so loyal to you.

If you don't go all-in, you're practically guaranteeing that your romance will be tense, distant, and disconnected. That's hard for anybody to sustain over time, so it actually *increases* your risk of divorce, and the accompanying tragedy and heartache, if you commit to the fence instead of to the man you sleep with every night.

But it's not going to *feel* safer for you when you first jump off the fence. The reason you climbed on the fence to begin with was because it felt less scary to sit there, contemplating your ability to get out if you wanted to. That seems reassuring, especially compared to being vulnerable with your man by doing the things that contribute to intimacy—like apologizing for your part in a conflict, letting him know you need him and miss him, and telling him that he makes you happy. That's the stuff that seems dangerous. Your knee-jerk reaction might be, "No way! I'm not going to be the one to apologize or let him know I'm all-in. Forget it!"

Nobody's saying you have to. You always have a choice and you always get to do what fits for you. But if what you want is to be intimate, choose the vulnerable approach. If what you want is more splinters in your butt, stay on the fence. I understand your hesitation because I've been there. But recognize that you're making the choice and you can change your mind at any time.

Now that you realize you have so much of the power (or at least you suspect on some level that it might be true), put what you've learned to the test. Prove me right or prove me wrong, but give your relationship the best chance to succeed before you give up. Jump off the fence right now and put all your energy and faith into making your marriage the most passionate, intimate, and nurturing it can be, instead of spending that energy worrying about whether you should leave.

When I say "succeed," I don't mean that you're giving it the chance to become just a *little* better. I'm talking about creating an exciting, gratifying, pleasurable romance. I'm talking about having fun together, looking forward to seeing each other, delighting in each other, and feeling really protected and secure. Maybe you've given up hope that you can have that, but I'm here to tell you that you can—just as soon as you jump off that fence.

Your butt will thank you.

Patrice had been sitting on the fence for years when she finally got the courage to get off—and leave her husband.

She'd practiced the Six Intimacy Skills for several months but eventually decided that her husband was both an alcoholic and physically abusive after he got drunk and threw her phone at the wall, breaking it. He'd hurt her hand wresting the phone from her grip as she videotaped him. This painful and dramatic incident gave her the clarity and motivation she needed to get out.

It wasn't easy, but she leased a nearby apartment and moved their kids and herself out of their home. She relished the prospect of feeling safe, away from her abusive husband.

But, of course, she wasn't completely away. They had two kids together.

Patrice continued to use the Six Intimacy Skills with her estranged husband, and he began responding—apologizing for what he'd done, expressing regret, and listening to her intently when she talked. He also took steps to address his problems with alcohol. They began taking walks together in the park. But whenever he became needy or domineering, she quickly remembered why she'd decided to leave him in the first place.

There was a record-breaking heat wave that summer, and while her husband's home had air conditioning, Patrice's did not. Soon, she and the kids were heading over to his place night after night to get relief from the dangerous heat. This went on for weeks, and Patrice worried that the kids were getting used to them being together again as a family—and that they would be crushed all over again when the temperatures finally cooled. When she reminded the children that they would soon be going back to their own apartment, she was met with tears and anger.

"I'm so mad that I put myself back in this position," Patrice told me when we spoke. "Why did I do this?"

"Maybe something is unfinished for you," I suggested. "Maybe *you* want to be a family again, too, but you're afraid you'll end up feeling trapped."

She reluctantly admitted that this was true. Her husband had made dramatic changes, and things seemed better between them than they ever had before. But their history made it complicated. "I just don't want to go back to the way it was. It's scary."

Patrice saw that she had put herself back on the fence—a familiar perch.

"How would it feel to run through the waterfall of fear and see what's on the other side?" I asked her.

By the next time we met, Patrice had done just that. She'd expressed to her husband her desire to reconcile, and he was overjoyed. Then, she told the kids they had to go back to their apartment...to get their stuff and bring it home for good. The kids cried, but this time they were tears of happiness and relief.

But Patrice wasn't doing this just for her children—though they had helped create the pain that led her to reexamine her decision. She was doing it because she was excited, exhilarated, and thrilled to be with her husband again. She was no longer sitting on a fence.

"I finally understand what people mean when they say, 'I can't wait to spend the rest of our lives together,'" she told me. "That's just how I feel."

That was over a year ago, and Patrice is still enjoying a playful, passionate connection with the man she married.

CHAPTER 22

How to Get Your Husband Back

What if *you're* not the one on the fence about your marriage? What if *he's* the one who's distant, absent, or sleeping in the other bedroom? It's painful to be married to a man who never has time for you because he's working a lot, has hobbies that keep him busy, or is constantly staring at his phone. Feeling rejected on a daily basis as he snuggles with the dog or the kids but offers you only disinterest or icy glares is not what you signed up for when you said, "I do." Even worse, it may feel like the decision to make your marriage last and thrive is out of your hands, especially if he's not even communicating with you.

In my experience, though, revealing your heart is a compelling force for attracting him back like steel to a magnet. That's proven true for our students, even when there's a crisis, like:

- *He's said he doesn't love her anymore, or that he never did*
- *They're separated*
- *He has another woman, or she has another man*
- *He's said it's over and that he won't reconsider*
- *He's filed for divorce*

Even when he's not willing to give the marriage a chance and isn't speaking to her, we see courageous students save their marriages with the counterintuitive but gratifying approach of practicing the Six Intimacy Skills with a coach and a community.

But talk about feeling vulnerable! I can't think of anything more painful or heartbreaking than hearing your husband say, "I don't love you anymore. Maybe I never did." Or, "It's over. I'm in love with someone else." Or—maybe even worse—to discover those things without being told. Even if he's just preoccupied with sports instead of paying attention to you, it hurts a lot to feel neglected or abandoned on the regular. A common way for any mere mortal woman to respond to being hurt is with anger, which is the opposite of vulnerability but feels so justified, and is practically involuntary.

That anger, combined with hopelessness about the marriage's future, has driven some students to give in to the temptation to find affection outside the marriage. They're so hurt, exhausted, and starving for attention that another man's interest feels like a tall glass of water in the desert. The temptation to enjoy feeling desired is enormous. Then they feel guilty and ashamed and sometimes even undeserving of winning their husbands back. But their infidelity doesn't have to be the end of the marriage. The way I see it, that painful situation arises out of a lack of training, not because they are undeserving or tragically flawed. When you have never been taught the Six Intimacy Skills, much less have a coach to help you implement them or a community to support you in doing so, your marriage can fall into a ditch, leaving you unsure of how to recover it. That can make you feel hopeless—and when there's no hope, honoring your marriage vows seems less important.

As a mere mortal woman, you may have experienced the pain of feeling like the one who has ruined your marriage. But you're not alone, and your marriage is not beyond repair, even if that's what your husband is telling you right now. I see too many miracles to doubt that your marriage and the connection with your husband can be completely restored. It can be!

One coach trainee shared her story of having cheated on her husband in the bad old days of her broken-down, hopeless marriage. She felt so ashamed about it. But as she shared about the incredible transformation in her home—how she and her husband were enjoying each other again, and how he was now her hero who made the bed just the way she liked it every day because he knew it would make her happy—the part where she stepped out of her marriage became just another part of her journey. Today, she and her husband are happy, connected, and passionate again. It's quite an impressive accomplishment, one that I admire very much. She's a beacon of hope that, no matter what's gone wrong in the past, your marriage can last and thrive in the future.

What Students Did That Got Him Back

When the risk of rejection already feels so high, being vulnerable probably feels like the last thing you're inclined to do. There are, however, specific actions you can take to give yourself real relief from that continuous ache of loneliness and to restore the connection and therefore your marriage, even if he won't talk to you. The pathway is through pure vulnerability, meaning it's free of complaints or criticism.

You might be thinking, "But my husband is repulsed by my vulnerability. He hates it when I cry, and he gets gruff or runs away." And that might lead you to thinking that the Intimacy Skills won't work with your man. I can see why you would feel that way. There's nothing worse than letting someone see your authentic grief or shyness only to have them respond with hostility or by abandoning you. We all want to avoid that!

But here's what I've learned from when my husband doesn't respond to me very well: There's something being reflected back to me in my husband-mirror. If my grief is also a perceived criticism or complaint about him, or if there's even a drop of blame in my sadness, it's not true vulnerability. Like drinking water laced with lead, it's no longer life-giving and sustaining. It's poison. My tears are an attack with the subtext "You let me down!" or "You disappoint me!" So I get a defensive response instead of a soft, comforting one because he is now wounded by my blame, shame, and criticism, and that will trump his instinct to protect and comfort me. Choosing blame also communicates that I've solved my own problem and nothing further is needed from him.

So that unpleasant reaction you're getting from your husband when you cry may not be because he can't stand your crying. If he reacts to your tears with distance or hostility, it's likely because he hears criticism. If the tears are about losing your dog, or from watching a touching commercial, or because you didn't sleep well, you'll know your vulnerability is pure because, chances are, he'll come close and offer comfort, try to make you laugh, or tell you everything is going to be okay.

It's so nice to know the distinction between true vulnerability and complaining with tears because instead of being mystified by his reaction, I can predict it, or at least reflect on it and understand why he responded with either indifference or protection and comfort.

Choosing to be vulnerable was one of the hardest, scariest things I had to learn when I discovered the Intimacy Skills. To this day, I still feel the instinct to pull myself together so I don't get mascara under my eyes and look like a fool, but when I just let myself fall apart, it creates experiences of connection and love with my husband, and with everyone I love, that I no longer want to live without. It's such an exhilarating mountaintop experience. So these days I strive for vulnerability instead of trying to keep a cool exterior.

Vulnerability has been the key to refreshing and restoring the connection between my husband and me. I've also seen it breathe new life into broken marriages for thousands of women who feared that their husbands were not affectionate or were otherwise defective and that their marriages were too far gone to repair. Many such women have shared their stories on *The Empowered Wife Podcast*, describing exactly what they did to get back to being happy wives.

Here are the recurring themes I hear from these incredible, inspiring women:

1. They Asked the Right Person About the Future

You'd like to know what the future holds, and it seems like he has all the power to decide if your marriage will last or fall apart, so the obvious thing to do is to ask him what his intentions are. The illusion is that getting his current outlook is going to provide you with some kind of security about what's going to happen. But the outcome you might want the most—him telling you that you're the most wonderful woman in the world, that he's lucky to have you, and that he'll never leave you—is just not going to happen this way.

If you've ever tried to get answers from him about his intentions for the marriage when you're feeling scared about losing it, you already know how icky it feels. That's because the urge to take his pulse on the relationship is the best indication that you're scared about the future, which comes through in your words, giving you an air of neediness and desperation. Those aren't attractive qualities, so if what you want is to attract him back so that he shows up attentively and affectionately all on his own, consider checking your own paper for clues about what the future holds.

But, you might ask, if he's the one who seems distant, disinterested, or disposed to divorce, how can you know the future of your marriage without asking what he's going to do? Consider asking the keeper of the relationship (that's you!) what *her* intentions are.

One powerful way to do this is to visit your imagined future self, maybe from a year from now. You can ask her how things went and have her tell you about how everything went your way!

One student and podcast guest, Annie, described asking herself the question "What are your intentions for the future of your marriage?" in a very deliberate way when she was separated from her husband, who was also pushing for divorce. It seemed like her marriage was over and that there was no getting it back. Doing this exercise took some imagination and all her faith, and even then it felt a little silly, as being vulnerable often does.

But check out what happened! This student asked herself a series of questions about what had happened in that year and wrote down her answers. Her future self (that is, her imagination and intention) told her that she and her husband were living under the same roof again, had completely reconciled, and were expecting a baby! It gave me chills to hear her vision during our interview on the podcast because here she was a year later, living the vision she had written down, including planning for another baby! You can hear her describe the process herself on episode 91 of *The Empowered Wife Podcast*.

Instead of turning outward to her husband in a panic-stricken moment and asking, "Are you going to leave me?" the key for her was asking herself the question, "What's going to happen to our marriage in the future?" and filling in her vision with her desires and intentions, regardless of what his position was that day. I hear this theme of creating and focusing on a specific intention and outcome again and again when I interview students who have successfully fixed their marriages.

I even heard the husband's side in episode 105 of the podcast, where my guest Antonio, the husband of a coach trainee, admitted he was inappropriate with another woman. He was resigned to what seemed like the sure end of their marriage. But things changed, he said, when his wife declared that he was *her* husband, and her intention was to keep it that way. That was the turning point allowing them to reunite and for the other woman to exit the scene.

2. They Got Happy and Smiled

While it may seem impossible when you're in heartbreaking pain, making yourself ridiculously happy, in my experience, is imperative to making your marriage last and thrive, just as we discussed in Chapter 3.

Do whatever you have to do to make yourself laugh or feel inspired, delighted, self-expressed, alive, and loved by family and friends, especially if your heartache makes you feel like your life is on fire. This can feel vulnerable too! But you can reclaim your life by deciding to have some pleasurable moments every day, even though it may feel awkward to be happy. It's an indispensable step to reclaiming what's rightfully yours: a gratifying life *and* a playful, passionate marriage.

You may be able to look back at the loneliest times of your marriage and think of the Charles Dickens line "It was the best of times, it was the worst of times." Even if it's already the worst of times, what can you do today to make it the best of times? Has your husband come to expect your anger or reprimanding tears? What if you surprised him by smiling when he sees you next? You may not feel like he deserves your smile, but what if this is more about you than him, anyway? What if you focused on your responsibility to yourself of having a happy life, regardless of what your husband is doing?

If he asks why you're smiling so much, you can say that recent events reminded you that life is short, and you've decided to pay more attention to your enjoyment. If you're worried that he'll think you're happier without him, you can always say you're happy to see him. As a fringe benefit to feeling good, you'll also be more attractive when you're smiling.

3. They Expressed Their Feelings—But Not to Him

At first, most of the women who would eventually make their marriages last and thrive after a breakdown did what anyone would do. They yelled, kicked, and screamed at their husbands, of course—they were hurting, angry, and sad! Those excruciating feelings deserve to come out and have their day in the sun, but your husband doesn't need to be the one who witnesses them.

Having some safe outlets will help you avoid blowing up or melting down at your husband. Get a relationship coach; join my community; write in your journal; or tell a bartender or your rabbi, priest, or other trusted adviser the whole sad story. Your feelings are valid. You're hurting, and you're human. We all need to be heard and understood—especially you, especially now.

It may feel strange to keep those critical thoughts to yourself instead of telling him about the pain he's caused you. It may seem only fair to blow up at him or have a meltdown. You may feel he deserves it!

But it's not him I'm concerned about right now; it's *you* I'm thinking about.

My blowups and meltdowns were a release in the short run but never made me feel better in the long run. Each one left me with an emotional hangover and the remorse of knowing I couldn't take any of it back. I didn't feel very dignified either. Even though I wanted to let my husband have it, I didn't like who I became in those moments, and those responses never got me closer to the kind of marriage I wanted.

Making the choice to be dignified in your talks with him will pave the way for a brighter future than raging ever could, and making yourself happy will give you the reserves to make that decision. If you're having a visceral reaction to this idea, which may sound a lot like sucking it up instead of speaking your mind, remember that this isn't the end of the story. It's only the middle, and the story will get much, much better. You always have the option to say whatever you want. I'm inviting you to experiment with a new way of doing things if that hasn't been as satisfying as you'd hoped.

4. They Suspended His Punishment and Listened

It's also natural to want him to hurt the way he's hurting you. Unfortunately, there's no real upside to making him suffer, even though your urge to retaliate can feel more tempting than a cinnamon roll.

Whether he's been rejecting you in little ways every day, moved out, or found someone else, it's incredibly painful to feel so betrayed by the man you married. There aren't words for how devastating that is. But he didn't do it because he *wanted* to hurt you. He did it because something was missing in your marriage. You've felt it too but didn't know what to do about it, and neither did he.

That doesn't make it right or okay for him to never come home or to break his vows. It just makes him human. If you can set aside his crime for the moment and stay focused on the worthy goal of making your marriage last and thrive, you'll give yourself a huge advantage.

Instead of telling him how hurt and upset you are, consider being on the quiet side and giving him the space to talk by providing emotional safety—no anger, judgment, or tears. For a whole evening (or at least for one hour), just say "I hear you" or "uh-huh," and nothing else.

One student did this at her marriage counseling sessions, and her husband said, "I keep waiting for you to interrupt me, but you don't!" She just smiled. It wasn't long before he moved back home.

5. They Cleaned Up Their Side of the Street

When you've been wronged, and he's the one who's behaving badly, it seems crazy to even think about apologizing to him! And to be clear, I'm not suggesting that you apologize, unless . . . there is something on your side of the street that you'd like to clean up. If there was anything about the way you behaved that was regrettable, then consider issuing a one-time apology.

I'm not suggesting that you apologize insincerely to make nice. But my experience is that there's enormous power in being accountable for my bad behavior, even when it seems teeny compared to his bad behavior, and even if my sins were in response to his agitations.

Look for ways you were critical or controlling and use the formula for a truly accountable apology by saying, "I apologize for being disrespectful when I ..." and fill in the blank. Watch your dignity return and the conflict between you melt away.

6. They Got Pleaseable

If your husband tries to make you happy in any way, big or small (and, from my experience, he *will* try), do your best to receive the gesture and convey your pleasure at his efforts. You deserve those efforts, and he'll feel good knowing he was able to please you.

With so much going wrong, it will feel strange to look for what's going right. But if you thank him—for continuing to pay the mortgage, for picking up the kids, for asking how you are—you'll be focusing on the things you want instead of the things you don't. And what you focus on increases.

But how do you signal pleaseability? Send a silly text. Do your happy dance. Laugh when he's funny, and reference the inside jokes you share. Bring your playful self to your interactions with him. You could even flirt with him! Flirting signals that you feel attractive. You might feel far from that, but flirting is a shortcut to getting back there. You'll trick yourself into feeling confident instead of insecure. And feeling confident is the same as being confident.

Dress up and doll up. Let him open the door, and thank him with a sweet smile. Have some fun with it. You might even seduce him. This is your husband we're talking about, so even if he's being intimate with someone else, he's yours, not hers. You might be tempted to retaliate by locking him out of the bedroom, but when you're trying to restore intimacy, why not start with physical intimacy? It's a great springboard.

Make every meeting a date. If you see him—even if it's at the divorce attorney's, the marriage counselor's, or just to hand off the kids—pretend it's a date.

7. They Got Cheerleaders

You probably know plenty of people who will tell you to throw him out or figure out where all the assets are in preparation for a divorce. That kind of advice is easy to come by but not very helpful when you're trying to fix your family. How would it impact your marriage story if you had cheerleaders to help you succeed instead? So many great come-from-behind-and-win-the-game stories have cheerleaders. You'll need yours too. Find a community that supports your vision.

There will be days when you think it's not worth it or that it's hopeless and stupid to try to save your marriage. When your husband says he's done, of course you'll feel temporarily discouraged, but your vision of being a happy couple and a loving family is worthwhile *and* possible.

When you find yourself on the fence about your marriage, seek out the people in your life who support your vision. Let them remind you why you're doing it all. I, for one, am cheering for you—for you to not only save your marriage but also make it magical again. I want that for you.

CHAPTER 23

Why Sex Is Better When You're Married (and What to Do If It's Not)

"It's become very fashionable to blame our hormones for loss of libido. But the truth is that although lots of research has been done, no one has managed to come up with anything very definite on the relationship between female hormones and desire."

—Christine Webber, Psychotherapist, and Dr. David Delvin, GP and Family Planning Specialist

How Sex Makes Marriage Great and Vice Versa

A woman on the news was being interviewed about her decision to have sex with her husband every day for a year, whether she felt like it or not. The big takeaway for her was that she had to be okay with her husband's view of her as sexy and get over her own view of herself as anything less than that. She said it was great for her to spend a year feeling desired every day, because it taught her that her own standards made her feel self-conscious. She also spoke about how close she and her husband became, how it deepened their bond and relieved so much tension.

Sex is the one thing that only you and your husband share. It's what separates your romance from every other relationship you have. You might talk intimately with your sister, and you might snuggle with your kids, but sex is only between you and him. Take that out of the equation and your relationship is no longer a romance—you two are co-parents, roommates, or business partners on a mortgage, but not lovers.

One reason marriage makes sex so much better is that you have total safety that makes it okay to be really vulnerable. Even if you feel awkward or embarrassed, your husband isn't going away. There's total permission to be yourself, whatever that looks like.

You also have plenty of time to practice getting it right. Sex is like anything else: the more you practice, the better you get, and the more satisfying the experience.

But what if sex is just one more area of your marriage that's not going well? What if one of you always wants it and the other doesn't? What if one of you never wants it? Can you ever get to where everybody's happy again and have this part of your relationship be as enjoyable as it's meant to be, rather than yet another source of conflict?

In my experience, you absolutely can—by practicing the Six Intimacy Skills.

Why Your Husband Lost Interest in Sex

When Gladys' husband spoke to an audience of women at her workshop about the Six Intimacy Skills, he started by saying, "Make a face as though someone just asked you to do something horrible, like eat a child." We all obliged and made horrified faces. He told us to look at each other, so we could see how unpleasant we all appeared. It was not pretty.

"That," he told us, "is how you look when you're controlling or disrespectful. You could be a supermodel, but no matter how hot you are, you're just not appealing to us in that moment."

It was a great way to illustrate what a passion-killer control is.

If the sex has gone missing in your marriage, and it's your husband who seems disinterested, control and disrespect are the likely culprits. If you're anything like me, you may have thought that the lack of sex was because he was no longer physically attracted to you since you'd gained weight or got older, but that is rarely the case. The good news is that the passion returns quickly when you clean up the disrespect and control and practice the Six Intimacy Skills outside of the bedroom.

What If You Just Don't Wanna?

If you're the one who's lost interest in sex, that can also be a side effect of the struggles in your relationship outside the bedroom. If your husband lets you call all the shots just to keep the peace, he won't seem very masculine to you—quite the opposite. If you've fallen into a mother/son dynamic outside of the bedroom, he's going to seem downright unappealing. If the two of you fight a lot and he's always saying mean things, you're not going to want to be as vulnerable with him in bed. All these issues clear up pretty quickly when you start using the Six Intimacy Skills outside of the bedroom.

But what do The Six Intimacy Skills look like *inside* the bedroom? All the same principles apply.

Self-Care

Your pleasure is very important. You have the only organ in the human body—the clitoris—that's sole purpose is for you to feel outrageously good. That's also a metaphor for your relationship and your life. You were born to feel good! The more you make your pleasure a priority, both in and out of the bedroom, the better things will be for both of you.

Respect

One way to respect your husband sexually is to honor his choices for himself and his own sexuality. You may not like it that he views porn or masturbates, for example. You may feel strongly that those are unacceptable behaviors and that you won't tolerate them. But relinquishing control means that you recognize where you end and he begins. Your husband is solely responsible for how he handles his own sexual urges. You certainly have influence, but letting him know you don't approve of porn or masturbating is a sure way to squander that influence. The more you insist that he must not masturbate or view porn, the more you're going to sound like his mother, which is not sexually appealing. It's only human nature that when you tell him it's not okay to do something, that something becomes even more alluring. Respecting your husband means letting him make his own choices without your comments or judgment—and trusting that they'll be wise ones.

If your husband is watching porn instead of being physically intimate with you, hearing that it's not up to you whether he watches porn might sound unreasonable or harsh. I know how painful it is to be married to someone who's not interested in hugging, kissing, petting, or sex—and not understanding why. I remember how hurtful and lonely that was. If you're thinking porn is the problem, that if it weren't for that stupid porn, you would be getting a lot more action in the bedroom, consider that there might be another reason entirely.

Control and lack of respect are more likely the real culprits. In my case, my husband simply wasn't attracted to me—not because he didn't find me physically alluring, like I feared. The turn-offs were the snippy comments coming out of my mouth and the way my eyes rolled back in my head when I didn't agree with what he said.

What I witness over and over is that when you bring respect back to the relationship, the sexual chemistry and desire returns in full force. If you're seeing yourself as competing with porn for your husband's attention, I have good news: Being made of flesh and blood gives you a huge advantage. But consider the possibility that he might not feel excited about being sexual with someone who doesn't respect him.

The good news is that bringing back the respect in your marriage can quickly change everything. In fact, it can bring the level of physical affection back to what it was when you first started dating. That's what women who practice the Six Intimacy Skills report.

If it sounds like I'm saying it's okay if your husband watches porn, please let me clarify: What I'm *actually* saying is that it's *his* decision. That choice is not on your paper. What is on your paper is the option to accept him or reject him.

You do have complete control over whether or not you treat your husband respectfully, and when you do, that's a powerful aphrodisiac. That could very well bring him to your bed. If you're respectful, willing, and available, how can two-dimensional women compete?

You might think it would be nice if you could make absolutely sure your husband never watched porn. But it's even better to focus on your own paper and use your feminine gifts of magnetism, which are strongest when you're respectful. Then, when he chooses you because he finds you irresistible, that's a much bigger rush than having him in your bed because you told him what to do. The only way to truly feel desired—and if you're anything like me, that's something you really crave—is to let him make his own choices. When you do, chances are, he'll choose you.

Relinquishing Control

Saying "We should" or "How come you never want to?" or even "Let's have sex" are all about control, which is never good for intimacy. It's still nagging, even if the topic at hand is sex instead of cleaning the garage. You're not going to get a good reaction, and you could end up feeling rejected when he doesn't respond well.

Petra complained that she wanted sex far more often than her husband did, which she couldn't understand, since men usually want sex more than women do. She complained to him that he was lazy about sex and tried requesting, demanding, and insisting they have more of it—but that only made her feel more frustrated.

It wasn't until she decided to take a different approach that things improved. She started by making a pact with herself to stop demanding or asking for sex at all. It wasn't easy because that was her habit, but it wasn't serving her. She decided to focus on seducing him with her body instead of saying a word.

She began to be receptive and enthusiastic whenever her husband initiated sex, even if she wasn't in the mood. She also expressed a lot of gratitude whenever they made love, no matter how the ball got rolling.

Instead of hearing her complain and feeling like he was falling short, her husband finally felt successful. As a result, he naturally started to initiate more physical intimacy. Petra felt so much more desired and relieved to know that her husband wasn't losing interest in her.

You're a magnet, and your husband is built to pursue and desire you. You are the sexier sex and the gatekeeper for sex. If you forget that and act like you don't have any special powers, sex can feel like a struggle instead of a fun party for two in bed.

Receiving Graciously

As a woman, you are built to receive. That's a great metaphor for your entire relationship, but with lovemaking, it's pretty literal. Receptivity is the essence of femininity. So the more receptive you are, the more feminine and attractive you will be, and the more masculine your husband will be in response.

Taking a seductive approach is not only more tantalizing and vulnerable, but also more gratifying than asking for sex directly. If you change into your sexiest undies to relax, you're letting your husband know you're receptive to having sex and giving him the opportunity to do something about it. Of course, you're also risking rejection. What if he sees that you're wearing something from your naughty collection and he just brushes his teeth and goes to bed? You'll feel rejected, which hurts, but I've never had a student die of rejection.

Think of this as an opportunity to express a desire without expectation. You can honor what you want (in this case without saying a word) without being attached to the outcome. The upside is worth it: If he sees that you're receptive and takes the opportunity to make love to you, you know for sure he wanted you, and that feels amazing.

Another way to be receptive sexually is to decide to make yourself available for sex whenever your husband desires you. You won't always start out in the mood, but that doesn't mean you won't end up there. There are plenty of things you do every day even though you're not in the mood. You might vacuum when you're not in the mood because you want an orderly house. Deciding to be receptive to sex whenever your husband wants it will make your marriage more passionate, and it will also make you feel good—sexy, desired, and happy. Sex is a mood booster, after all!

Only you know for sure what's right for you, but try to receive the passion your husband brings whenever he brings it. Consider experimenting with just giving an automatic yes whenever he's asking, so you don't miss an opportunity to have all that pleasure and connection with him.

If that doesn't work for you, consider being receptive to lovemaking at least once a week as a way of acknowledging the importance of this special relationship and keeping the passion in your marriage alive.

Be Vulnerable

Vulnerability around sex is much more attractive than criticizing or complaining that he doesn't initiate or isn't doing it right. You'll never feel as vulnerable as when you're seducing your husband with your feminine magnetism, instead of initiating the way a man would.

Your husband just wants to make you happy (in this case, by bringing you to orgasm). It can't hurt to tell him what you would love in bed, even if that feels scary and secret.

Express Gratitude

The more your husband feels appreciated for his efforts, the more he'll be inspired to treat you like his queen. Why not thank him for making you orgasm? Why not thank him for making you feel sexy? What you focus on increases, and in the bedroom you have a chance to focus on feeling gratified, beautiful, and desired by acknowledging those things out loud.

If you feel that the lovemaking is lacking overall in some way, perhaps a spouse-fulfilling prophecy (you'll learn about those in Chapter 24) is just the thing to inspire him to pay more attention to the things that make your toes curl.

How to Tell Him What You Want in Bed

One great way to make your sex life more fun is to let your husband know exactly what you want—from bubble baths or a slow dance to making out in the car. But having a conversation about what's going on *in* the heat of the moment can take you both *out* of the moment, and that makes it a lot more challenging to express your desires in the bedroom.

If you have a fantasy you want to act out, a position you want to try, or something you want more of, a great way to approach the topic is to wait until you're alone with your husband somewhere else—in the car, out to eat, or anywhere you can have a private conversation. Start by saying something positive about the last time you made love or about your sex life in general. You might say, "I love how you seduced me last night," or "I had a great orgasm on Friday. You really get me going," or "We've been having such great sex lately." Or maybe just, "I'm so glad we finally got to do it this weekend."

Next, you can say, "You know, next time, I would love to . . ." and fill in the blank with your desire. By giving him a compliment or expressing gratitude first, your desire is less likely to land as a criticism and more likely to sound like an opportunity for him to feel more successful and manly.

This can be a really fun, titillating conversation—whispering it in his ear and saying it with no expectation is likely to get the sparks flying. It's fun and bonding to share a secret, and it heightens the anticipation.

Another great way to teach your husband what you like in bed is to communicate nonverbally—whether by moaning, whimpering, or screaming—but *only* when he's doing something that feels good to you. If he stops doing the thing you like or if he's doing something you don't like, be silent. He'll get the message. If you continue to moan after he's stopped or when what he's doing doesn't feel that good, he'll have a much harder time figuring out what you like. Men love feedback, and the way to say "That's not doing it for me" is to go silent. The only way he knows he's delighting you is when he hears you enjoying yourself. Don't give him the wrong signal!

Why Sex Goes Missing and How to Get It Back

If you don't want to have sex ever, something's wrong. There's a popular myth (and a diagnosis with a corresponding drug treatment) that lack of desire is caused by hormonal shifts, but there's no evidence to support that, despite lots of studies on the subject. The likelier explanation is that your lack of desire is a symptom of feeling resentful toward your husband.

It could be that you're hurt and angry from years of arguing or feeling neglected. Using the Six Intimacy Skills will help remedy that in a hurry.

It could also be that you just don't like feeling that out of control. Sex is a vulnerable act. You're not composed when it's happening. And you can't make yourself hurry up—that never works. To women, the whole thing can feel a little uncivilized when we're not in the mood. But sex is not only proper, it can make you feel amazing on a lot of levels.

Husbands just want their wives to be happy, and that's never truer than in the bedroom. I'm happy to report that my husband has memorized a complicated set of procedures that reliably bring me to orgasm. Your husband would probably be glad to do the same. He'll go to just about any lengths to make you happy in the bedroom if you tell him what you want. If you don't know, that's something for you to figure out. What gets you going? What turns you on most? Only you can determine that, so it's well worth it to spend some time experimenting until you find the yellow-brick road to orgasm and can show your husband how to get you there. If you're not climaxing, that's a big loss for both of you. He wants to know that he made you feel good and you want that pleasurable release. If lovemaking feels like a tedious road to nowhere, it will naturally move to the bottom of your to-do list, so make it your mission to climax. Your husband will gladly join the mission if you express your desire purely. Keep going until you get to Oz.

Here's another possible cause for sex that's gone missing: Maybe you've turned your husband down so often that he thinks it's a waste of time to try. But that means you don't ever get to feel physically desired. What a waste to miss out on getting to feel your magnetic powers of attraction and the pleasure you were born to enjoy during sex.

Refocus Your View with Gratitude

Gratitude has magical powers. It turns an ordinary meal into a feast, an ordinary man into your hero, and an average relationship into a lifelong romance.

Refocusing your view with gratitude may be the most powerful intimacy skill of all because it does double duty. First, it shifts your focus from what you don't like to what you do like, and since what you focus on increases, just doing that makes a dramatic, positive, immediate change in your relationship.

Second, by expressing gratitude, you're actually causing people to respond to you differently. If you make someone who has done you a small favor feel like he did you a big one, he's more likely to want to do things to please you in the future.

When you can't please someone, it's human nature to get discouraged and give up. Expressing gratitude will make your husband feel appreciated and inspired to want to do more to please you.

PRESCRIPTION

Express gratitude to your husband three times day. It can be for ordinary things like taking out the trash, making coffee, or stopping at the store to get milk. Or it could be for

big things like working hard to support the family, moving
where you want to live, or giving you three great kids.

If you find yourself focused on or complaining about
something your husband does that gets on your nerves,
consider creating a spouse-fulfilling prophecy to affirm what
you want to experience instead. For example, instead of
saying "You're always grumpy," come up with an affirmation
that feels like a stretch but comes from your faith instead
of your fear, such as "You're usually in a good mood."

CHAPTER 24

The Most Powerful Intimacy Skill of All

"When I feel lacking, I don't need new things—I need new eyes with which to see the things I already have. So when I woke up this morning, I walked into my kitchen wearing fresh perspectacles."

—Glennon Doyle Melton, Author and Blogger

Double Your Pleasure with Gratitude

When you practice intimacy skills, you concentrate on changing yourself and your attitude, and you give up trying to control anybody else. In that process, you end up becoming a better version of yourself. One powerful way to do that is by expressing gratitude.

Practicing gratitude means you take stock of your life by listing the things that are good. Adopting the attitude of gratitude—even when things don't seem to be enough—opens up possibilities that didn't seem to exist before.

One of my coaches, Sheri, who now has a wonderful relationship with her husband, reflected on the days when she was stingy with her gratitude. Before she learned the Six Intimacy Skills, she would tell her girlfriends, "I'm not going to throw him a parade just because he helped the kids with their homework." Her relationship ended up in crisis when they separated and nearly divorced. Today, Sheri takes a very different approach. She realizes that her husband's efforts make her load lighter, and she's not afraid to thank him for it. Knowing that she appreciates his efforts inspires him to do more, and that's part of what creates a strong connection between them.

One of the common complaints that I hear from men is "My wife doesn't appreciate the things I do." That's so easy to fix by expressing gratitude! But sometimes we're afraid to be grateful because we think we won't get what we want if we appreciate something that doesn't meet our expectations.

When my husband made the bed years ago, instead of saying "Thank you," I would say "Now how about fluffing the pillows?" Back then, I was afraid that if I thanked him for taking out the trash, he would think it was optional and stop doing it. It turns out that just the opposite is true. The more I appreciate John's efforts, the more motivated he is to do things that make me happy.

A young attorney I know, Rita, couldn't think of one thing to thank her husband for. I suggested she thank him for working hard to support the family. She objected because she also worked hard to support their family. But just because you're doing your part doesn't mean you can't thank him for doing his part. Everybody likes to be appreciated, and Rita's standard of living was certainly better because of her husband's efforts than it would have been without him.

Three Gratitudes a Day

Isabella was not enthusiastic when I suggested that she express gratitude to her husband at least three times each day. She said, "I already do everything around the house—the cooking, the laundry, everything! He never thanks me for that, so why should I thank him?"

But Isabella agreed that she would experiment with gratitude, so she thanked her husband for taking out the trash, for watching the baby so she could go to Zumba, and for killing a spider in the bathroom. A couple days later they were sitting down to dinner and he said, "You've really taught me that we need to appreciate each other more, and I wanted to thank you for making dinner tonight." She nearly fell out of her chair.

The point of this exercise is to remind yourself just how fortunate you are. If your husband works hard, runs to the store when you're out of milk, and wears snore strips so he doesn't keep you awake at night, then you have a good guy, and that's something you can be grateful for. Even if you don't *feel* grateful, you can still decide to *be* grateful.

Instead of focusing on how her husband didn't appreciate her, which she couldn't do anything about, Isabella took action. When she became willing to change her own behavior, she brought the entire relationship to higher ground. Becoming her best self helped her realize how much she appreciated her man.

That's what the Six Intimacy Skills are all about.

Sometimes a student will say, "My husband does help around the house, which I really appreciate. The problem is, when he does the laundry, he doesn't hang things up properly, so they get all wrinkled. I'm wondering if I can thank him for doing the laundry, but still ask him to hang things up right in the future."

That's like asking if you can criticize him and still be grateful, and I don't know of a way to do that. It's as if you're saying, "How can I go swimming without getting wet?" It can't be done. Saying "Please hang things up right" is the same as saying "You're hanging things up wrong." And that's not very inspiring or motivating.

Either you're grateful for something and you accept it the way it is, or you complain about it. It's one of the two, but you can't do both. Otherwise, you've couched your complaint in really nice words, but it's still a complaint, and it's still going to cost you the intimacy you crave. It's also going to negate the pleasant effect of your gratitude.

Expressing gratitude means letting your husband know that you appreciate him. So thank him for doing his job, even if it's not exactly what you had in mind.

Another option is to reject his efforts entirely, maybe by doing the laundry yourself. If you're anything like me, you have an opinion about how everything should be done, and you have probably taken things over because you didn't like the way they were being done. That gets lonely and overwhelming pretty fast. So if what you want is to feel like you have a true partner who helps out so you don't have to do all the work, consider just going with expressing your gratitude.

That doesn't mean, however, that you *never* get to say what you want. In fact, you always get to say what you want! I just don't recommend that you complain, because that doesn't get you the outcome you're wanting. One approach would be to find something that your husband put on a hanger the way you like it and then comment on that. You might take something out of the closet and say, "I love how you hung this up for me. Look! Not a single wrinkle!" I call this "Catching him doing something good." This allows you to stay in gratitude and focus on what you do like. It always gets a better response than complaining, and it puts the focus on things you like, things you want more of. It lets your husband know you're pleaseable and builds up his confidence in his ability to make you happy.

If you think your husband never does anything the way you want him to, consider that the word "never" is pretty extreme. So is "always." Maybe he *mostly* does things a certain way, but it's unlikely that he *always* or *never* does. And as long as he *sometimes* does things the way you like them, you have a chance to focus on the positive, choose your gratitude, and create a completely different culture in your relationship. It might seem like a strange way to look at things, but it's really a matter of seeing them in a way that serves you and your relationship.

The Gratitude Experiment

Bestselling author and motivational speaker Zig Ziglar once told a story of a woman from Birmingham who wanted him to help her with her problem, which was that she hated her job. Zig nodded, then asked her to get out a notebook and write down the things she was grateful for about her job.

She just looked at him in disbelief, then explained again, "No, you don't understand—I hate my job! I'm not grateful for anything about it! The people are just awful!" But Zig insisted this gratitude list was the next step, so he waited and she resisted and he waited and she refused and he waited.

Once more she said there wasn't one single thing she was grateful for. Zig asked, "So this is a volunteer position then?"

The woman looked at him like he was crazy and said, "No! I go there because I have to support myself! I go there for the money!"

Zig said, "So you don't *like* to be paid?"

This made her even more agitated, but she admitted that she did like being paid.

Zig said, "Good—that can be the first thing on your list."

She wrote that down, and they continued to work on her list. It turned out that her job paid her above average wages and also came with a generous medical plan, so those things went on the list. Her employer contributed to her retirement fund, so that went on the list. Her office was close to her house, which meant she didn't have to travel far every day. They kept adding more things she was grateful for about her job, until there were twenty-two things on the gratitude list about a job she absolutely hated.

Next, Zig instructed her to read the list out loud in front of her mirror every day. She agreed, and Zig left Birmingham for his next destination.

A while later he was back in the area speaking again, and he saw the same woman in the front row. Zig said she was smiling so big that she could have eaten a banana sideways. After his speech she came up to him and said, "I just want to thank you for your help. I've been reading my gratitude list in the mirror every day for months." Zig asked about her job and she said, "It's much better! You can't believe how much the people there have improved!"

Of course, it may be that the woman's coworkers *had* improved, but one thing we know for sure is that her *attitude* toward them improved. She was focused on what she liked. She was grateful for what she had. That makes all the difference.

Try your own gratitude experiment for your marriage. Start by making a list of things you appreciate about your husband—in honor of Zig, try to come up with twenty-two of them. If you're having a hard time, think about the things about him that you were attracted to in the first place. Was he gentle? Did he make you laugh? Was he ambitious? Smart? Accomplished? Easygoing? Reliable? He probably still has those qualities, but you may not have been focusing on them recently.

Once you finish your list, try giving him three gratitudes a day, just like Isabella did with her husband. You can thank him for ordinary chores like taking the trash to the curb or for being a loyal husband for all the time that you've been together. Be a detective and try to find as many things as you can that he does to lighten your load or make you smile, and make sure he knows that you appreciate them.

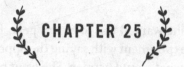

CHAPTER 25

The Power of the Spouse-Fulfilling Prophecy

"...Expectancy is the atmosphere for miracles."

—Edwin Louis Cole, Author and Minister

That's *Just* Like You

We affirm things all the time. Often we don't even realize it. We say things like "I'm terrible with money" or "I have intimacy issues," which may be just the opposite of the experience we want. But what we focus on increases, and when we're focused on things we don't want, we end up with more of them.

That's one great reason for abstaining from self-criticism. You're actually making a negative affirmation whenever you put yourself down. Every time you say "I'm so disorganized" or "I'm really out of shape," you're focusing on and expanding those outcomes.

Affirmations also work on the people around us. Everybody knows how damaging it is to tell a kid he's stupid, for example: It's a negative affirmation and he might believe it, even if it's not true.

Affirmations also affect adults. Author and performance coach Lee Milteer taught a course on how to create a desirable outcome (i.e., better health, more money) by using the power of autosuggestion. During Lee's course, one woman realized she had been unwittingly affirming that her husband was always losing his temper, which was *not* what she wanted. What she wanted was to have a peaceful, calm home. She decided she would experiment with saying the opposite of what she had been saying, to see what would happen. She went home and waited for him to lose his temper. She didn't have to wait very long.

As soon as he started raising his voice and swearing, she used her new affirmation, which was "It's not like you to lose your temper." When she said that, her husband looked at her funny. Their young son said, "Yes it is, Mom! He *always* loses his temper!" because that's what he'd heard his mom say for his whole life. But the woman stuck to her guns and continued to affirm that it was unlike her husband to lose his temper.

Not long after, the couple went to a restaurant and the service was slow. The husband started to fume, saying he had a good mind to get the manager and let him know how long they'd been waiting. Suddenly he stopped and said to her, "But it's not like me to lose my temper, is it?"

You're Mr. Moneybags

I too have been guilty of using the power of a spouse-fulfilling prophecy to affirm something I didn't want. I used to tell my husband to ask for a raise at work, for example. This let him know in a not-so-subtle way that I thought he should be making more money. It's pretty embarrassing to admit that now, but even worse is that it wasn't serving me at all. What he heard was the subtext: "You don't make very much money." That's not a good affirmation because it was the opposite of what I wanted. And we ended up in a position where he was out of work and not making *any* money. What a mess!

Once I connected the dots between what I was saying and what he was hearing, I decided to change it up and create spouse-fulfilling prophecies. I started saying things like "You've always been such a good provider"—and looking back, he really had been. Then, just for fun, I started calling him Mr. Moneybags.

It sure felt like a stretch to say that at the time, because I had a lot of fear that we were going to run out of money. But I decided to ignore that feeling and focus on the outcome I wanted.

Shortly thereafter, my husband started a business, which has become extremely successful. He's run it for more than a decade, and he has consistently been a very good provider. He's much more successful now than he ever was when he worked for other people, and he has much more flexibility and freedom to boot. He's also much happier.

I still call him Mr. Moneybags, and now it doesn't feel false at all. If I say he's a good provider, it's because I think it's absolutely true. I now have plenty of evidence to support that.

Once I made the suggestion on Facebook to try a spouse-fulfilling prophecy of saying "You're always on time" instead of "You're always late." One person responded, "You are encouraging people to lie!" But here's how I see it. If I say "You're always late," nobody accuses me of lying. Complaining, yes—but not lying. But can it possibly be true that someone is *always* late? Isn't that also a lie? It's certainly an exaggeration, at least.

So if you're going to exaggerate anyway, why not stretch the truth in the direction that serves you best? Why not focus on what you *do* want instead of what you don't?

Our perspective changes depending on what we focus on. If we focus on the lack, that's what we create. If we focus on gratitude, we get more of what we're thankful for. Your perceptions of your spouse may seem very real, but they actually start with your own view of the world, which only you have control over. Choose your focus wisely.

Interestingly, when you decide to change your focus, you can always find evidence to support your new view. Imagine a court of law, where you are going before a judge and jury to make a case. Could you gather evidence that your husband is thoughtful, loving, and smart? Of course you could. Could you gather evidence that he's a big loser? Of course you could. Nobody's all one thing or another. We all have our good points and bad points. Which case do you want to make to the judge and jury? Which one will serve you better? You always get to choose.

Two Weeks to a Great Husband

Sara was convinced that her husband was useless. She told me he was overweight and too out of shape to play with their kids, that he wasn't making enough money to support their family, and that he never seemed to want to spend time with them either. It wasn't hard to see why the guy might be keeping his distance, because I could hear her disgust and hostility in everything she said about him. I'd probably keep my distance from somebody who felt that way about me too.

Sara was already in the habit of reading something inspirational and journaling every morning, so I suggested that she incorporate writing down three things she was grateful for about her husband into that daily routine. We also agreed that she was going to pick a spouse-fulfilling prophecy that she could write in her journal and affirm to her husband. She decided on "You're a great husband," although she was moaning and groaning about having to say it. She said, "It doesn't feel true at all!" But she agreed to experiment with it anyway, just to see what happened. She didn't think it was going to change things.

When we spoke again two weeks later, Sara had written her gratitude list faithfully every day and repeated her spouse-fulfilling prophecy in her journal and to her husband. I asked her how things were going and she said, "I'm just so happy that my husband forgives." When I asked her what she meant by that, she said, "I realize I've been very unpleasant to him lately, even though he's a great husband. I apologized to him and he was so sweet and forgiving. I felt really grateful that he didn't hold it against me that I was so nasty."

She also related stories of him being romantic, having success in his new business, and helping her handle the kids when it was time for some discipline. He sounded like a completely different guy.

I couldn't resist teasing her by asking, "Is this the same loser you were married to two weeks ago?" She said, "I know! I guess I just needed an attitude adjustment. He really *is* a great husband. I couldn't see it, but that wasn't about him, it was about me."

Her daily gratitude served as evidence for the case that her husband was thoughtful, generous, devoted, and hardworking. She could have used her journal in a court of law to prove that he was a good man and a great husband. Or she could have stuck to her old, tired complaints and proven to the jury that he was an overweight, underearning waste of space.

Sara not only started focusing on what she appreciated about her husband, she began to get more of what she wanted from him because she had changed her attitude. You can bet he was responding to her differently; who wouldn't? Knowing that someone respects and appreciates you is likely to help you feel more relaxed so you can be yourself. Feeling like you're being picked on all the time can make anyone defensive.

Gigi was affirming that her husband never wanted to spend time with her when I introduced her to the concept of the spouse-fulfilling prophecy. That weekend they had planned to spend Saturday together, but then he announced that he had made plans with his friend Matt to go cycling instead. When he told her that, she was so hurt that she automatically reverted to her old affirmation. She said, "You *never* want to spend time with me!" and stormed out of the room. A few minutes later, she remembered about her new spouse-fulfilling prophecy and decided to give it a try even though they were now in the middle of a fight. She went back to him and said, "I'm sorry I said that. I know you want to spend time with me. I'm sure you'll work it out somehow." Imagine her surprise when, a few minutes later, he said, "I called Matt back and told him I can't go cycling today so that we can spend the day together."

Gigi told me she was shocked at how quickly she got what she wanted with the power of a spouse-fulfilling prophecy.

What negative affirmations do you currently have about your husband? Is he always cranky? Is he stingy? Is he lazy? Is he messy? It's time to create a spouse-fulfilling prophecy that serves you better. You can decide to focus on how he's easygoing, generous, industrious, tidy, or anything else.

What Will Your Spouse-Fulfilling Prophecy Be?

Often our students feel awkward using a spouse-fulfilling prophecy because it's completely different than what they're used to. Yours will probably feel awkward too at first, or even dishonest. That's just because you're stretching into a new perspective. Any change—good or bad—will always feel strange in the beginning. But what have you got to lose by trying to affirm what you want to experience?

A friend of mine who was engaged to a wonderful guy was complaining about how her fiancé was being inconsiderate to her during a very busy period at work. She was unhappy that he never washed the dishes and she was always stuck doing them, which she thought was rude. I suggested that she catch him doing something good to help her change her focus by thanking him when he did wash dishes. She could also let him know how happy it made her when he did them. But it was a no-go for her; she insisted he *never* washed a single dish. She said, "Look, my fiancé is awesome, but he's not like your husband. John is much awesomer."

I took that as a huge compliment, because what I heard her saying was that I focus on how wonderful my husband is. And she's right—I do focus on that, constantly talking about how often he does things that I like. And because of that, John is very willing to do more things that make me happy because he feels appreciated. In my experience, this is a much awesomer way to live.

You can focus on the outcome you want for your marriage even on the brink of divorce, as Regina discovered.

When her husband served her with divorce papers, she was devastated and terrified, but she decided to speak only her faith, not her fear. She said to him, "I don't even need to read them. I know you have been generous and fair. You're the kindest man I've ever known. I don't want to have anything to do with these papers."

Regina attended a meeting with her husband and the divorce attorney for the sole purpose of being able to say, "Whatever you think," and "I trust you." Her husband had started out charging hard, in a hurry to dissolve the marriage and move on. By the end of that meeting, he was telling her, "I'll get new papers to you, but there's no rush."

Regina's approach made what could have been a thirty-day divorce in her state into a process that stretched on for more than eight months, time she used to show her husband her newfound respect, gratitude, and vulnerability.

She called on him to be his best self, and that's how he began showing up. It was only a matter of time before they were connecting again.

Sometimes it really is darkest before the dawn.

In this abridged excerpt from *The Empowered Wife Podcast* episode 116, I interviewed Frances, whose blended family was falling apart. She and her husband were both done, and they each had their own divorce attorneys.

FRANCES: My husband and I have been married for twelve years now, and we have both been divorced before. We both have a Christian faith, so it was something that didn't sit well with either of us.

We got together quite quickly, and we got married, and within two weeks we were in marriage counseling. Putting together a blended family quickly is a tricky thing to do.

The first issues that we had were about his interaction with my children and my defending them. In my mind, he could do nothing right. In his mind, my kids could do nothing right. So we were fighting all the time. I thought things would improve once my children left, but we were still fighting.

He said he could set the clock for when we would have a huge argument. They would be ones with one of us packing our bags and leaving. Finally, we were packing them for the last time, and we each had divorce lawyers lined up. I thought we were done!

I was devastated because I was ashamed to think that I was going to be divorced again, and I was ashamed of what my children would think of me. I did not want us to divorce, not deep down. But I was so angry, I didn't know what else to do about it.

It was really hard because, in between the fighting, we'd settle back to something that was really quite loving and nice. But not great because you could feel the tension build up around that two-week mark and something with me, usually, exploding.

In the past, my husband hadn't sought divorce. He would wait till the storm blew over, and then I'd perhaps apologize, and I would demand an apology from him. And we'd tiptoe our way forward and settle down. But there were often phases where he wouldn't talk to me for a week or two weeks. And we had massive cold wars, no intimacy whatsoever. Then we'd settle down a bit.

And the funny thing is, I've realized over the last two years, where I've been following your program, that I would get some self-care, and then I would feel better about myself. So I would approach him, and we would muddle our way through, and it would be okay for a while. It's taken a long time to recognize that this is what was happening. I might chat with girlfriends and then I'd be like, "I feel quite happy towards him. Now maybe I'll reach out to him." He was always willing when I would reach out because he didn't really want us to end either.

But this time I was scared because he had a lawyer and he said, "We're done!" And I did not know what I was going to do about it. It was really very dramatic. I was sleeping in the spare room already. I'm on my knees, and I'm praying to God: "Please help! Please help!" And then I was on my Facebook feed, and up pops Laura Doyle.

I thought, "Here we go! Another thing that says, 'We will fix your marriage.'" I decided to listen, and you were telling your story. And I sat there, and I went, "I've done everything that Laura did! Everything!" I've tried to have my husband diagnosed with a mental illness. I've yelled at him, I've been disrespectful to him—everything you could imagine. And I felt like this is what I needed to do.

When I heard him get up in the morning—I was awake nearly all night—I went straight away, and tentatively, I said, "You don't want a divorce, do you?" And he burst into tears and said, "No, I don't!" And I said, "Neither do I," and I got up and snuggled his knee.

I said to him, "I am so sorry that I have treated you so disrespect-fully and I didn't realize," and he said, "Thank you." I said, "I want to make changes," and he said "Yes," and that was the start of the journey.

That was nearly two years ago. And it's taken time, but it is truly a miracle where we're at now, an absolute miracle. Because I started fol-lowing your program. The first thing I did was I found your TV series, and I started watching that. I go out every day with my headphones on and listen to that or your podcast, or read your books, and then I looked up coaching as well. Where we were then and where we are now is just miraculous.

I've always recognized the fact that it only takes one person to change your relationship. To apply the skills that I've learned, and to have the coach to actually point out my blind spots, to recognize how controlling I was—that was one of the biggest changes.

And also, I've been brought up in a family where the wife pleases the husband and puts herself aside. And I was listening to a session that Coach Kathy was leading one day, and she talked about the fact that nobody is responsible for our own happiness except for ourselves. And it was like the lights went on, and I went, "Oh! I've been expecting him to make me happy!" If I went for a walk along the beach and he didn't want to come, I'd be angry with him. Because I expected that he would want to come with me. I was controlling all the time! And then I realized that if I want to go for a walk, I should go for a walk! You can invite him if you want, but don't expect him to come. Don't expect him to make you happy. Go because that will make *you* happy.

That was like a real release for me, to not put that pressure on him or on our marriage, but to realize I am my own person, and I can choose to do things to make myself happy—and guess what happens along the way?

Because I *stopped* pressuring him, he actually started to want to come.

I don't need to fight to defend myself, and he doesn't have to fight to defend himself. And it is so peaceful and so relaxed and calm. We're both saying, "This is nice!" We even say we don't fight anymore because I can't remember the last time we had an argument.

LAURA: Really? How long has it been?

FRANCES: Probably a year.

One of the big blowups happened just over a year ago, and it was really significant because we were on holidays in a lovely beach town that we go to regularly. We'd been in lockdown for a long time, and I booked a few days to go away to this town because it's the end of the school year. I'd been teaching online, and it had been really tough, and I just needed a few days to go away. He came along, and we were walking on the beach that day, and he was chatting to me about something just normal, and I noticed something I can't remember that was in the water, or whatever it was, and he flew off the handle at me and said, "You don't listen to me" and "I was talking! Why did you interrupt me?" I was devastated, and he stormed off, and I didn't know what was going on. I didn't realize I had taken the bait, whereas now I would have handled it much differently. I would have said something like, "I love you, honey," and just kept walking. I wouldn't have accepted the invitation to the argument.

So this year, we went to the same town at the same time. Twelve months after what happened last year, I am now sitting on a deck at the same beach, and I'm here feeling loved and adored and happier than I've ever been. We've been through a whole year of me practicing the Skills and learning and choosing and selecting. Now, even if I did interrupt my husband, it would never end up in that mess that it ended up being a year ago because I don't take the bait. I've learned to say "Ouch," I've learned to express my desire in a way that inspires, I've learned how to apply the Skills so that we're both in a really happy place.

I tell him that "You're my hero" because he is, and I tell him that he's my favorite human. I often look back and I think, "God, you were going to toss him aside. How stupid! Somebody else might have gotten him by now!"

LAURA: You sound like a very different woman than the one who had the divorce attorney lined up. How are you different?

FRANCES: I thought my husband was against me. So every time he would say something, I would always take it in a negative way.

For example, while we were out of town recently, there was a step, and it was the same color as the pavement. And my husband, being the caring person he is, said to me, "Watch the step."

In the past, because I am a very independent person and I know how to look after myself, I would have said to him, "Do you think I'm stupid? I can see a step. I can get down the step myself." Now I turned to him this time because I've realized that that's him showing how much he cares. I actually said that to him. I said, "Thank you, I know that you're showing me you care." And I think I might have even said to him, "In the past, I would have thought you were treating me like an idiot, but I know that's not what you mean." So I had to deliberately choose to put on different perspectacles.

Every single time I was having a bit of a tricky moment, I would Google "Laura Doyle husband" or "Laura Doyle self-care" or something. I would type it in, and I've listened to at least one hundred podcasts. I would simply put in what I needed and something would come up, and I would go, "Okay, all right," and I recognized that I needed extra self-care to make myself happy. I needed to put on different "perspectacles" by writing a list of appreciation.

So I started with them, and I still do that every day in my journal because I love to journal. That's one of my self-care acts. And I will do things about what the day ahead is, or what the day behind was, and ten things I appreciate about my husband. It's completely changed how I see things, and it helps me to look for evidence of the things that I believe to be true about my husband, and I often put those down as a win in my journal.

It's changed my perspective completely, and in the early days I looked at applying the Skills as learning a new language. I didn't realize how I spoke to him in the past was causing him to be defensive and to close up and to not be able to respond in a way that I understood either, but now we understand, and we can communicate, and it's great.

LAURA: It's beautiful. I'm really impressed with your discipline about your daily gratitude list. That's magical—I call it the "drop and do ten." Whenever you're having emotional turmoil, you do your ten gratitudes. You talked about how it has changed your perspective, your perspectacles. Now, I wonder if your husband has also changed?

FRANCES: Yes, and he said to me he can see how much [I've] changed, and he has said that it makes him want to be a better person for me as well. He's definitely changed, and it's amazing from where we were even a year ago. It's just miraculous, but I think the important thing to note is it does take time—because I created a toxic place, and now we have a safe place, and that doesn't happen overnight because my husband had to build trust and faith in what I was implementing and believe that this was going to stick, that I wasn't going to turn back to the Wicked Witch of the West, and I was going to keep doing what I've learned. And I am committed to do this for the rest of my life because I can see the Skills working not just in my marriage, but in my relationship with my children, with my mother, with friends, with my staff, with colleagues, and it makes a difference.

He supports me in anything that I want to do. I couldn't see that he was doing that before because perhaps I wasn't listening, and I didn't have different perspectacles. I didn't value what he was doing—I thought he had an ulterior motive for something like that.

Now I can see that he supports me in any choices I make or anything I want to do. He is kind and caring. I respond very well to that as well. Like, if I need to step down, instead of snapping back at him when he tells me to watch the step: "Thank you." I have a little laugh on the inside because I think, "Oh, my goodness, what a difference that is."

I see him differently, and he steps up to what I see in him. He said to me he wants to be a better person because of the changes that I've made. He was always a good person, but now it shows more and I look for it more, and I see it more and I'll say it to him. I will thank him for everything he does for me, whereas in the past I had this stubbornness in me: "He doesn't thank me, so why should I thank him?"

I've got a friend who's quite elderly, and when I was first going through the Skills, I talked to her about them. She said to me, "Is it going to damage you or hurt you at all to say 'thank you' to him and appreciate him?" And I thought, "I am not giving anything away by doing that. What does it matter if I do it?"

I think one of the first things I thanked him for was hanging out the washing or doing the washing. I didn't do the washing for the next six months. I didn't touch it. He did it every single time it needed doing, and it was like, "Whoa!" At first I probably thanked him just because I thought I had to, to get this thing happening. Now, I do it very authentically because I do really value and appreciate him.

CHAPTER 26

The Connection Framework

"People often say that motivation doesn't last. Well, neither does bathing—that's why we recommend it daily."

–Zig Ziglar

Maybe things aren't that bad in your relationship. Maybe there are just a couple of things you'd like to improve.

Or maybe your relationship feels like an exhausting struggle. Like mine did.

Either way, there are millions of women in your same situation who are hurting and don't know what to do.

What we've seen again and again, thousands of times over, is the same solution: the magical power of the Six Intimacy Skills. The incredible response from women who practice the Six Intimacy Skills with the Connection Framework validate that it works not just for me, the women in my living room, and our coaches, but also for women all over the world from every walk of life. Husbands that come and share on *The Empowered Wife Podcast* further confirm the incredible outcomes of their wives' courageous stands for their marriages.

Now that you have an understanding of the Six Intimacy Skills, I'm sure you can see why I'm so passionate about getting them in the hands of every woman who wants to make her marriage last and thrive.

If you're anything like I was, you probably wonder why nobody ever taught them to you before and wish that someone had.

When I first discovered the Intimacy Skills, I felt like a veil was lifted, and I could finally see clearly how I actually control the levers for the culture in my house. I could either make it loving and fun, or else distant and tense. It was all up to me! When I realized that, I think I walked around with my mouth hanging open in surprise for the rest of the day.

You're probably also feeling inspired and hopeful about what's possible for the future of your relationship. Maybe you've already made your relationship shinier because you've applied what you've read and seen good results. It's so exciting to see a way to get the marriage you've always dreamed of having.

But even once I had this knowledge, it wasn't easy to just break my old habits and start practicing the Six Intimacy Skills. My journey was bumpy, like a roller coaster. First my marriage was up! Then it was down. His face lit up to see me! Then we had a huge blowup in the car again. In order to develop the consistent new habits I needed, what I did—and what I now see that I had to do—was pass on what I'd learned.

I started out by controlling my friends. I'd say, "Here's what you should do. Apologize for being disrespectful when you said he was a slob." I was clearly not very good at treating my friends like the experts on their own lives yet, but somehow it worked. The habits I wanted to cultivate started to sink in at a whole new level when I heard myself talk about the Intimacy Skills, focus on them, and apply my best thinking to another woman's situation. Hearing her wins and excitement helped motivate me to do the things I was inviting her to do. And that's when I was able to make my marriage magical again and feel confident that I could keep it that way.

That's why, when I first wrote down what I had learned about how to have a playful, passionate marriage over twenty years ago, I included my phone number and my email in the book. I figured a few women might have some questions. To my surprise, that book became a *New York Times* best seller and was published in thirty countries. Thousands of women reached out, asking for help with implementing the information.

Problem was, I wasn't ready for that response.

Women were emailing, calling, writing letters, and messaging me their questions about how to practice the Six Intimacy Skills, which can be a little tricky to apply by yourself. A book alone wasn't doing it for them, and I was so passionate to help them that I tried to respond to all of them one by one, just like I had been doing in my living room.

I realized I needed help, so I trained a few women to teach workshops and help other women apply the Intimacy Skills, including Kathy Murray, who is now one of the top relationship coaches in the world.

But for the most part, I was trying to help everyone by myself, and I very quickly got overwhelmed and exhausted. I didn't have any structure to support an avalanche of women who were struggling in their relationships, and it wasn't humanly possible for me to serve them all.

So I stopped. The only good option I could see was to excuse myself to go to the restroom and just never come back. And that's what I did. I rationalized that everything was right there in the book and that anyone who wanted to fix her marriage could just read it. I put my feet on the desk and told myself, "My work here is done."

But the truth was, I was scared, and I ran away. I stopped talking about the Six Intimacy Skills with other women because I felt inadequate to help them.

Around that time, my marriage stopped being as shiny as it had been when I was helping other women with their marriages. My brain started to replay some of the old jingles about my husband, including familiar hits like, "I'm smarter than you are" and "I'm the only responsible adult in this family." No wonder we weren't laughing together or enjoying as much physical affection as we had been when I was staying inspired by sharing my own experience and hearing uplifting stories from courageous women who were fixing their marriages.

Then came the day I ran into Lisa (not her real name). She had been coming with her friend to the support group at my house to learn about the Six Intimacy Skills before we outgrew my living room. In the beginning she had shared about how she felt like she had to do everything and that her husband acted like another one of her kids. She was not feeling loved or in love. But as she heard what the rest of us were doing and started treating him with respect and showing more gratitude, she reported that her husband seemed so much more confident and relaxed. Then Lisa's husband got a promotion and was making her laugh again, and she was starting to remember why she had married him. She was crying when she shared how she was feeling so in love with her husband and that he was coming home from work early just to be with her. Lisa was a very early success story who helped me realize that the Intimacy Skills would work for anyone who practiced them.

Then I lost touch with Lisa for several years while I was hiding out, so I didn't hear how things were going with her until I ran into her again with her husband, Steve. I was excited to see her because of the warm connection and bond we'd shared from working on our marriages together, but we were only a few minutes into the conversation before I realized something had changed.

This was not the same Lisa who had been so vulnerable and in love with her husband. This Lisa was a different woman. She was complaining about her husband and insulting him right in front of him and me. She rolled her eyes when he was talking. She seemed disgusted with him, and you could see he was a little stooped over and just looked tired. This was the same great guy she'd been so happy about and so in love with years ago in my living room! But now, Lisa had amnesia.

I was crushed because I had believed that if a wife knew the Intimacy Skills as well as Lisa did, she wouldn't go back to being disrespectful and controlling—not once she knew the cost and what she could gain if she practiced the Skills. I thought she would find the Intimacy Skills so self-reinforcing that she would keep practicing her self-care, expressing her gratitude, and trusting her husband. But I could see with my own eyes that this wasn't the case for Lisa. She was back to feeling exhausted and lonely in her relationship, and she couldn't make her way back to the magic by herself.

She wasn't the only one. Around that time, Marlene called me. She had taken my workshop to work on her relationship, and now she was begging me to coach her because she knew she was shooting holes in her own marriage bucket. She told me she was struggling: "Laura, I know The Six Intimacy Skills are the answer, but there's nowhere to go to get support."

Then there was Kathy Murray. Something interesting was happening at her house too. Her marriage, once on the brink of divorce, continued to thrive. The first time Kathy experimented with one of the Intimacy Skills, she and her husband slept in the same bed for the first time in six months. So she fired the marriage counselor she had been seeing for the past year and hasn't stopped supporting other women with the Six Intimacy Skills since. Twenty years later, she still gets tears in her eyes when she talks about how wonderful her thirty-year marriage is.

Unlike Lisa, Marlene, and me, Kathy carried on with helping women in their marriages, and that kept the magic of the Intimacy Skills alive for her.

So my story about how I wrote the books and therefore my work was done? It was painfully obvious that wasn't true—the books weren't enough. We all needed something more, something to keep these lessons alive in our lives. Even I did! Otherwise, it's like knowing a language that you rarely use. Without other women to talk with and listen to who are equally committed to practicing the Intimacy Skills, amnesia starts to set in.

What we see is that life happens. Maybe a pandemic hits, and now you're homeschooling on top of working. You and your husband start to get on each other's nerves, being together all the time. If there's no recent reminder, no fresh story of accountability and gratitude to draw from, no inspiration to practice what you've learned, then the Intimacy Skills won't be easy to reach for.

But where are you going to get that group of like-minded women you can share with openly— and know you're not going to be judged for admitting you threw a bag of cereal at your husband in anger? Or that you're staying with him even though you know he has another woman? What if your best friends tell you to leave him when what you want most is to have a lasting marriage and a safe, happy home for your kids?

In my first book, I outlined a format for women to get together and support each other, but it didn't work. There just wasn't enough structure to the circles, and the leaders weren't trained coaches, hadn't had their own transformations yet, and didn't know how to provide a sacred space.

It was obvious that, in order for the mission to end world divorce to succeed, more structure was needed. So, despite a lot of free-floating terror, I started a relationship coach training school a decade ago. Then I connected students who were struggling in their marriages with trained, certified coaches who are experts on the Six Intimacy Skills. And that worked!

That's how the Connection Framework was born.

The Four Pillars for Lasting Playfulness and Passion

There are four pillars to the Connection Framework. Each pillar is critical to having a marriage that lasts. In fact, what we've found in helping thousands of women is that most women need all four pillars to make their marriages last and thrive.

Pillar #1: The Six Intimacy Skills

You already know about the Intimacy Skills, which are the exact phrases and steps I gathered from women who had happy marriages and that I used to save my own marriage. They started a worldwide movement over twenty years ago. I see them as tools, not rules, that you can use in all of your interactions with your husband regarding parenting, finances, physical intimacy, in-laws, vacations, and holidays. They're the behaviors that actually work, and they form the foundation of the Connection Framework.

For years, I believed that if I could just get women these skills, they could save their marriages too. It's a great start, because having the right information is vital. But my big takeaway from doing this work all these years is that applying that information is what leads to transformation, and the other three pillars support that application. Many women want support with implementing the Intimacy Skills, and rightly so. That's why we created the other pillars of the Connection Framework.

Pillar #2: A Like-Minded Community

There's nothing quite like having a community of like-minded women who are passionate about having a great relationship and believe that marriage is important. Because it is!

We've seen that having a community provides inspiration and connection and accelerates our transformation. I couldn't sustain my new practices long enough to make them a habit until I was uplifted by the other women practicing the Six Intimacy Skills with me. Community has made all the difference for thousands of other students as well.

Everybody deserves a safe environment in which to be seen, heard, and understood, and our group of students and coaches is extraordinary in that regard. We talk about very personal, private, and embarrassing experiences we're facing, which is scary, but it makes us feel more connected than ever. We celebrate vulnerability and authenticity. We provide as much anonymity as we can because it's extremely fortifying to connect at that intimate level, which requires tremendous emotional safety and training.

It's something you really have to experience for yourself. To give you a taste of what it's like, I've included the recordings from a Five-Day Adored Wife Challenge in your portal (exclusively for book readers) at skillsforlove.com. Thousands of women participate in this free challenge, which we offer twice a year.

Now that I know what it's like to have a tribe of women who all value having a strong family and becoming their best selves, I consider being a part of this tribe essential to my happiness.

Community is imperative, in my experience, but what will really take you to the next level of your self-development, and therefore of your thriving marriage, is having a coach.

Pillar #3: A Trained, Certified Relationship Coach

A Certified Laura Doyle Relationship Coach is a highly trained woman who stands for your marriage and for your greatness. She'll help you see what's blocking you from having the marriage you want, but she won't tell you what you should do (like I did when I first started). Our coaches recognize that they only know a little about your life, and they trust you to be the expert. Your coach will bring a big listening ear, share her own experience of what's worked in her relationship, and ask you powerful questions so you can have your own breakthrough and insights about what will work for you. Having a certified coach in your corner is a huge asset for any woman who wants to create a playful, passionate marriage.

One of the things we're most proud of about our coaches is that each and every one has had her own transformation with the Intimacy Skills and the Connection Framework. She was lonely and neglected, or close to divorcing, or the sizzle was gone, or he was leaving her. She was struggling in some way. And then, she had a breakthrough. She learned how to stay on her own paper, to honor herself, and to create a peaceful, loving relationship. And those transformations are what make her uniquely qualified to show another woman how to do the same thing. She's been down that trail already and knows how to guide you to get where you want to go.

Then our coaches invested in immersive training. There are coaches in the world who go to weekend seminars and pay a thousand dollars to get certified, but not our coaches. They were students who were impacted by this work themselves, and then invested a lot of their own time and money to complete a year-long training with us. They became experts in the Intimacy Skills and the unique coaching methodology that springs from them. Our coaches are pretty special because of their ability to maintain a sacred, safe space while helping you make an action plan to address your specific challenge.

And it has to be that way—because what I've learned over the last twenty years is that it takes a *lot* of training to effectively coach on the Six Intimacy Skills and provide the Connection Framework. I used to think women could just support each other once they read the book, but that didn't work. At all.

Sometimes students try to coach without having had training and structure. It's illegal to practice therapy without a license, so we always invite students who feel called to help others with the Intimacy Skills to get trained and certified so they can be wildly successful. No matter how well-meaning, many untrained women fall into the trap of telling someone what to do (like I used to), compromise emotional safety, or revert to a familiar therapy model, which is very different from coaching. When any of that happens, it can spoil the whole experience of practicing the Intimacy Skills and burst the fragile hope of a new student. When your family's future is hanging in the balance, that's especially tragic. Your marriage is too important to leave in the hands of someone who may be passionate but isn't specifically trained. Our coaches are trained, supervised, accountable, and get ongoing instruction and support. We have Certified Laura Doyle Relationship Coaches coaching in numerous languages all over the world. The way you can tell you're getting the real thing is by looking for the exclusive Certified Laura Doyle Relationship Coach seal.

A lot of women have read my books—hundreds of thousands—but only a fraction of them have had the opportunity to get the guidance from certified coaches, trained by me personally, to make sure they get it right.

You won't know what's possible and waiting for you in your marriage unless you gain the actionable insights that you can only get from practicing the Intimacy Skills alongside our coaches and community.

But there's one more opportunity that I wish for every woman who wants a playful, passionate marriage to have.

Pillar #4: Paying It Forward

Paying it forward by sharing my experience practicing the Intimacy Skills with women who were just never taught them is one of the most satisfying, moving things I've ever done. But besides being gratifying, sharing with and listening to other women is also the secret to staying inspired in my own journey and ensuring my lasting transformation.

I'm forever grateful that I've had the honor to work with thousands of committed, determined, and courageous women in real relationships who not only fixed their families but also became more calm, confident, and happy along the way. They send me thank-you messages saying, "This saved my marriage." Or, "Here's a picture from our anniversary that almost didn't happen. Thank you!" The plot twist here is that they saved my marriage too and helped keep it shiny all these years. Sometimes I wonder if I'm giving as much as I get. When you pay it forward, it comes back to you tenfold.

We see this with students too. They pay it forward by celebrating each other's wins and offering empathy in group coaching or at coach-led workshops. Some women tell their relationship story on *The Empowered Wife Podcast*, while others simply talk privately with their coach. Many students decide they never want to leave this work, so they pay it forward by training to become coaches themselves.

Coaching other women is a powerful way to coach myself. Showing other women what to do helped me do the things that make my own relationship playful and passionate. I love watching women slowly uncross their arms and get the same OMG look on their faces that I had. They also tell me their deep, dark secrets, which is a huge honor.

Just by reading this book, you're also in a position to pay it forward by sharing with women who have never heard of the Six Intimacy Skills—because most women still haven't. If you've had even a little success with the Six Intimacy Skills, you have a precious gift to give them. Even if your marriage is still a work in progress, you can accelerate your own journey to being a happy wife by paying it forward. You might introduce a friend or a colleague to this book, or the podcast, or the blog. You could write a book or podcast review and inspire a woman you've never even met, or comment about the Skills on a blog. The women whose lives you'll touch might have wins that will be your future inspiration and contribute to the end of world divorce.

You're probably thinking, "I need the Connection Framework!" And you're right. If you're wondering about the next steps for getting support for your marriage, read on to the next chapter.

CHAPTER 27

Ending World Divorce

"A small body of determined spirits fired by an unquenchable
faith in their mission can alter the course of history."

—Mahatma Gandhi

Life Begins Where Your Comfort Zone Ends

I didn't start out as a world-renowned marriage expert—far from it. I
used to be just another unhappy wife on her way to a painful divorce.
But a divorce wasn't what I wanted, and it certainly wasn't the best
thing for me. If I had divorced, I would have missed out on having the
relationship of my dreams. It's sobering and heartbreaking to think
about where I would be now if I had given in to the illusion that my
husband was the wrong guy, when he's actually the perfect man for me.
I suffered needlessly because I didn't have the right skills, and I'm not
the only one. There are millions of women in the same predicament.

I've made it my mission to end divorce all over the world, but I can't
do it by myself. I'm inviting as many women as I can to be a part of it.

For a long time, I resisted stepping out in such a big way because
some people are offended by what I say. I've wondered, "Who am I to
try to change the world anyway?" But having found the courage to
save my own marriage, write very personal books about it, talk about
it on TV, travel abroad speaking about it in front of live audiences, and
start a coach training school and podcast, I've learned that life begins

where my comfort zone ends. I'm afraid every day, but so what? I'm doing what I know I'm supposed to do, and it's a thrill and an honor.

So far we're serving women in nineteen languages and thirty countries. I have certified relationship coaches in the United States, the United Kingdom, Ireland, Canada, Australia, New Zealand, Latvia, the Netherlands, India, and Mexico, and more are joining us every year. My coaches work with me because they too now have the kind of relationship they've always dreamed of, and they want to be a part of helping other women have the same thing. They tell me, "I believe in this. I want to do it too."

I'm not alone in this mission, and knowing that keeps me going. Let the critics criticize. They're just doing their job. I've got a job to do too.

Every time a woman learns the Six Intimacy Skills with the support of the Connection Framework and transforms her marriage and her family, that's cause for celebration. Getting to be a midwife to that process is the most gratifying work I've ever experienced. My team of relationship coaches and I feel it's a sacred, miraculous process that we have the joy and privilege of witnessing.

Here are just a few examples of women who have shared the story of their journey with the Intimacy Skills and Connection Framework on *The Empowered Wife Podcast.*

Abby's husband left her and said there was zero chance that they would reconcile. He was doing the paperwork to file for divorce while his mother was cheering him on. He said so many hurtful things, she wasn't even sure she wanted to save her marriage, and she didn't really think she could. But after four months of practicing the Six Intimacy Skills, he came back and told her (and his mother) that he wanted to love her deeply. They have big plans for their future together, including starting a family. (Episode 37)

Rachel's husband checked every box for narcissistic personality disorder, which she knew meant he would *never* change his selfish ways. Their weekly marriage counseling sessions were ugly fights, so she got a divorce attorney and started making plans to leave him. But instead, she discovered the Six Intimacy Skills and started practicing them. Today she says her husband loves, honors, and respects her, and they have an amazing life together. Same husband! (Episode 70)

Rivkah felt like she'd married the wrong person and that she and her husband just couldn't connect; she constantly felt criticized and defensive. After thirty-six years of marriage, she felt like she was just going through the motions and didn't feel loved like she always wanted to be. But then she started a practice that changed her experience completely. Her husband is no longer critical, and he tells her he has the wife of his dreams! And she has the husband of her dreams. (Episode 88)

Ch'vaun's marriage was lonely and felt like a roller-coaster ride. She knew that trust and respect were missing, but she didn't know how to get them back! But when she learned the Six Intimacy Skills and what respect really looks like to her husband, she says he went back to doing all the great things he did when they fell in love. She says she could cry because she feels so loved in her marriage now. (Episode 93)

Those are just a few examples of the transformations that we see every day. There are many more stories on *The Empowered Wife Podcast.* Yours could be next.

Each of these women made a giant step toward ending world divorce by creating intimacy, passion, and peace in her own marriage. That's step one, and it's a big one.

Practicing the Six Intimacy Skills in this book is a start, but if you're ready to take your relationship to the next level, I invite you to work with one of our Certified Laura Doyle Relationship Coaches. We find that many of our best success stories come from those who have joined our community of like-minded women with a shared vision for having an amazing marriage.

When you spend time with other women who support each other in feeling desired, cherished, and adored every day, you give yourself a better chance of succeeding with these new skills and getting what you've always wanted in your marriage. If you don't know anyone in your life who can support you that way, joining us will feel like you've found a tall, cool drink of water in the desert.

So much of the magic, joy, and celebration happens within the tribe of women who bear witness to and identify with your challenges and victories. There's no need to go it alone.

A student who was working with one of the coaches on our team called recently to say, "I just had to tell you what a difference this is making in my life. The one-to-one coaching is so powerful and amazing! I just had to thank you." That was the whole purpose of her call.

I look forward to hearing your success stories too.

Fringe Benefits of Practicing the Six Intimacy Skills with the Connection Framework

Spending time and energy practicing these new habits is going to lead to a much stronger connection with your husband. But that's not all! Here are some additional ways women have said that practicing the Six Intimacy Skills has improved their lives:

- *I became my best self and feel that I'm more authentic than ever before.*
- *I regained my dignity.*
- *I made friendships with other women like I've never had before. I've been a loner, but now I have the deep bonds with others that I've always craved.*
- *I stopped hiding. I left a prestigious job and paycheck that didn't feed my soul. It wasn't what I'm called to do, and through this training, I got the courage to let it go.*
- *I'm more confident because I now have such a stable marriage. I have a lot more energy and a lot less stress.*
- *I get an absolute thrill and feeling of being in the flow when I make a difference in someone else's life by sharing what I've learned. It's a powerful natural high for me.*
- *I found that we have more prosperity.*
- *I get more help from my husband and have more time for things I enjoy.*

Before I discovered the Six Intimacy Skills, I couldn't do most of the things that I wanted to do. I felt really trapped. I had to work hard at a job I didn't enjoy, and I was also responsible for everything at home.

As a longtime student of the Six Intimacy Skills with the Connection Framework, it's just the opposite: I get everything I want and more. I get to do inspiring work. I have a romantic, thoughtful husband. I have better, closer relationships with my family and friends. I live by the beach and play a lot of volleyball. I have better self-care, and I'm much happier.

I want all of that for you too.

My coaches and I are so committed to and excited about this work that we get sad when we see a woman not following her heart and not getting support. My coaches and I want you to be one of the women who gets the full benefit—every drop of it. If *I* can adopt these habits and get the marriage I have now—along with tens of thousands of women worldwide—then so can you. We're here to support you.

Even if we've never met and this is the first you've heard about the Six Intimacy Skills and the Connection Framework, I see a world of possibility for you. It takes more courage to get help than to do nothing and continue to limp along, but I don't think you'd be reading this book if you weren't courageous and ready to honor your desire to improve your relationship.

So much is possible for you. I'm standing in that possibility for you right now, and I won't give up until you have the relationship of your dreams. I know you can be great, and I want to celebrate that with you.

My Gratitude

If this is not the first time our paths have crossed, I want to thank you for your incredible support. I'm elated that you've enjoyed my books, podcasts, videos, and courses and shared them with so many women around the world. I don't take for granted how powerful you have been in supporting me and this message. You've made it possible for me to do the work that I do, and I couldn't be more grateful.

Here's to your intimate, passionate, peaceful marriage. You deserve it!

Acknowledgments

I'm so grateful for Glenn Yeffeth, who saw my vision and has been a dreamy publishing partner. I also want to thank my talented, honest editors, Erin Kelley and Alexa Stevenson, who turned out to be right about everything and carried me along when I needed it. Oriana Leckert made this a better book with her perspective and clarity, and so did Lydia Choi. I so appreciate Jennifer Canzoneri for her tireless marketing genius, and Sarah Avinger for cleverly capturing the essence of the book in the cover design. And I'm especially grateful for the loyal, passionate Kathy Murray for providing structure, support, and encouragement. I'm very lucky to be supported by this team!

None of what I do would be possible without the support of the amazing John Doyle, who bravely lets me share about his private life with the whole world and has taught me so much about what it means to love and be loved.

About the Author

Laura Doyle is a *New York Times* best-selling author, marriage expert, and the founder of Laura Doyle Connect, an international relationship coaching school that certifies coaches and guides students in practicing The Six Intimacy Skills™ to make their marriages last and thrive.

Her books are translated into nineteen languages and published in thirty countries. Laura is also the host of *The Empowered Wife Podcast* and the *Empowered Wives TV* series on Amazon Prime. She is on a mission to end world divorce.

She has appeared on *CBS Evening News*, *Dateline NBC*, *The Today Show*, *Good Morning America*, and *The View*. She has been featured in the *Wall Street Journal*, the *New York Times*, the *Los Angeles Times*, the *Washington Post*, the *London Telegraph*, and the *New Yorker*.

But the thing she's most proud of is her playful, passionate, 33-year marriage with her hilarious husband John, who has been dressing himself since before she was born.